A Practical Guide to

Builders
Questions
and
Answers

D1584651

by

Peter Roper

A BTJ Book

Published 1985

© International Thomson Publishing Limited

ISBN 1 85032 002 0

A 'Building Trades Journal' publication

Typeset by Avon Communications Ltd, The Sion, Crown Glass
Place, Nailsea, Bristol BS19 2EP

Printed and bound in Great Britain by John Wright & Sons
(Printing) Ltd, at The Stonebridge Press, Bristol

CONTENTS

INTRODUCTION

This book is a simple yet practical guide to solving many of the problems which arise during a building or improvement project. It is not intended to answer every problem in depth but to offer assistance to professionals and enthusiasts alike.

Whenever any project is being undertaken, whether it be concreting a path or solving a problem with central heating systems, there is a need to obtain confirmation that your remedy is correct. This book aims to offer that advice.

The questions are based on those received by Building Trades Journal's advisory service over the years and represent those which are constantly being asked.

Chapters are presented in an order running through the entire building process from foundations through to the roof and cover advice on the construction itself as well as good site practice and care and maintenance of plant and machinery. Safety in work and equipment is vital and this subject is covered along with a section on legal requirements.

Everyone who gets involved with construction either full-time or part-time will recognise the value of this book in speeding up the work process by preventing problems arising before work starts.

The advice and opinions given in this book are provided on the understanding that neither the author or publishers, nor its officers or advisors, may be held responsible for any 'neglect misstatement' which may be contained within it.

The author would like to thank all the panel of experts and advisors who have contributed to Building Trades Journal's technical advisory service over the years for their help in providing the basis for this book.

1 Foundations

Q1 : *What kind of foundations are usually used for framed buildings?*

A : The most commonly used type of foundation for this kind of building is the independent strip foundation. This is a square or rectangular slab of reinforced concrete, carrying a single column, with a base area sufficient to keep the soil stress well within the allowable bearing capacity of the soil.

At the bottom of the slab, reinforcement is placed in both directions to resist bending stresses set up by the double-cantilever action of the slab about the column base.

In the case of reinforced concrete columns the critical plane for bending is the face of the column, but in the case of steel stanchions it is the centre of the base plate.

If the column area gives a size of base relative to the thickness required for shear resistance such that the load can be spread entirely by dispersion at an angle of 45 deg. over the whole area of the slab, the reinforcement need only be a nominal amount.

At least 50 mm cover of concrete should be given to the reinforcement to protect it from attack from the soil.

Q2 : *What factors can cause soil movements?*

A : Cohesive soils or clays are affected by ground water. In moist and wet conditions clays expand, in dry conditions they contract. This will occur during seasonal changes when the level of the ground water rises and falls. The greatest danger occurs during dry periods when the clays may shrink, causing considerable ground movement.

Tree roots from growing trees may have the same effect; roots will absorb ground moisture which if unchecked may cause shrinkage of the clay and other ground movement.

Another source of ground movement is mining operations below ground level. They may cause subsidence of ground soils that may affect the support of the building.

Q3: *Clarification is required on details concerning three kinds of foundations.*

In Eire, traditional strip has been altered from 3W to 2W — W = width of wall. As known in structural work, this is not wide enough to allow the load to be distributed over an adequate area, i.e. shear in concrete is about 43 deg.

Deep strip would appear to have relatively small cover, i.e. adequate cover from temperature change, normally recommended as 900-1000 mm.

With a raft, it is necessary to maintain a continuous recess in the ring beam 225 mm high by 160 mm wide. The width would equal the external skin of masonry plus 50 mm cavity.

This is to keep the raft ring beam below finished ground level which is generally 300-350 mm below finished floor level.

As far as the width of the actual cavity is concerned, some technical advice has been received from a company on cavity insulation. The firm is promoting the use of 40 mm sheets kept against the inner leaf of the cavity, but suggests one big change in the structure, ie. the firm maintains a 50 mm cavity outside the insulating board, thereby increasing the actual cavity to 90 mm.

A: Regulations governing building may vary, and from time to time be altered and amended. Usually, minimum sizes are stated and there is nothing to prevent these sizes being exceeded, but they must not be reduced.

A foundation having a two-width spread (Fig. 1) may be adequate, depending on the load carried, the safe bearing capacity of the subsoil and prevailing conditions.

The Building Regulations 1976 (which apply to **England** and **Wales**, apart from the inner **London Boroughs**), require that the thickness of the foundation "T" should be at least equal to the

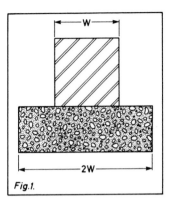

Fig.1.

projection from the wall face "P", and in no case may "T" be less than 150 mm (Fig. 2).

Since the angle of dispersion of the load in the concrete is 45 deg., making "T" at least equal to "P" ensures that if the concrete should fail under the compession induced by the load, it will crack at an angle of 45 deg. from the base of the wall (Fig. 2) and the area bearing on the soil will be retained.

The underside of the foundation concrete must be taken to such a depth that it will not be affected by shrinkage of the subsoil. In clay soils particularly, the effect of moisture changes (most marked towards the outer periphery of the building) may cause settlement to occur (Fig. 3).

A depth of 900 mm to 1000 mm is usually considered adequate as at this depth any volume changes likely to occur are too slight to seriously affect the foundation.

N.B. Where fast growing trees (e.g. poplars) are nearby it will be necessary to go deeper. It is recommended that a tree should

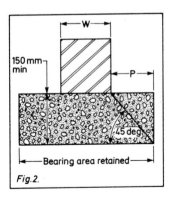

Fig.2.

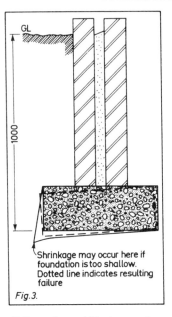

GL

—1000—

Shrinkage may occur here if
foundation is too shallow.
Dotted line indicates resulting
failure

Fig.3.

not be nearer to a building than 1½ times the mature height of the
tree.

Deep, or narrow strip foundations, are sometimes preferred
(Fig. 4) and may be suitable for normal two-storey construction.
Quite often the trench need only be 380 mm wide, and is filled up
to ground level with concrete.

This type of excavation is best carried out by machine, because
of the narrow width of the trench. The method overcomes the
difficulty of bricklayers working in a narrow trench, and compares
favourably in cost with the common traditional 600 mm wide strip
foundation.

The 75 mm layer of ashes, coarse sand or gravel provides a
clean, level surface on which to work, improves conditions in wet
weather and aids thermal insulation.

The top of the strip may be taken up to ground level, or finished
slightly below if required. The proximity of the surface of the
concrete to ground level does not matter, providing it is adequately protected against frost during placing and the subsequent
hardening period of the concrete.

Raft foundations may be used where the subsoil is of low
bearing capacity, or where relative settlement may occur.

The design of rafts is complex and where heavy loads are
involved and complications may ensue, the advice of experts

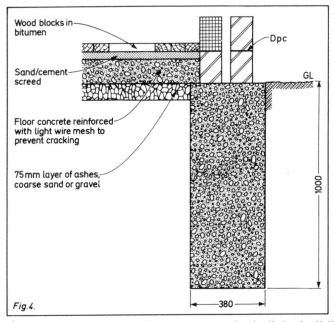

Fig.4.

should be sought. However, for a comparatively light building, a light raft, usually thickened beneath the walls may often be the most suitable foundation.

Fig. 5 shows an example of a raft foundation suitable for a light building. The reinforcement may consist of mild steel rods laid in both directions or welded steel fabric reinforcement.

The outer periphery of the raft should include some additional heavier gauge reinforcement near the top of the slab for a width of 1.5 m or so. This acts as a cantilever and guards against any shrinkage of the ground below.

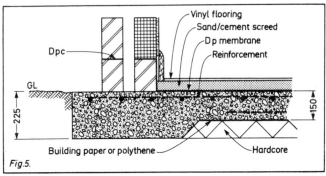

Fig.5.

The suggested cavity 90 mm wide seems excessive. It should be not less than 50 mm wide, or more than 75 mm wide.

There are proprietary systems for lining the inside leaf of the cavity with suitable insulating sheets, but this does not normally affect the cavity width.

Q4: *How do you waterproof the foundations of a bungalow which is to be built on the banks of a river?*

A: There is no point in making the foundations as such waterproof. Use a good, dense concrete—a well graded mix rather than one of any particular ratio—and vibrate it into the foundations so that it will be thoroughly dense and compacted. Use Class B engineering bricks below the dpc.

If you intend using a timber joisted suspended floor then do not waterproof the void below. Whatever you do, water will get in, and if the walls and floor are waterproof the water will not be able to get out again.

Provide plenty of ventilation and use joists and boards which have been properly treated with preservative.

Keep the floor well above ground level; if the ground tends to get flooded, keep the floor above flood level.

On ground like this, a concrete ground floor is to be recommended.

If the ground is bad, make sure that the foundations have adequate spread and use some reinforcement if necessary.

Q5: *A bungalow, 19 m by 7 m internally, is to be built by traditional construction with a roof of trusses at 600 mm centres and internal partitions of non-loadbearing light-weight blocks, 100 mm thick including plaster both sides.*

As shown in Fig. 6, the partitions will be built directly from the top of the oversite slab to the underside of truss.

(a) Is the concrete slab thick enough to resist movement or cracking?

(b) As reinforcement will be necessary in the concrete slab, what width and weight of steel mesh will be required?

(c) What fixing is required between trusses and block partitions?

(d) What is the best method of transferring the load of a 50 gall. storage tank between trusses to minimise the dead loading on each truss, bearing in mind that all partitions are non-loadbearing?

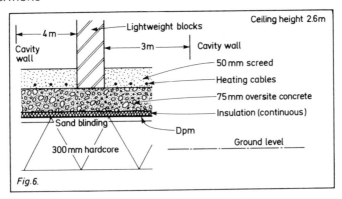

Fig.6.

Would Thermalite, Celcon or others be recommended as sufficiently light for my purposes?

A: Questions (a) and (b) concerning the thickness of the base and its reinforcement are related. This concrete oversite slab for which the thickness suggested was 75 mm would be too thin especially as reinforcement has to be covered. As reinforcement can be regarded as a necessity to prevent uneven settlement and cracking, the minimum thickness of concrete is 100 mm.

The reinforcement for this can be assessed on the basis of 0.12 per cent of the cross-sectional area. Taking dimensions of 100 mm deep, and 1 m of width (1 000 mm) the area of mesh would be a minimum of

$$\frac{0.12}{100} \times 100 \times 1000 = 120 \text{ mm}^2.$$

Tables show that A142 square mesh fabric to be suitable.

The slab can best tie into the outer walls (inner leaf) and as this tends to settle under greater pressure the bending near the perimeter of the slab tends to be hogging and so the reinforcement should be placed near the top of the slab and be continuous to a point approaching any partition. Where the partition exists the bending is the reverse way and a strip of fabric 1 m wide is best placed under the partitions, full length, at the bottom of the slab (18 mm cover), with the top reinforcement overlapping a little.

Be sure that the damp-proof membrane is thick enough and the blinding of the hardcore smooth enough for the membrane not to puncture, and see that the joins are welted.

Now comes the question, not raised by querist, but important, about the position and type of thermal insulation and water-proofing membrane over it.

The insulation, not stated as to type, was shown as positioned below the concrete. If below, then the concrete will take a considerable amount of heat and warm up and remain warm acting as thermal storage. If placed above the concrete, but below the screed, the screed only has to warm up and this it will do much more quickly. It depends therefore on the user as to which position it is put in.

If below and of polystyrene, it will squash up somewhat and should be 50 mm thick, or it may be of wood fibreboard 25 mm thick or woodwool slab 50 mm thick. If placed above the concrete then 25 mm polystyrene is sufficient or 25 mm wood fibreboard.

One more point in this connection. It is advisable to put a damp-proof membrane above the insulation if wet concrete is to be placed on it, in addition to the membrane below. It is possible to obtain wood fibreboard, coated with polythene which should be satisfactory as the one membrane. (See Fig. 7)

(c) The fixing required at the top of the partitions to the trusses depends upon which way the partitions run with respect to the trusses. There is no probelm with those which run at right angles. The partitions which wil run up probably—if 11 blocks high—about 25 mm above the base of the trusses, can be notched at the correct points to fit the trusses and this will tie them together. In the other direction noggin pieces can be notched and fixed by connector or nails through the bottom booms of the trusses. These noggins should be flush to take the (presumed) plaster-board ceiling. (See Fig. 8).

(d) The 50 gal. tank when filled may weigh about 540 lb. Placed on 100 by 50 mm bearers across two trusses this imposes a load

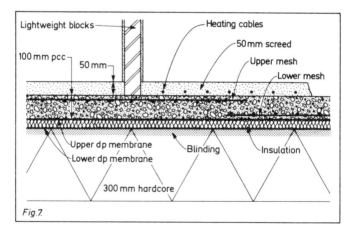

Fig. 7.

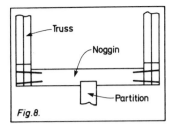

Fig.8.

something like 270 lb. as approximate point loads on each. It would be better to extend the bearers to rest across four trusses (three spans of 400 mm each), their length being 2 m.

As the centre two trusses, assumed dead level on top, would be expected to take more weight than the outside two, one might consider packing up the bearers at their ends to compensate and impose more load. But calculation of free upward deflection of each 400 mm end shows only 1 mm deflection so less packing than this is needed.

(e) As regards lightness of the blocks the slight difference in density between blocks is immaterial in considering the load on the foundation. Thermalite or Celcon as suggested would be light enough.

Q6: *An all-timber conservatory with a corrugated Filon roof is to be built with a raft foundation.*

The slab specification is terrazzo tiles bedded on a 150 mm RC raft poured on 1000 gauge dpm over blinding on 150 mm hardcore. The finished floor level will be only 50 mm above ground level at one point.

Advice is required on the materials for hardcore, materials for blinding, position of the dpm and the necessary reinforcement.

The sewer pipe will be laid in an excavation under the building and enclosed in concrete. How long should this be left before the slab is placed?

A: Hardcore consists of irregular pieces of broken brick, stone or broken concrete, which are hard, preferably do not readily absorb water, are durable and do not deteriorate.

It is important that the hardcore is clean. Old plaster mixed in with broken bricks, and clay mixed with stone will encourage dampness and provide an easy path for water to rise by capillary action. Certain impurities notably sulphates, can cause chemical action to take place with resulting cracking and crumbling of the concrete slab.

The Building Regulations, part 'C', lay down the requirements for ground floors as follows:

i. Such part of a building (other than an excepted building) as is next to the ground shall have a floor which is so constructed as to prevent the passage of moisture from the ground to the upper surface of the floor.

ii. Any floor which is next to the ground shall be so constructed as to prevent any part of the floor being adversely affected by moisture or water vapour from the ground.

iii. No hardcore laid under such floor shall contain water-soluble sulphates or other deleterious matter in such quantities as to be liable to cause damage to any part of the floor.

Before concrete is laid over the hardcore it is usual to 'blind' or seal the top surface of the hardcore. This may be done by spreading a thin layer of coarse clinker, or ash, or a coarse sand over the surface. Sometimes a fairly weak concrete mix is used for this purpose.

The object of the blinding layer is to prevent loss of grout from the concrete and of the more expensive concrete itself by running down into the voids in the hardcore. This blinding coat will vary in thickness and may be 50 mm in parts.

The blinding material, particularly if ash or clinker is used, must be reasonably free from sulphates. A layer of building paper or polythene sheet laid over the blinding as shown in Fig. 9 is an excellent additional precaution.

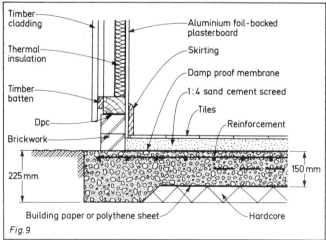

Fig.9.

Design of rafts vary considerably. In the case in point only a comparatively light structure is to be carried, and the raft need not be heavily reinforced. A light raft construction is shown in Fig. 9.

The reinforcement may be of mild steel rods laid in both directions or welded steel fabric. In the conditions specified BRC fabric reinforcement would be suitable. A range of gauges is available, but a comparatively light gauge should suffice in the circumstances.

The outer periphery of the raft should include some additional heavier gauge reinforcement near the top of the slab for a width of 1.5 m or so. This will act as a cantilever and guard against shrinkage of the ground below.

Take a sketch of the proposed construction along, and have a word with the local building inspector.

The concrete cover to the drain pipe need not cause any protracted delay. The slab can be placed almost immediately, perhaps an interval of a day might be allowed before continuing with the slab.

Q7: *Advice is required on the size and reinforcement (if any) for a strip foundation for a three-storey extension.*

Details of the extension are given in Fig. 10. From calculation, a figure of 90 kN/m total load was obtained, which is beyond the scope of the tables in Building Regulations.

The subsoil is firm, sandy clay and as the building is on sloping ground the foundations will be stepped.

A: The given conditions for the foundation design are:
Loading 90 kN/m run, soil: firm and sandy clay.

The type of soil can be taken as Class IV of the Building Regulations, and the loading goes beyond the figures and sizes in the 'deemed-to-satisfy' examples.

The highest loading given of 70 kN/m is stated to require 850 mm width of concrete, giving 82.5 kN/m² for bearing pressure. For the lighter loadings the pressures work out at 80, 83.5, 89 kN/m². It is therefore reasonable to take the least figure of 80 kN/m² as the bearing pressure and work to this.

The required width
$$= \frac{90}{80} = 1.125 \text{ m}$$

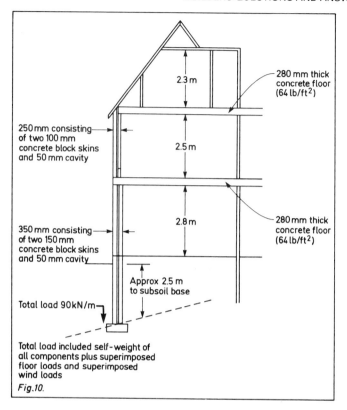

The wall width is 0.350 m and so the projection on each side is ½ (1.125 — 0.350) = 390 mm.

For unreinforced concrete the depth of concrete should therefore be equal to this figure. As this depth may seem excessive the question of reinforcement and thereby saving depth of concrete must be examined, and then the choice according to economy, etc., can be left to the querist.

For calculation, the design is rather like an inverted double cantilever and having a loading of 80 kN/m², projection 390 mm. Assume concrete of cube strength 21 N/mm² and working to only 7 N/mm², the calculation is as follows:

The bending moment about the edge of the wall

$$= \frac{80 \times 0.39^2}{2} = 6.1 \text{ kNm}$$

See Fig.11.

$$d_1 = \sqrt{\frac{6.1 \times 1000}{7/4 \times 1}} = 59 \text{ mm}$$

Add to this a cover of 40 mm and half the diameter of mesh bars, say 5 mm, giving 104 mm, say 125 mm.

Now check for shear on the edge line of the wall.

$$\frac{0.39 \times 80}{La} = 0.7$$

From this La = 45 mm.

As d_1 can be reckoned as 60 mm at the least, this is satisfactory.

To calculate the steel necessary.

Assume 125 mm slab and high yield steel (stress 230 N/mm²)

$$A_{st} = \frac{M}{p \times La_{st}} = \frac{6.1 \times 10^6}{230 \times \frac{3}{4} \times 70} \text{ (La increased)} = 500 \text{ mm}^2$$

The mesh C 503 meets this requirement.

Place the mesh in a slab which though calculated as 125 mm thick would better be 150 mm thick nominally to allow for unevenness of base. Allow at least 40 mm (say 50 mm) below for cover. This thickness of 150 mm compares with 390 mm for unreinforced concrete.

Note: depth below ground level. As the ground slopes the concrete must be stepped. The question of depth in the soil to its underside at the shallowest is determined by whether the clay is regarded as 'shrinkable' or not.

If shrinkable, then 1 m depth is regarded as necessary. If not, and this soil is described as firm sandy clay, then the depth in the soil could be less.

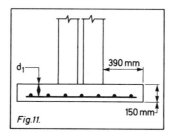

Fig.11.

Q8: *Advice is required on how to assess the likelihood of settlement in a bungalow after the felling of a mature sycamore tree when construction reached dpc level.*

What precautions should be taken to strengthen the building in the area where the ground has been severely disturbed (see Fig. 12).

The soil from the excavated area 6 m to 8 m from the south west corner of the bungalow was essentially the same type down to a depth of 3 m. In its undisturbed state the soil was firm and dark brown to black in colour. It could be easily moulded in the fingers and retained its shape.

The tree stood 24 m high, was 4 m in girth and had a spread of 20 m. It had to be felled and the root buried after construction reached dpc, when extensive fungus infestation was found at the main fork. The stump was eventually buried 3 m deep and 2.4 m south of its original position.

A 150 mm sewer pipe laid at a depth of 2 m runs across the south west corner of the bungalow and was surrounded with weak concrete on the advice of the building inspector.

A: There is no known way of "guesstimating" the probable movement of a building due to its resting over dead tree roots which are decomposing, other than a case history which is nearly identical.

It is not clear from the description of the soil that it is silty or peaty, but either will retain a lot of moisture and therefore the whole site is liable to slow movement with the seasons.

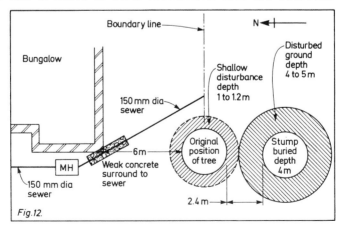

Fig.12.

The distance of the tree centre from the structure will mean the spread of roots will probably extend under the kitchen and dining area. The size of these will probably be fairly small - 100 mm at most.

Hence as a construction problem the safest approach at this point of building, ie, if up to dpc now, will be to introduce mesh fabric reinforcement into the top of the floor slab and thereby endeavour to ensure equal settlement over the whole plan area. The mesh should be A141 or better, lying 15 mm below the top of the slab which should extend over the inner wall skin.

If construction has progressed above this level the only simple remedy is to lay the mesh on top of the slab and screed over. The screed would need to be 40 to 50 mm thick. The probable overall average settlement of the bungalow will be of the order of 10 mm to 15 mm and should be uniform over the site.

It is doubtful whether the gradual rotting of one or two 100 mm roots and some smaller ones would cause the corner to subside more than the rest, as the foundation concrete would span across these small areas and the building is only lightly loaded anyway.

To embark upon expensive precautions such as underpinning or soil stabilisation "just in case" is rather like a hypochondriac going to a doctor and demanding a surgical operation for an imagined appendix or undiscovered ulcer—it is a thing that is just not done. Underpinning, in any case, would be difficult at the main bungalow corner owing to the presence of the sewer.

One has to bear in mind the difference between dying roots and those of a growing tree. A growing tree keeps taking water from the soil over a wide area and this may affect the stability of a building nearby. Moreover, the physical growth and expansion of roots causes an almost irresistible pressure near the roots, so again affecting stability. These effects are not present here, so apart from the one safeguard mentioned that may still be possible, nothing should be done.

Q9: *What checks should be made to ensure the safety of excavations for foundations and, more importantly, the safety of operatives.*

A: The digging of an excavation on a site may be a man's first and last job. If the sides collapse, there may be no escape. There is almost no ground which will not collapse under certain conditions. If there is any doubt whatsoever about the safety of sides, they should be timbered or battened. Timbering materials should always be provided on site.

If the excavation is more than 1.21 m deep you should check
— is the timber provided strong enough to support the sides of the
excavation?— is the method of putting in timber a safe one?
— is the angle of batten appropriate?
— is the excavation inspected daily, and the timbering weekly?
— is there safe access to the excavation?
— is there a barrier to prevent persons falling in?
— is the stability of the excavation being affected by vehicles
which come too near?
—if vehicles tip into an excavation, are secured stop blocks
provided?

Q10: What is the legal position when the foundations of a house are apparently damaged by water which flows from adjoining sloping land which is owned by the local council?

A: In general for a legal claim to succeed when some harm has
been suffered, it is necessary to show that there has been some
fault on the part of the other party.

From the facts given it is uncertain whether the water is draining
from the adjoining land by flowing above or below the surface and
whether it is water flowing naturally because of the slope or
whether it has been increased by some works carried out on the
adjoining land.

Where water flows naturally, whether above or below the
surface, there is probably no liability on the council since the law,
in general, does not hold a landowner liable for harm caused by a
natural act on his land. If the water was flowing naturally
underground it would also probably be difficult to prove that the
damage had been caused solely by water coming from the
council's land.

In addition, the court might take the view that a person who
builds a house on a sloping site ought to take account of the
possibility of water flowing down the slope and provide for this
possibility in the construction of the house.

If the flow of water has been caused by or increased because of
works carried out by the council on its land then the council would
probably be liable for any damage caused. A claim could be made
for nuisance and negligence.

2 Brickwork

Q11: *What is a Flemish bond brick wall?*

A: A Flemish bond wall consists of alternate headers and stretchers in each course with the headers being laid centrally over the stretchers in the course below.

Q12: *In brickwork, which is the most commonly used bond?*

A: Stretcher bond is the most common. This is simply a half-lap bond where all bricks present their stretcher faces to the face of the wall.

Q13: *What is the cause of staining often seen on the surface of brickwork?*

A: The staining to which you refer is usually due to effluorescence. The watersoluble salts found in clays and clay materials are mainly sulphates, which in moist conditions dissolve to form solutions which are absorbed into materials by capillary action and travel towards the surface, where evaporation of the moisture takes place, leaving behind concentrations of drying salts.

Q14: *Can you tell me how to erect a quoin in stretcher bond and Flemish bond for first class work?*

A: A half brick quoin should be racked back as shown in Fig. 13. The drawing assumes a stopped end on one return, alternatively both sides may be racked back as on the right. When stretcher bond is used it is necessary to rack out for a considerable distance, if scaffold height is to be achieved, and a "profile" or "Dead Man" as shown will help to ensure that the wall is straight and level.

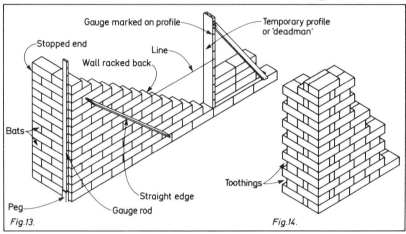

Fig.13.   Fig.14.

A gauge rod should be used at the quoin to check the correct height of the courses. In practice the height of any features occurring along the wall such as sills, window heads, air bricks, etc., are marked on the gauge rod. These heights can then be indicated on the quoin so that when the wall is 'run in' to the line the bricklayer will know when he is at the correct height.

The quoin is checked for plumb with a plumb level as the corner is built up, and should be checked for straight by holding a level or straight edge against the wall as shown.

A quoin in Flemish bond may be erected as shown in Fig. 14. In this case one or two bricks may be toothed as shown on the right in order to avoid racking out the corner too far.

Continuous toothings in one unbroken line as shown on the left should be avoided as these may constitute a weakness if carelessly filled.

Q15: *An area of 3 m by 3 m is to be paved with slabs in Tudor bond, could you describe the sequence.*

I want to use 600thmm by 600 mm, 600 mm by 300 mm and 300 mm by 300 mm slab combinations.

A: I am not familiar with 'Tudor bond' for paving work and inquiries have failed to identify it.

There is a wide range of bonding patterns used for paving work, often varying with particular localities.

I have sketched one or two designs (Fig. 15) that might be suitable.

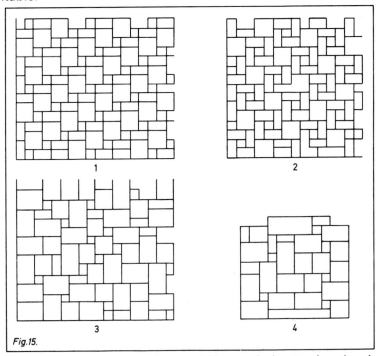

Fig.15.

No. 1 is an arrangement that could be carried out using the sizes mentioned. **No. 2** is an alternative pattern for the same size slabs.

Nos. 3 and **4** show two other bonding patterns.

Q16: *An extension to the third bedroom of a detached house is to be supported on brick piers 13½ in. by 18in.*

Solutions are required for the following:

Detail D (Fig. 17)—note 3 ft. difference in levels between house ground level and adjacent garage which belongs to another property.

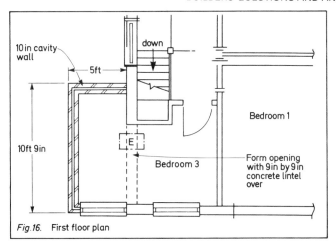

Fig.16.   First floor plan

Details A and B (Fig. 16) and Detail E (Fig. 18)—it is proposed that in each case the supporting beam is to consist of two 6 in. by 3 in. rsj's surrounded by concrete. Is this suitable.

A: Let us first consider the loading on the most heavily loaded beams and design for these. (Using imperial measurements).

The longest span is about 10 ft. (Detail B Fig. 16) and the imposed load consists of cavity wall, part floor slab and roof slab. It is as well to calculate and not judge without same.

The calculation based on assumed construction (concrete floor and concrete roof slab, 10 in. cavity wall) I make out to be as follows.

Wall 10 ft. by 9 ft. by 75 lb./sq. ft. = 675 lb.

2 slabs and coverings, total 10 ft. by 5 ft. by 80 lb./sq. ft. = 4000 lb.

Imposed load on floor and roof 50 sq. ft. by

$$(40+20) = \frac{3000\ \text{lb.}}{7675\ \text{lb.}}$$

Add weight of encased beam $= \dfrac{325\ \text{lb.}}{8000\ \text{lb.}}$

or 3.6 ton

Querist suggests 6 by 3 in. rsj's. I do not think this size exists. Nearest is 6 in. by 3½ in. by 11.5 lb., safe load on 10 ft. being 6.8 ton or 13.6 ton on two. This allows more margin than

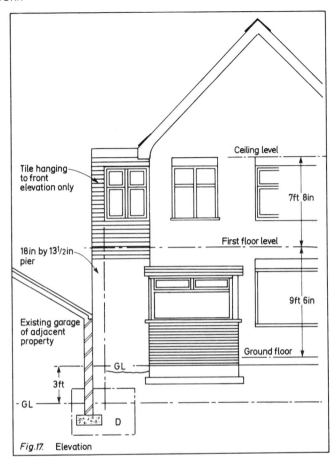

Fig. 17. Elevation

necessary. I suggest 5 in. by 3 in. by 9 lb. safe load 4.4 ton, 8.8 ton on two. Both of the figures quoted are for high yield steel.

For pairs of the same sizes in mild steel the safe loads quoted are (when doubled) 9.8 and 6.4 ton respectively. It would seem then that the smaller size in mild steel is sufficient.

The same size could just as well be adhered to for beams A and E, with similar casing. I indicate the kind of casing in Fig. 19.

An alternative would be reinforced beams of similar width namely 10 in., but slightly greater depth, say 9 in. to include cover, the concrete strength being 1500 lb./in^2.

The effective depth of 7½ in. gives sufficient strength. The steel require at the bottom would be 4 No. ¼ in. or 20 mm bars of mild steel or 3 No. of high yield steel.

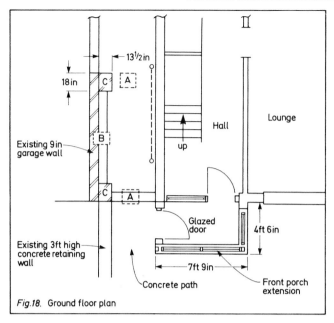

Fig.18. Ground floor plan

The detail D of the base for the piers I give in Fig. 20.
Taking the level of the existing base of the garage as being
suitable, as it is 3 ft. below ground, form a new foundation over the
haunch of the garage foundation as shown, each pier base being

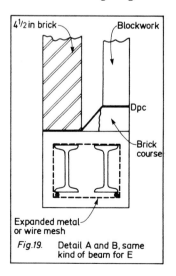

Fig.19. Detail A and B, same
kind of beam for E

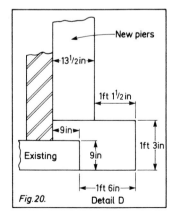

Fig.20. Detail D

3 ft. long. Bearing pressure works out at not more than 0.52 ton/ sq.ft. which is quite light for normal soil. This figure was worked out by taking 3.5 ton as the load on one pier to include self-weight and dividing by the area under the new concrete and old haunch only, being 3 ft. by 2¼ ft. or 6¾ sq. ft.

Q17: *Advice is required on the best way to fix York stone paving vertically to brickwork.*
A second problem relates to a recently completed job where roof tiles were laid on an extension adjacent to existing tiles. Although the new tiles are the same, the existing ones are about 40 years old and the new tiles stand out glaringly alongside.
How could the new tiles be toned down?

A: Fixing York stone paving to brickwork, should be put out to a sub-contractor expert, as if this is high enough to fall on anyone it might prove fatal and the builder become involved in costly litigation.

Local stone masons who do this class of work also have supplies of suitable 'hidden' fastenings, which when the job is completed are obscured from view, and furthermore, are usually, these days, of stainless steel or other rust-resisting metal.

Further, side cut mortises are provided in the stone work for these, and to carry out the required cutting is a very skilled job, and supports have to be provided, in a similar manner, at the bottoms of all openings.

With reference to the second question, the correct way to do any work on roofing which involves additional tiles against old tiles, is to strip the old work and mix them with the new, and relay, taking great care that the finished roofing does not present any form of pattern, if practicable. Unfortunately it is not stated what the difference is, but in a job I had some years ago they had to match perfectly.

The work involved two cottages, one thatched and falling down, the other roofed with a very rare type of interlock, about 170 years old. The existing roof was dark, almost black, and the tiles from a recent demolition were red.

In this case the red tiles were tinted and broken down in colour with a diluted thin tar and benzol mixture. The new roof built, the tiles taken off and mixed with ours and relaid over the whole area.

Based upon years of experiences in re-roofing ancient buildings, remember handmade tiles may be the same pattern, but remember as there were so many makers, they often were of non-standard lengths and widths, but with skill they can usually be mixed.

Q18: *It would be of great interest if you could list the Codes of Practice which relate to bricklaying.*

A: CP 101:1973: Foundations and substructures for non-industrial buildings of not more than four storeys.

CP 102:1972: Protection of buildings against water from the ground.

CP 111:1970: Structural recommendations for load-bearing walls.

CP 121:Part 1:1973: Brick and block masonry.

CP 122: Walls and partitions of blocks and slabs.

CP 131:1974: Chimneys and flues for domestic appliances burning solid fuel.

BS 5628:1979: Code of Practice for the structural use of masonry.

Q19: *Could you tell me how I can remove the unsightly sucker feet marks left on brickwork after I have pulled some ivy from the walls of my house.*

The brickwork is 25 years old and is in dark red sand faced type of brick in a soft cement.

A: Usually the feet marks can be removed by brushing. Before you start you should check the mortar joints to make sure that they have not been damaged by invasion of the ivy. Before starting to brush, damp the wall - but do not soak it - then use as little (warm) water as possible.

Use a stiff close-packed natural bristle brush. If the marks are hard to remove do not become aggressive with the brushing, use a domestic detergent (eg. washing-up liquid).

If there are still problems you can use a dilution of magnesium silico fluoride (1 part to 40 parts of water); if you do have to resort to this, first damp the brickwork with clean water, and wash down with clean water, when you have finished the job. Wear gloves and take care not to get any of the solution in the eyes.

Q20: *What is a sleeper wall?*

A: This is a wall erected at intervals between the main walls to provide intermediate support for ground floor joists. The joists may be supported at each end by the inner skin of the cavity wall or by the partition wall.

The intermediate sleeper walls reduce the joist span and allow smaller section timbers to be used, thus reducing cost considerably. Sleeper walls are usually built up on the oversite concrete and are a honeycombe construction designed to allow free circulation of air under the floor.

Q21: *What are the main types of mortar used for brick and blockwork?*

A: Lime mortar: a mix of 1:2 lime and sand which has good working properties if thoroughly mixed, but develops strength very slowly and is consequently used little today.

Cement mortar: a mix proportion of 1:3 cement and sand is required to give a good workable mortar. It may be suitable for high strength engineering brickwork but is too strong for most ordinary work. Leaner mixes of cement and sand become harsh and unworkable.

Cement lime mortars: the addition of lime to a cement mortar will improve the workability considerably and allow a lower cement-sand ratio to be used. A lower strength mortar will be the result, having most of the properties of cement and lime mortars.

Plasticised cement mortar: to improve the workability of weaker cement-sand mixes, air entraining additives are used as an alternative to lime.

Masonry cement mortar: this consists of a mixture of Portland cement with a fine mineral filler and an air entraining agent.

Q22: *What problems can occur if bricklaying is carried out in cold weather?*

A: Water in the mortar mix and in wet bricks expands on freezing, disrupting the bond and causing spalling and cracking of the mortar, resulting in a loss of strength in the brickwork.

Cement in the mortar mix is slower setting and gains strength less quickly when the weather is cold, consequently, the brickwork will take longer to develop strength.

Differences in drying conditions may vary the final colour of the mortar. In addition, heavy rains, occurring before the mortar sets, can wash the mortar out and badly stain the surface.

These effects can be overcome by using mortars suitable for cold weather and by protecting materials, working areas and completed work.

Q23: *During cold weather, what precautions should be taken to protect materials for bricklaying?*

A: Bricks and blocks should be kept dry by stacking them clear of the ground on their delivery pallets or on slatted platforms which will allow a free airflow underneath. The stacks should then be covered on all sides with well secured tarpaulins or polythene sheeting. Where they are to be used under conditions of artificial heating, they should be stored under such conditions for 24 hours before use.

Cement and ready mixed mortars should be stored well above ground level on a timber platform, preferably inside. If this is not possible, cover completely with weighted tarpaulins or polythene sheeting. Cement must be used in order of delivery. Damp cement should be discarded.

Cover sand immediately after delivery with a water-proof sheet - over insulation if necessary, to prevent freezing. Tarpaulins or polythene sheeting should be supported about 50 to 150 mm clear of the sand for improved thermal insulation. Dirty sand should not be used because it slows the hardening time and weakens the mortar.

Q24: *How does one keep the cavity clean and free from mortar droppings during construction?*

A: One method is to use the cavity battens or sweeps. These are wood battens placed on the first level of wall ties which catch the mortar droppings as the two skins of the wall are built up to the next new wall tie height.

Before placing the next row of wall ties, the batten is lifted out by means of the wire or cord handles provided, cleaned off and replaced on the wall ties and the process repeated.

At the base of the wall, below dpc level, holes may be left to allow for cleaning out the base of the cavity. Similar cleaning-out holes can be left above door and window openings or any other place where the cavity is bridged to allow for cleaning any surplus mortar droppings off the dpc.

These holes, normally one brick long and two courses high, have to be made good when the wall has reached its full height.

Q25: *What forces should be taken into account when constructing a gate pier and what is the normal method of construction?*

A: To start with, a gate imposes considerable lever action on the pier from which it is hung, acting through the top hinge. The weight of the gate must be considered as well as the possibilities of it being slammed shut by a person, or the wind, or even having children swinging on it.

The minimum size for a gate pier is 1½ bricks square. This is built as a Flemish bond unit and the centre either filled with concrete or a half-brick built in.

Reinforcing rods cast into the foundation concrete and passing up through the pier give greater stability for a pier of over 1.5 m high.

Piers two bricks square or over are usually bonded in Flemish or English bond. If iron or steel hinges are built into the brickwork and later corrode, the corrosion expansion can split the pier or cause it to expand. Galvanised types can be used but the galvanising may wear and rusting may occur on the moving parts. Stains from the rusting metal can discolour the brickwork.

Q26: *How are temporary openings formed in walls?*

A: Openings may have to be formed in walls during construction and made good later, although it is best to avoid this if possible.

Making provision for the installation of large items of plant or equipment, or providing access to the interior of the building for construction purposes, may involve a large temporary opening in the wall.

This would involve toothing the sides of the opening to allow for making good later and fixing a temporary lintel in place.

A weak mortar mix is generally used for bedding and building over a temporary lintel in order that it may be removed easily when the opening is made good. The toothing must be built accurately and left clean, and when building in later, care must be taken to ensure that the toothing is packed solidly with mortar.

Smaller openings, perhaps for pipes, are usually formed by building bricks or blocks in sand at the required position. After the wall has set and hardened, the bricks set in sand are removed and an accurately formed hole remains.

Q27 Is it possible that block partitions on suspended timber floors may crack?

A: They may crack if carried on a floor which may deflect, for example, a timber joisted floor. Unless the span is short and deflection negligible, the blockwork above may crack. Mesh reinforcement may help but cracking may be localised around door openings.

Allowance for movement may be needed at junctions with other walls. It would be best to consider alternative designs such as avoiding blockwork or re-locating it over a supported area.

CP121 states 'where a wall is built on a floor which may deflect ... and create non-continuous bearing ... the wall should be separated from the floor ... and should be strong enough to span between the points of least floor deflection. . . .'

Q28: I intend building an extension in brickwork to a stone walled cottage. How can I prevent dampness?

A: 1. The cavity wall could be tied to the stone wall with 90 mm wide galvanised expanded metal strips 250 mm long built in at 450 mm vertically and the stonework joints cleaned out and the expanded metal grouted in, ensuring that the joint is not dry, to enable a good key to be obtained.

The vertical joint provided with a patent expansion and contraction joint filler.

As an added precaution the cavity wall ties would be at 250 mm vertically as for a reveal as near as is practicable to the end of the cavity wall.

2. As an alternative to No. 1 a patent channel tie system could be employed 'Tymore', 'Furfix' or similar.

3. Referring to the penetration of damp at the joint. I would suggest:—

i) Three coats of bitumen emulsion for a band 1 m wide up to full height of the existing wall. The last coat of bitumen emulsion to be dashed with sharp sand to act as a key, or

ii) A vertical chemical dpc (with appropriate current Agrément Board Certificate) vertically up the existing wall.

Q29: *How can I best bond an extension to an existing stone building of two storeys to prevent dampness at the joint?*

A: I would introduce a vertical dpc into the cavity and frame of the cavity wall brick extension.

I suggest that a lead core bitumen dpc is chased 25 mm into the stone masonry or if possible follow the vertical masonry joints within the width of the cavity. The dpc should extend into the cavity 75 mm clear of either brick leaf.

The brickwork should be tied into the main structure, preferably block bonded and the joint pointed with mortar.

I would not use mastic which has been found to have a limited life, particularly in the proposed exposed position and I would not use softboard as detailed.

If the foundation is deeper than the original foundation and of sufficient size no movement should occur.

Q30: *How can I prevent settlement cracks appearing in a brick extension to a stone built cottage? Advice on tying in is needed.*

A: The most suitable answer would be to employ the wall extension profiles such as "Furfix". The profile which consists of a 'U' section in stainless steel or galvanised metal is plugged to the existing bricks or blocks built into the section.

The design permits the use of standard butterfly ties and mortar on the ends of the brick is pushed through perforations to provide a sound key.

Personally I would prefer to set the new wall face in about 12 mm from the stonework existing, which provides a much better location for a bead of polysulphide mastic caulking which would bond well in the right angle formed.

31: *I have just had a small extension built on to the house. My query is, what is the correct mix for mortar?*

The extension was built with strong mortar up to the blockwork, which was rough-cast: then the mortar seemed rather weaker.

I would like to build a bedroom on top later on but I wonder if the mortar is strong enough.

The rest of the house was built with sand, lime and brick: would cement-sand mix have the same strength as the lime mix which has stood for 40 years?

A: You do not say what type of blockwork was used for your extension, but the fact that it was given a roughcast rendered finish suggests lightweight-aggregate or aerated concrete blocks.

It is normal practice to use a somewhat weaker mortar for lightweight masonry than for bricks or dense blocks.

Whether the extension would carry the additional weight of an upper storey depends much more on the design and construction of the walls, and on the foundations, than on mortar strength; you should consult your local authority Building Control Officer or a chartered surveyor.

Q32: *On an external brick wall horizontal, vertical and diagonal cracks have appeared. What could the possible causes be, and what remedies are recommended?*

A: The cracks may be caused by a variety of reasons including subsoil movement (including change of water content), foundation movement and failure, expansion of the brickwork, chemical action on the brickwork, failure of the wall ties or the spread of the roof structure having the effect of pushing out the walls.

Clues to which of these may be responsible could be whether the cracks are widening or lengthening, whether a building development is taking place nearby, whether mining is carried out in the area, if the weather has been particularly wet or dry or if there is a tree close to the affected wall — or if one has been felled recently.

If the cracks are stable, fill them with a compressible filler which prevents water penetration and allows for further movement. The tenant can remain while repairs are carried out.

If they are unstable they are structural defects and may involve excavation, underpinning and rebuilding parts of walls. It may be necessary to move the tenants while the work is done.

Q33: *Should movement joints be provided in long runs of brickwork? If they should, how far apart are they placed?*

A: The requirements for clay brickwork are one 10 mm joint per 12 m run for normal conditions. Short returns (600 mm of half brick thickness) are vulnerable and should be avoided in long runs unless a movement joint is provided.

Calcium silicate brickwork requires a joint every 7.5 to 9 m, depending on shape and openings. These are elaborated on in BRE Digest 157 which also gives appropriate mortar mixes.

The separator can be bituminous felt or polystyrene built-in or, say, precompressed foam plastics inserted into an open joint. The joint must not be bridged by mortar.

3 Walls

Q34: *Could you explain the method of calculating a wall 15 ft. long by 6 ft. 6 in. high? How many blocks or bricks and how much sand and cement is needed to construct such a wall?*

A: Area of the wall is length×height — 15 ft.×6 ft. 6in.=97.5 sq. ft. Assuming a wall is one brick (9 in.) thick, including allowance for cutting and waste=100 bricks. Therefore, 11 sq. yd., 9 in brick wall=11×100=1100 bricks. (Keeping the calculations imperial).

Concrete blocks and the like in various thicknesses are generally sold by the sq. yd. Allowing 10 per cent for cutting and waste, this means 1.1 sq. yd. of blocks for each sq. yd. of wall.

Therefore, 11 sq. yd. block wall=11×1.1=12.1 sq. yd. of blocks. Mortar quantities are as in Table 1.

Table 1

	1 sq.yd. wall	11 sq.yd. wall
One brick wall	0.06 cu.yd.	0.66 cu.yd.
3 in. block wall	0.01 cu.yd.	0.11 cu.yd.
4 in. block wall	0.013 cu.yd.	0.14 cu.yd.

Table 2

	Cement mortar		Cement/lime mortar		
	(1-2)	(1-3)	(1-1-4)	(1-1-6)	(1-1-8)
Cement — tons	0.54	0.40	0.28	0.20	0.16
Sand — cu.yds.	1.00	1.10	1.00	1.10	1.20
Lime — tons	—	—	0.14	0.10	0.08

The quantity of sand, cement, lime etc required will depend on the specified mix. See Table 2 for quantities for component materials. They are for one cubic yard of mortar of various mixes.

Assuming 11 sq. yd. of one brick wall, 0.66 cu. yd. cement mortar (1-3) is required, then the materials required are as follows:
Cement—0.66×0.40=0.264 tons (6 cwt)
Sand—0.66×1.10=0.72 cu. yd. (¾ cu. yd.)

Q35: *How can I obtain an even exposure to the aggregate in an in-situ concrete wall?*

A: One cannot expect to achieve a uniform distribution of aggregate by using a concrete which has been designed simply to comply with a given strength grading.

Such mixes generally contain a higher sand content than is wanted for exposed aggregate work and, if the coarse aggregate has too high a proportion of small-sized material, it will give an uneven appearance.

The best results are obtained by using a selected, single-sized coarse aggregate with just enough sand to fill the voids between the aggregate particles. Obviously, to achieve good results, trials with the chosen materials are essential to determine suitable mix proportions.

Q36: *What reasons could there be for newly applied rendering having developed a pattern of fine cracks over the whole area.*

A: The most likely causes for the cracking are:

1) The sand is too fine, so that it requires quite a lot of water to produce a workable mix—this leads to a high shrinkage as the rendering dries out.

2) Shrinkage also results from the evaporation of water from renderings exposed to warm, drying winds or to the sun within a few hours of them being applied. In hot dry weather, protection from drying out is essential for the first few days. Sheet polythene should be used for this and is best arranged to hang just clear of the face of the wall to totally enclose the area concerned. If it forms a tunnel, air can blow through and increase the evaporation.

3) Excessive working with a steel trowel will bring fine material to the surface and this will have a different rate of shrinkage.

Q37: *Irregular cracks have appeared in rendering to brickwork on an external wall. In a couple of places the rendering has actually come away from the brickwork and if*

it is tapped around the cracks it sounds hollow. What could the cause be, and can anything be done to cure the problem?

A: You should check to see whether the cracks correspond to cracks in the brickwork itself. If they do, then that is the most likely cause of your problem; repair the cracks in the brickwork and make good the rendering.

It may be, however, that the cracks have been caused by shrinkage of the cement-based render. Once the cracks begin to appear, the rendering is open to water penetration.

Possibly, chemical action may have affected the back facing of the rendering resulting in cracking and falling off.

It is difficult to make good extensive cracking and break away without total re-rendering.

To prevent water penetration and chemical attack, weather cladding, such as tile hanging or shiplap boarding is necessary. Painting with a cement-based paint or a textured coating may help.

Q38: *What can you tell me about the mortar bee? I saw this bee mentioned on TV some time ago and I have now come across my first case of this insect in 30 years in the building trade. I believe it is responsible for the collapse of a garden wall which I have been asked to rebuild.*

The wall is one brick thick, some 2.1 m high and originally built in a weak lime mortar. It was built in Flemish bond but most of the header bricks are half bats. I take the wall to be some 100 years old.

A: A couple of years ago, in response to a number of inquiries about damage resulting from the burrowing of the masonry or mortar bee, the Building Research Establishment issued an information paper on the subject.

This explains that the damage complained of is most frequently in soft mortar joints, especially those of older buildings, but can occur in comparatively new buildings in which the mortar is particularly weak. Soft bricks and stone have also been damaged on occasions.

A number of wild bee species whose normal habitat is earth banks and soft exposed rocks are capable of causing damage to buildings by burrowing. The most common species is *Osmia rufa*. They are all solitary types in as much as they do not form distinct social colonies although many individual bees will often attack the same area if it provides particularly suitable conditions.

The damage is caused by the female bees boring into the material to form a system of galleries or tunnels in which to house the pupal cells of the next generation.

The gallery construction takes place during the early spring and the burrowing and emergence activities are completed by early summer.

Only a single brood generation is raised each year so, although the bees may be evident during the summer because of more frequent flights, the building fabric will not suffer further damage until the following spring.

The gallery system constructed by a single bee will not cause any significant deterioration of the building's fabric. However, the brood raised in one year may over-winter within the galleries and in the following spring enlarge them or construct new ones.

Over a period of a few years large numbers may become established in a small area. In these circumstances damage can become much more severe and in extreme cases has been sufficiently bad to require some rebuilding.

In cavity walls the bees may construct cells within the cavity and on occasions have caused nuisance by gaining access to the interior of buildings.

As the bee's boring activities are limited to comparatively weak materials the most effective method of preventing further damage is the repointing of the walls in which the mortar joints are being attacked.

The joints need to be raked out to a depth of at least 15 mm and then pointed with a mortar that is not too strong for the brick, but sufficiently hard to discourage the bees.

For brickwork a 1:2:9 (by volume) cement/lime/sand, or 1:8 (by volume) cement/sand with plasticiser should be adequate provided it is used when frosts are unlikely. If there is a risk of frost a 1:1:6, cement/lime/sand or 1:6 cement/sand with plasticiser should be used.

For some stonework or brickwork where the stone or bricks are fairly weak a 1:1:6 mortar may be too strong, and it would be better to use a 1:2:9 or 1;9 with plasticiser and ensure that the work is done in a frost free period.

Pointing is generally best carried out during late summer or autumn. This avoids both frost and the activities of the bees. If the work can only be done in spring an insecticide solution should be injected into the gallery entrances, and the wall sprayed with the same solution after pointing to prevent attack on the mortar before it fully hardens.

In cases where the borings are in the actual stone or bricks a regular spray treatment may be the only effective method of control unless protecting the whole surface with an additional coating, such as a rendering, is an acceptable solution.

Q39: *The faces of a few sawn sandstone blocks with which a country cottage is constructed have exfoliated and some of these and other blocks have been attacked by mining bees.*

Rendering the whole of the outside of the cottage has the disadvantage of hiding the attractive sandstone and an alternative remedy of treating the surface with Ioda Phenphos suspension concentrate would have to be repeated annually.

A: This is really no great problem if attended to at once. August is the time of year mining bees can be expected to be working again.

The bee makes a hole which is quite visible, and after the hole is made lays its eggs at the bottom, and puts in a supply of nectar and pollen. Some bees actually fill the hole with food. Obviously, these holes are all made by the female.

The burrowing bee (Anthophora occidentalis), well known in the USA makes only one entry hole, but branches off from this and forms several cells, each of which at the bottom contains the larva and just above this the supply of its own pollen and honey.

The majority of Apoidea are solitary bees, each female making its own nest, and unlike the ordinary bee, there are no castes (i.e. worker, queen, or drone).

Some individuals line their cells with wax-like substance, others do not.

On the completion of the process the hole is blocked, or closed, and the mother goes on to start the process all over again.

Some species may be in flight only a few weeks having spent their earlier life cycle in their cells, as eggs, larvae, pupae, and young adults.

This type of bee has a life cycle of 12 months, but others have several generations yearly.

While normally solitary bees, their nests can be inhibited by two females, but in rare instances over 40 have been observed.

Cure, can only be obtained by constant lookout for the entry holes, and taking suitable action. Attempt to clear the hole down as far as practicable, and this can be done by means of a short steel flexible wire in an electric drill.

There are two important points to be observed, the wire must be well soldered in a short length of copper tube so that it is safe and a tight fit in the chuck. Also, the wire must not be long or it will tend to whip round onto the operator. As a further safety measure, only start and stop the drill while the wire is in the hole.

Make up a very strong cement mixture of about 1:2 mix with the correct colouring such as Cementone yellow, but here a word of warning, make up a small mix, taking great care to measure everything carefully, using about 100th of colour, and put a test dab on a stone where it will not show, then keep doubling the colour, for say four mixes, with four test dabs protected against the wet to thoroughly dry out for accurate colour test.

Start filling the holes with the required mix, tamping it down well. Unless this is well done the work will be wasted as the young bees will work their way out.

Some time before, damp down the wall with "Ajax" water to help adhesion, but here another word of warning make sure it is not blue Ajax, but clear. Use a cheap plastic banister brush for the "wetting" process as it can be used with considerable force to hit the mixture into the holes, it will last for years. Dried out later, it can be used to brush off any extra cement, and if tapped onto the cement will give it a natural look.

Having managed to get the colour matched, it is now only a matter to repair the rest of the stonework.

Make sure that the stone is thoroughly damped down, and do not carry out the repairs in sunshine, and or heat.

Everything depends upon the owner, but it is preferable to cut out the blocks which have exfoliated, and perhaps, a block can be recovered from an area which is not exposed.

A craftsman who is daily dealing with reconstructed stonework very often can reproduce matching work, but this is the exception rather than the rule. If any alterations are to be made in exterior openings try and save some of the removal material.

Often a look around the garden will produce material which has laid there for several hundred years, on exceptionally old property, where normally there is no hope of getting today matching material where it has been worked out.

Q40: *How should one go about inspecting wall ties in existing cavity walls, and how can ties be located?*

A: The most satisfactory method is the removal of bricks or other units from the outer leaf overlying suspect ties so that the ties can be inspected for corrosion. Ties within a cavity can often be inspected by removing bricks at returns or by use of an endoscope (a fibre optic device for remote inspection).

However, while part of the tie in the cavity may appear unaffected, it could be severely corroded where it is buried in the outer leaf; such inspection may not, therefore, reveal a loss of connection between leaves.

A large number of metal detectors and cover meters are on the market and many of the more sensitive types will locate ties to within about 50 mm. Before buying such equipment it is a good idea to check it out on a wall in which tie positions are known or can be verified.

Q41: *What methods are normally employed to clean stonework?*

A: Periodic cleaning can be carried out by hosing the building with water and then brushing down with a stiff brush. This is an effective method if done on a regular basis.

For more serious staining water spraying can be employed. This is done with the application of a fine spray of water directed on to the coated stone surfaces. Because the calcium deposits are soluble they soften and can be brushed off.

The length of spraying required may be from 15 minutes up to several hours before the deposits become soft enough to be removed.

Steam cleaning is another method. In this process steam is applied from a jet under high pressure on to the surface of the stone, where it softens and removes calcium sulphate deposits fairly quickly.

A dry process which can be used is sand blasting. This is carried out by blasting fine angular quartz particles under pressure from a nozzle on to the surface of the stone. The force of the particles striking the surface will remove the deposits.

Q42: *What is the difference between partition walls, party walls and compartment walls.*

A: Partition walls divide a building up into rooms and corridors. They may be a load bearing part of the structure or non-load bearing; permanent or temporary, demountable types which can be moved to give different room layouts within a building.

The party wall is a wall which divides two adjoining properties and which is common to both owners.

Compartment walls divide a building into fire resistant compartments. The walls must have fire resistance as set out in the Building Regulations and any permitted openings for ducts, pipes and chimneys, etc. must be protected against passage of fire.

Q43: *Several sections of a dry joint stone wall—the joints are filled with top soil—have collapsed during recent heavy rain.*

Quarried from Westleigh, Somerset, the stone is quite large and is in irregular shapes.

Fig. 21 is a cross section of the 1.6 m high and 43 m long wall.

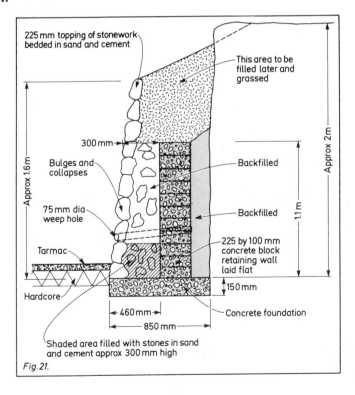

225 mm topping of stonework bedded in sand and cement

This area to be filled later and grassed

300 mm

Bulges and collapses

Backfilled

Approx 1.6 m

75 mm dia weep hole

Backfilled

Tarmac

225 by 100 mm concrete block retaining wall laid flat

1.1 m

Approx 2 m

Hardcore

150 mm

460 mm

Concrete foundation

850 mm

Shaded area filled with stones in sand and cement approx 300 mm high

Fig. 21.

A: Querist has a very difficult type of stone for walling, under any conditions, especially when only erected dry, but this type of stone makes a wonderful "pitching" (base) for roadways taking heavy traffic. I have used thousands of tons for this purpose, but never walling.

The work is being carried out in Devon which is the second wettest county in England, beaten only by Lancashire. To make matters worse "clay" has entered into the construction. Any works involving clay either as a base or backfill are much more likely to bring trouble to the owner and/or builder. So much so that in some instances the aluminium content of clay which keep it stable is lost when the clay is moved, and is artificially replaced by driving large quantities of heavy aluminium rods around the site and connecting them to a direct current in a manner similar to electro-plating, a costly undertaking only carried out by experts.

Querist is not alone in this type of failure as I saw, in Devon, an attractive looking wall, mason built, come down a few days after completion and block a road. Unfortunately, querist has made matters worse by adding a backfill in which clay and large stones are combined, especially at a time of inclement weather.

This type of stone, because of its configuration, is not really suited to this method of construction and a number of points would add considerably to its strength, if correctly carried out.

The whole of the stonework will have to be replaced, as any weak points, if left, will again eventually bring down, sooner or later, the rest of the wall, and it might be a costly matter if someone is caught by falling material. So until the work is rectified post warning notices of possible danger on the structure.

The wall will look most attractive if a mortar is made up of sand-lime and cement, (make sure the lime is well slaked and has no lumps). To this mixture add an approved colouring to give a yellow-sand effect when dry. Make up a sample mortar and dry some on a piece of metal under a grille to get the final colour (when the mixture is dry) and submit this for approval to the client. Keep this sample until the work is finalised and approved.

The joints look best if they are finished "soft", not the type of finish associated with brickwork, in fact an "old world" effect can be obtained by leaving drainage holes and planting them with rock plants. If the wall is on private property away from a public highway, and gets sun, strawberry plants can be added, to advantage to the owner.

While rebuilding, add ties back into the concrete block retaining wall. This can be done with an electric drill 18 mm (percussion) using Cyntride tipped drills.

Never include any backfill which contains clay, and it is always asking for trouble to include any unsupported stones larger than 25 mm because by their weight they will work down in the wet base after rain and cause a considerable build-up of pressure behind the wall. "Balanced" stones on the face will soon be dislodged, to eventually bring about the collapse of the wall either in places or totally.

If the method of construction was carried out under instructions, I should try and get some of the cost of the additional work back, but remember it might be said that a professional man should not have carried out the work in this manner in the first place.

If the stones, as laid, are higher than in depth then the mortar should form a backing so that they are at least equal, this applies to this type in particular. By Fig. 21 it looks as if a water trap exists at the bottom of the wall, unless the top of the shaded area slopes to the to the face work.

4 Concrete/Formwork

Q44: *I know approximately how much concrete I need for a job, but how does this work out in terms of bags of cement and quantity of aggregate?*

A: The quantity of each material needed to produce a particular amount of concrete depends largely on the mix, but a rule of thumb measure for this is that the volume of concrete or mortar is about equal to the volume of combined aggregate used in the mix.

For a 1:2½:4 mix, about 1 m^3 of concrete is produced by mixing six bags of cement, 0.5 m^3 of damp sand and 0.8 m^3 of coarse aggregate. The 1:2:3 mix yields about 1 m^3 of concrete from seven bags of cement, 0.5 m^3 of damp sand 0.75 m3 coarse aggregate.

Q45: *Is there a treatment for slippery concrete?*
Two cows belonging to a client have slipped up and broken their legs on concrete made with limestone chippings and dust about 20 years ago.
At the same time, something is required to remove green mould from concrete and brickwork.

A: Most concrete surfaces will suffer from the topping becoming smooth with wear, but if the concrete was made with chippings that are angular in shape and not round as gravel or pebbles there is a chance of cutting into the surface slightly to roughen it.

Diluted acids will do this, but great care is needed to keep a good circulation of air in the place and to well scrub off with clean water afterwards.

Builders' merchants stock cleaning fluids with an acid base; Disclean is one brand name. This is mainly used for cleaning mortar and cement stains from brickwork so it will take a certain amount of the surface off the concrete and roughen it slightly. Rubber or polythene buckets must be used and so must gloves and goggles, and the place will have to be well cleaned out afterwards.

A better bet is to hire an electric hammer complete with a tool holder with "combs" or a brush hammer tool. This will scarify the surface and so do away with the smooth surface by mechanical means. This may make dust, but it does mean that the place can be used by animals immediately after working on the floor.

The acid-based fluid will also do away with the lichen and algae, but one of the household bleaches such as Brobat or a similar hypochlorate compound will do just as well, querist will most probably use one of these or his customer does, on the farm for cleaning and sterilising. Depending on the thickness of growth it may need two coats, but it should be possible to dry brush off the growth after a week or so, then give the surfaces another treatment and it should keep clear for some time.

There are specialist firms which make these types of fluids for use in concrete swimming pools and fish ponds.

Q46: *Screeds laid in hot, dry weather on a previously laid and very dry concrete sub-floor, are showing hairline cracking.*

The new work varied in thickness from 40 mm in the centre of one room to 75 mm towards the edges. Overall, the concrete was about 60 mm.

A mix of 4:1 sharp sand and Portland cement was used and nothing was added to the water. The sub-floor was liberally soaked with water and the concrete laid as wet as possible. The floors were then trowelled off and a nice job made.

Could anything have been done to avoid hairline cracks by using an additive or a different mix?

A: Cement floor screeds can present problems unless certain basic requirements are followed rigidly and this applies particularly in hot weather periods where the surfaces can dry out before proper hydration has been completed.

I suggest that the undermentioned points should be observed if a good, even, sound, screed is to be found on completion.

1. The aggregate should be washed coarse flooring sand, a grade that does contain grit; with no silt.

2. The mix for such a thickness as 50 mm could well be made at 1 cement: 4 aggregate.

3. If there are likely to be varying thicknesses of screeds in the same area of screeding and if the sub-floor is very dry, it would be wise to well dampen down the concrete first and just prior to laying the screed brush over cement slurry, but this must not be allowed to dry up before the topping is laid.

4. The mix should be placed as dry as possible to lay it down and make a finish properly, just sufficient water to allow the mix to be squeezed in the hand without any water actually dripping from it. This will, of course, make it hard work in trowelling up the surface, but more poor concrete and screeds have been laid as a result of too much water than not enough water. All one does when the mix is wet is to work the cement to the surface, thus making the top part nearly all cement and therefore very liable to dusting with the lower part weak and nearly all aggregate.

5. In hot weather the screed/or concrete needs protecting with hessian or building paper to prevent it drying out too quickly, as this will mean that the water will evaporate out of the mix before proper hydration and set-up of the cement has taken place.

With a screed of aboout 50 mm, it needs to be a dry mix.

Use a heavy tamping board to get the screed well hammered down before trowelling, and only use a steel float if the floor coverings are to be thermoplastic or rubber tiles or sheet.

Prevent the screed from drying out too quickly and if necessary damp down with water the next day. Keep windows and doors closed to prevent drying air from blowing across the floors in certain areas.

Q47: *During warm weather, early last summer, I was pouring a storey height columns and wall. On stripping the formwork I found a darker scabby surface along the top 100 mm of the units. Can you explain the reason and how to prevent recurrence?*

A: If the formwork was examined on stripping, the 100 mm band would have shown small particles of the matrix adhering to it. The probability is that the mix when placed was fairly wet, the pour completed without undue delay so that most of the concrete was still plastic at the end of pouring.

Furthermore, if the tip of the formwork was left uncoverd, allowing water evaporation from the top to take place, the concrete would have settled under its own weight, and shrinking away from the formface has resulted in a slight plucking.

A suggested remedy is to vibrate the formwork at the top 0.3 m with a percussion hammer or even a rubber mallet, and then seal off as well as possible with polythene sheeting.

Q48: *A new concrete garage drive and adjacent footpaths have dried out a very light colour. Is there any way of toning or staining to reduce the glare?*

A: Yes, there are proprietary preparations including paints that are suitable for use on concrete or you can prepare one yourself, as follows:

Cream to rust colour: The recipe as given is a 10 per cent solution which can be diluted further to give lighter shades, particularly on white cement concrete; alternatively, several applications (to almost dry surface) will intensify colour.

Dissolve 500 g of commercial ferrous sulphate in 2500 ml of near boiling water—when completed add further equal quantity of cold water. Spray and then brush the solution over the dry plain or exposed aggregate concrete surface until absorbed, allow to dry so that further absorption can take place before repeating, finally wash off into a convenient sump hole with clean water.

Green blue: Dissolve copper sulphate, quantities as above—no need to heat the water, and apply in the same way.

Remember, the stains can work on other materials so be careful when applying.

Q49: *What are the main reasons for using release agents, and what are the main types?*

A: The main purpose of treating formwork with a release agent is to make it easy to strike the form from the concrete face. Only a few special form face materials, such as expanded polystyrene, do not need to have a release agent applied.

There are a number of different types of release agent and the various form face materials such as timber, steel and glass fibre require different release agents. It is therefore important to make sure that the right one is being used.

The three most common types of release agents are: neat oils with surfacants—mainly used on steel faces,but can be used on timber and ply; mould cream emulsions—for use on timber and ply, a good general release agent; chemical release agents which can be used on all types of form face—recommended for all high-quality work.

Because of their absorbency, new and untreated timber and plywood should always be given a coat of the appropriate release agent at least 36 hours before being used. A second application should then be made before using for the first time. For all further pours, a normal application is all that should be necessary.   Do not use oil from a container which is not clearly labelled, unless you are sure that it is a release agent. Release agents are prepared by the manufacturers to suit various requirements and their instructions must be followed carefully.

The most common fault with release agents is for too much to be put on—this can stain the concrete. On the other hand, if not enough is applied, striking is made difficult and both concrete and form face can be damaged. The right amount is a thin film applied uniformly by brush, roller, or best of all, spray.

Q50 : *How does water-repellent Portland cement differ from ordinary cement?*

A: Water-repelent Portland cement is ordinary Portland cement to which has been added a small quantity of a water-repellent additive. It has similar properties to and is used in the same way as ordinary Portland cement.

Water-repellent cement is not normally necessary in concrete since resistance to the passage of water is obtained primarily by good control of the mix and thorough compaction. It does not make concrete proof against water vapour.

Its main advantages are obtained when used in the backing coat of renderings in order to reduce and control the suction caused when applying finishing coats.

Q51 : *How much time should generally be allowed to elapse between pouring concrete and striking the formwork and what precautionary steps should be taken when carrying out this operation?*

A: Formwork can be struck when the concrete has gained enough strength to be self-supporting and also to carry any other loads that may be put on it.

The job specification will normally give guidance on when forms can be struck and these times may be governed by the size and shape of the member, the concrete mix, and the weather.

For walls, columns and beam sides, the forms can usually be struck within 12 to 18 hours of placing the concrete, but since the concrete will still be green it is easily damaged and so care must be taken. This is particularly important during cold weather when it may be necessary to leave the forms in position longer than normal.

When the time comes to strike, ties and clamps should be loosened gradually, a little at a time, to prevent the last tie from binding. As you remove bolts, ties and screws, put them in boxes—do not throw them down in the hope of recovering them later.

If the forms do not immediately come away they should be carefully prised loose using hardwood wedges. Nail bars used to lever forms from the concrete invariably damage both the concrete and the form. Blocking-out pieces are best left in as long as possible since they protect the edges; and also they eventually shrink, which makes their removal easier.

When striking soffit formwork, release the props evenly in small stages starting at the middle of the span and working out towards the supports. If you strike from the supports and work inwards, gross overloading of the props towards the centre of the span can result because of the slab or beam deflecting under its own load.

"Crash striking"—where large areas of formwork are dropped in one go—should never be allowed. It is dangerous, and not only does it cause damage to the formwork, but the structure itself can be damaged from the sudden loading.

When lowering large sections of formwork, take care to see that they are not damaged by scaffolding or other projections and that they finally rest on a level surface so that they are not twisted or misshapen.

Always withdraw or hammer down projecting nails as the formwork is struck from the concrete. Nails projecting from the timber cause untold injury on construction sites.

Make sure that other trades are kept away from areas below those where striking is being done.

Q52: *What is rapid-hardening Portland cement?*

A: This cement is chemically very similar to ordinary Portland cement but is more finely ground and, because of this, develops strength more rapidly at early ages.

The term rapid-hardening should not be confused with quick-setting. Concrete made with rapid-hardening cement stiffens and initially hardens at a similar rate to that of ordinary Portland cement: it is after the initial hardening that the strength gains more rapidly.

This quicker rate of strength development enables formwork to be struck earlier. For this reason rapid-hardening cement is often used by precast concrete manufacturers or when a job on site has to be finished specially quickly.

This cement produces more early heat than ordinary Portland cement and so can be used to advantage in cold weather to offset the effects of low temperature. It should be stored and used in the same way as ordinary Portland cement.

Q53: *What are clamp vibrators?*

A: These are vibrators which are fixed to the external sides of shuttering and when operating vibrate whole sections of shuttering.

They are very useful when casting large sections of concrete, but special provision should be made to reinforce the shutters and supports to withstand the vibrations. They are also used on shutters for precast work.

Q54: *How does one make concrete for building-bases and pools waterproof?*

A: Good quality concrete rich in cement is virtually waterproof but with the passage of time, dampness may seep through. There are admixtures formulated to make concrete water-resistant but the most effective way of ensuring that water does not penetrate is to lay it over a polythene membrane.

Lay sand over the sub-base, put the membrane over the sand and place the concrete on top, making sure that the polythene extends up round the edges of the slab.

Q55: *How thick should one make a concrete drive?*

A: Thickness of concrete driveways depends on two factors; the type of load they have to withstand and the sub-soil in the area.

If the sub-soil is firm – a stony or sandy soil – 100 mm of concrete would be sufficient for drives that support cars or light vans.

If the sub-soil is poor – soft clay or very light soil – the slab thickness should be increased to 125 mm, and if the drive is to have commercial vehicles parked on it, the above thicknesses should be increased by a further 50 mm. These recommendations are based on the 1:2½:4 mix.

Garden paths or bases for paving slabs need only be 75 mm thick but it is advisable to use the 1:2:3 mix.

Q56: *How should formwork be cleaned after it has been struck?*

A: Formwork should be cleaned as soon as it has been struck and not left until it is needed again.

Timber and ply forms should be cleaned with a stiff brush to remove dust and grout; a timber scraper should be used for stubborn bits of grout. Do not use steel scrapers on ply or faced ply. With grp and other plastics, a brush and wet cloth are all that should be needed.

When steel forms are to be put in store or are not going to be needed for some time, they should be lightly oiled to prevent rusting.

Timber and untreated ply should also have a coat of release agent applied for protection if they are not going to be re-used immediately. At the same time, any depressions, splits and nail holes should be repaired with plastic wood, or similar material, followed by a light rubbing down.

Unwanted holes should be over-filled with a suitable filler such as plastic wood and then sanded down to a smooth surface.

Q57: *Could you let me have the name of any product on the market that will remove cement from paving slabs? Cement has been allowed to get onto coloured paving slabs.*

A: If it is dry cement powder on the slabs, this can be readily removed by brushing with a stiff brush and then washing the surface of the slab with water.

However, if it is rock hard mortar on the slabs this is more difficult and can often leave a stain on the slab when removed. First you may like to try a small cold chisel and a hammer if the mortar blobs are large enough and of a suitable shape to give a purchase to the chisel. This method could remove the bulk of the mortar.

To take off the residue a drilling sanding disc could be used or perhaps formic acid such as that used for kettle de-scaling. The acid should be dabbed on the mortar with a soft brush but take care not to get acid on the surrounding surface of the paving slab. Obviously, the normal precautions when dealing with acid should be strictly observed.

After a time remove the mortar which has been softened by the acid and then brush on some more. Repeat this process until all the mortar has been taken off and then wash the slab thoroughly with clean cold water.

Q58: *How should one make a concrete slab for foundations for a garage?*

A: The minimum thickness for a garage floor slab on a firm sub-soil base is about 100 mm; in poor loadbearing sub-soil it should be 125 mm.

Footings beneath walls should be made twice the thickness. The transition between floor slab and wall footings should be gradual and not squared-off.

If the building is prefabricated, the manufacturer's recommendations for foundations should be followed.

Q59: *How should dry lean concrete be cured?*

A: Just like ordinary concrete – and in fact more important because of the small amount of water in the mix – loss of moisture has to be prevented in order to stop the surface of the lean concrete from becoming weak.

This is best done by the spray application of a bituminous emulsion or a cut back emulsion. Spray it on at the rate of about one litre for every m^2 so that the lean concrete surface is evenly and uniformly covered.

Because it is important that the curing membrane is applied as soon as possible, make sure it is done within one hour after compaction has been completed. By using simple masking board, you can avoid spraying kerbs if they have already been laid. After applying the membrane, blind it with a thin layer of concreting sand.

Alternatively, and only for small areas, curing can be done by covering the lean concrete with plastic sheeting, but do make sure that it is properly held down at the edges to prevent its being blown off; any joints in the sheeting should be lapped at least 300 mm. Keep the sheeting in place for seven days.

Generally, lean concrete should not be laid during frosty weather because additional protective measures will have to be taken. If it is laid during the cold weather, then insulation quilts or loose straw held down by plastic sheeting will have to be used.

Q60: *What treatments can be used to repair concrete floors with faulty dpc membrane, or a floor with no membrane at all? Is it possible to carry out a chemical injection similar to that for dpc's?*

A: There is no really effective way of chemically injecting in this case.

Assuming the problem is not too severe, that is, that the hydrostatic pressure is not too great, the answer could be to paint the floor with a good epoxy coal tar paint – two coats will normally do. If the pressure is too high it will force the paint up before it has cured.

First you should check the degree of dampness on the floor. One way of doing this is to leave a rubber mat on the floor overnight, making sure the floor is dry first. Check the next day, and if the moisture content on the mat is fairly low it should be all right to paint.

The painting should be done in warm weather. Heat the room and completely dry out the floor before starting to paint. Once the paint has been applied, keep the room temperature up high for 24 hours to allow it to cure.

Q61: *What is the purpose of underpinning and under what circumstances is this type of work likely to be necessary?*

A: Essentially, underpinning transfers the load carried by an existing foundation to a new foundation at a lower depth.

It may be necessary when settlement of the existing foundations has occurred due to such factors as uneven loading, movement of the sub-foundation due to moisture movement, action of tree roots or deterioration of the foundation concrete by sulphate action or similar.

Underpinning may be carried out to increase the load-bearing capacity of the foundations, either to allow for the building on of additional storeys or to allow for an increase in the superimposed loads of the structure – many renovation jobs require this type of work.

It may also be undertaken to allow the level of the adjacent ground to be lowered, for example, when constructing a new basement.

Q62: *What is the cause of grout fins? Should they be removed, and if so, how should this be done?*

A: Grout fins occur at leaking formwork joints either between or within individual pieces of formwork. With board-mark-finished surfaces (fairly rare these days), such fins are not often detrimental and may even be considered a desirable feature, but on most other surfaces they are unwanted.

If they are not objectionable when viewed from a distance of about 2 or 3 metres they are best left untreated, especially if they are narrow and do not protrude from the surface by more than about 2 mm.

However, such grout losses and water leakages are usually accompanied by a darkening of the surface and where leakage is excessive there is likely to be a sandy-textured surface, some 5 mm or more in width, each side of, and along the length of, the fin.

Where the grout fins have to be removed this is best done by hand, striking very carefully with a hammer and bolster held at an angle to the root of the fin to remove it cleanly. This may leave a line of sandy-textured concrete which, if no more than about 2 mm wide, is usually best left untreated.

If the fin is also accompanied by surface darkening and a wider sandy-textured area, and has to be disguised it is possible to take remedial action.

Q63: *Are there any instruments which can be used to give details of the density and thickness of concrete when applied to the surface of, say, a floor slab?*

A: Thickness: When the far side of the floor cannot be reached, e.g. placed on the ground, there is no instrument that measures its thickness as yet on the UK market.

Some years ago in the USA a radar set was shown measuring thickness on road slabs, but this was unlikely to be cheap or easy to use.

Where it is possible to hold a steel plate against one side of a floor, wall or door less than about 300 mm thick, a sensitive cover-meter can be calibrated to estimate its thickness.

Density: A nuclear gauge can be used accurately and in a few minutes to give density and moisture contents of fresh concrete and hardened concrete, although for density it is desirable to lower the probe into a hole in the concrete.

Such a gauge cost between about £1500 and £4500 and requires a locked store for overnight storage of the radio-active sources, (one source for each property being measured). The operator must have a day's training in its use.

Q64: *At what age should concrete be tooled?*

A: It is difficult to lay down a hard and fast rule for when to tool concrete, as it depends largely on the mix, the type of cement and aggregate used in the mix, and the time of year when the concrete is placed.

The important thing is not to begin tooling too soon, as otherwise there is a danger that particles of coarse aggregate will be dislodged, causing pitting of the surface.

The maximum size of aggregate also influences the age at which tooling should be started: aggregate of 10 mm maximum size is more likely to be torn out by early tooling than 20 mm and larger aggregates, because it has a smaller surface area for the matrix to hold on to.

Concrete made with ordinary Portland cement should normally be tooled when it is at least three weeks old, the actual time being governed by site conditions. For example, it is often found advisable to delay the tooling until other trades have finished their work, when the danger of the surface being damaged or stained by rust or mortar drippings can be avoided.

To obtain the most consistent finish, tooling should be carried out when the areas of concrete to be tooled are as nearly as possible the same age.

Q65: *What is sulphate-resisting cement and in what circumstances should it be used?*

A: Sulphate-resisting cement is mainly used in concrete exposed to sea-water or concrete below ground level where sulphates are known to be present in the soil or ground weather.

The durability of concrete and its resistance to all forms of chemical attack depend primarily on its being dense, impermeable, and well compacted. Lean mixes tend to be more permeable than rich mixes and when sulphate-resisting Portland cement is used the cement content of concrete using 20 mm maximum sized aggregate should not be less than 280 kg/m^3 and the water/cement ratio should not be higher than 0.55.

It will usually be found necessary to increase the cement content above this figure if the water/cement ratio is not to be exceeded, in order to provide a reasonable workability so that the concrete can be compacted.

The strength properties of this cement are similar to those of ordinary Portland cement and it should be used and stored in the same way.

Do not use calcium chloride or admixtures containing calcium chloride with this cement because the resistance to sulphate attack is thereby reduced.

Q66: *In order to get a good construction joint it is important to have the surface of the hardened concrete free from laitance. Can you suggest the best ways of removing laitance from horizontal surfaces, i.e. the tops of walls and columns?*

A: There are a number of ways of removing laitance from the tops of walls and columns. The main objective is for the surface to have an exposed aggregate appearance.

The easiest way is to brush off the laitance while the concrete is still fresh but has stiffened slightly. The timing is quite critical because it depends on the weather and the mix – in warm weather concrete stiffens quicker than in cold weather and a rich mix stiffens quicker than a lean one. The best time will usually be about one or two hours after the surface water has evaporated.

Use a small brush to remove laitance while gently spraying the surface with water. It is worth having two brushes to hand – one with soft bristles and one with harder bristles in case the concrete has stiffened more than expected.

Make sure that you brush gently so that you do not undercut or dislodge pieces of the course aggregate – just the tips of the aggregate should be showing.

Another method is to remove with a jet of combined air and water. This can be done up to about six hours or more after placing, but timing is again critical and will depend on the pressure as well as the concrete and weather. If you use this method too early you will dislodge the coarse aggregate particles.

If the laitance has hardened but is still green – say the following morning – a wire brush and some washing will usually be enough to remove it. Wash it well afterwards to remove the dust.

If the surface has hardened enough for wire brushes to be ineffective, then mechanical scabbling must be used. Small hand-held percussion power tools, such as those used for tooling exposed aggregate finishes, or a needle gun are the best to use.

The danger with this method is that it can shatter and weaken coarse aggregate at the surface or loosen the larger particles, so do not do it until the concrete is more than three days old and then only carefully.

Wet or dry sand-blasting is usually only suitable when very large areas have to be treated.

An occasionally used method is to spray a retarder on to the surface of the concrete to 'kill' the set, so that the laitance can be brushed off the following day or later. This method is not recommended because it is difficult to be sure that all the retarded concrete has been removed – if it has not, fresh concrete cast against it can be affected with a resulting poor bond.

Once a surface has been prepared and cleaned, keep it clean. When washing, try to avoid laitance running over and down the surface of the concrete.

Q67: *Are there any time restrictions on placing and compacting concrete?*

A: Many specifications place limitations on the time permitted to elapse between mixing the concrete and placing and compacting it.

Concrete can be placed and compacted at any time after mixing provided that it is still workable by the compacting method available, even if some loss of workability has taken place.

For example, if a poker will sink into the concrete under its own weight and the hole closes up as the poker is withdrawn, then that concrete can still be compacted.

No fixed time limit can be applied to all concreting operations because the actual time will depend on the stiffening of the mix which in turn depends on the richness, on the temperature (both ambient and of the concrete itself) and on whether a retarder has been used.

On cool damp days, most concrete is still workable three to four hours after mixing, whereas on warm dry days, and especially with rich mixes, 30 minutes may be the limit.

Q68: What is the best way of storing formwork to prevent damage to the various components?

A: After all formwork has been cleaned, and oiled where necessary, panels and components should be properly stored and protected until they are wanted again. Unless they are going to be re-used immediately do not leave them lying around because they will only be damaged or used for something else (timber has a great ability to 'walk' off site!).

The main rule about storage is to avoid any damage. More damage happens to formwork when not in use than when it is being erected or struck.

Care taken in stacking formwork panels prevents damage and avoids unnecessary repairs. The orderly storage of formwork and components is essential if later work is to proceed without delay.

Panels and plywood sheets are best stored horizontally on a flat base so that they lie flat without twisting and should be stacked face to face to protect faces.

Large panels are usually best stored on edge in specially made racks.

Loose wailings and soldiers are best numbered and stored with their respective panels. Numbers painted on panels make their identification easier.

If formwork is not to be used immediately, the stacks should be protected from the sun and weather by tarpaulins or plastic sheeting in such a way that they are still ventilated.

Small components, such as bolts, ties, wedges and keys, should be kept in boxes; larger components like clamps and props should be stacked off the ground to prevent them becoming covered with mud.

Fire extinguishers in working order should always be easily accessible to storage areas.

Q69: Can you tell me what kinds of curing compounds are generally available and how do they work?

A: Curing compounds are liquids sprayed onto concrete and have the advantage that they can be used on both horizontal areas of fresh concrete and vertical surfaces after the removal of formwork.

Most commercially available curing membranes consist of a resin in a solvent such that, after application, the solvent evaporates leaving behind on the surface of the concrete a thin continuous film or membrane of resin which seals in most of the water in the concrete.

The resin film remains intact for about four weeks, but then becomes brittle and peels off under the action of sun and weather.

They were developed for roads and airfield pavements which are difficult and impractical to cure satisfactorily by any other means, and they are now used extensively for curing structural concrete but there are some occasions when they may not be suitable.

Most proprietary makes are available in various grades, usually a standard grade having what is termed a curing efficiency of 75 per cent and a better grade having a curing efficiency of 90 per cent. Both are pale amber/straw in colour.

In addition, both grades are usually available either with a white or aluminiumised pigment or containing a fugitive dye; the white and aluminium powder pigmented types are specifically for external paved areas where the pigments reflect the sun's rays, so reducing the amount of heat absorbed by the concrete from the sun.

Those containing a fugitive dye make it easier to see where the membrane has been applied and that it has been applied uniformly. The dye quickly disappears after application and will not stain the surface provided that it is not applied to a dry concrete surface.

Special non-toxic compounds are available for use on concrete which is to contain drinking water.

Generally, and certainly in Great Britain, the pigmented higher efficiency grades should be used for external paved areas with the non-pigmented lower efficiency grades being used on structural concrete. It is essential on any job to make sure that the right type of curing membrane is used. Because the resin film breakdown is caused mainly by bright daylight, concrete surfaces which will not be exposed to such conditions should not be treated with a curing compound if they are to receive additional concrete (as at construction joints), renderings, screeds or paint type decorative treatments which require a positive bond.

Q70: *Can you outline the methods of providing fixings into concrete. There are so many products, it is difficult to choose the correct one.*

A: There can be little of less use than an insecure fixing in concrete! Much of the work in providing fixings and fastenings is carried out in adverse conditions of wind and weather. Fixings are attempted above, between and below tidal level using the massive armoury made available by the supplier of proprietary methods and sytems.

Fixings have generally been unremarkable until latter years with the advent of powder actuation – the use of resin anchors and of course, the use of sticky stuff.

Consider the problems of fixing and fastening to concrete and you are faced with technologies varying from the 'stoneage technology' of the concrete material to the sophisticated technologies of metallurgy, plastics, synthetic resins and explosives as well as the pure mechanics of the simpler systems.

There is an immense lack of knowledge of the simple facts of fixing technology.

The problems of selection are immense, made more complicated in many instances by popular misconceptions.

This is an area where the 'law of Dr Sodde' and 'O'Henry's precept' are proved and reproved daily on construction sites across the country. For those unfamiliar with O'Henry his precept stated that 'on the whole, Soddes law was optimistic!'.

Consider the base material, concrete. Concrete is a mobile material affected not only by temperature, humidity and stress, but also by creep, and the combination of these factors. Concrete is rarely, in spite of specification, true to line and level or plumb.

There are inherent inaccuracies in concrete construction, those arising from movements, and induced inaccuracies arising from men and their methods of construction. 'Dr Sodde' has so arranged things that these inaccuracies combine to make fixing and fastening a problem, the solution of which requires all the combined skills of the designer, constructor and the practitioner.

One major hurdle which must be overcome by all concerned in their attempts to provide sound fixings, is the 'seven tonne syndrome'. Take any system and the catalogue will state the capacity of the fixing – however achieved as being seven tonnes (or 70 KN, or some other figure!). It is essential that we realise however, that this capacity will only be achieved when the concrete in which the fixing is made has achieved a specified strength.

The strength of concrete most usually quoted is the magic 28 day characteristic strength, and this 28 day strength is that used as the basis for the establishment of the capacity of the greatest number of fixings – concrete does not always develop the magic strength for a number of reasons!

Not all concrete is alike – although in the minds of many construction workers concrete is concrete. Concrete may in fact be produced in densities ranging from 800 kg/m^3 to something approaching 4000 kg/m^3. The characteristics of fixings made (where possible) into these concretes will be wide ranging indeed!

All fixings are designed with a particular function in mind, their means of introduction into the concrete varies from being cast into the fresh material to being drilled in or fired into the concrete from a pistol. The fixing is required to be located with some degree of accuracy and having been located must stay there.

Many are the obstacles to the achievement of this apparently simple aim. Reinforcement is frequently present and remarkably its position often coincides with that of the intended fixing. Some concrete is strong enough to resist the strongest charge or the toughest drill.

Fixings are frequently specified at minute centres or too close to arises. The forces, to be sustained by the fixings are often of a different nature to that anticipated in the early stages of design; intermittent loading, loads which introduce some element of bending as well as tension, all these problems come to a head at the time of decision making.

What can be done to reduce the problems to surmountable proportions?

1. Compare like with like.
2. Consult the supplier.
3. Take note of recommendations regarding compatibility.
4. Establish test criteria.
5. Ensure jig-setting of cast in components.
6. Protect threads and plug holes.
7. Observe requirements of cover for both reinforcement and fixing.
8. Specify torque for threaded connections.
9. Take advantage from the reinforcing steel in the concrete to supplement the cast in fixing.
10. Read the instructions.

Q71: *I understand that observations have shown that generally poker vibrators are not used as efficiently as they should be. Could you outline the correct use of these tools?*

A: A study by the Cement and Concrete Association indicated that pokers do often run wastefully, or at a reduced efficiency, for about 7 per cent of their operating time, this being made up of 15 per cent out of the concrete and running, 35 per cent wrongly positioned in the concrete, and 20 per cent vibrating already compacted concrete.

It is, therefore, essential to plan the compaction in advance, along with the placing method and technique, so that both operations are done as economically and as quickly as possible.

There are a number of points to be considered. Make sure you can see the concrete surface – lights may be required in deep sections. Put the poker in quickly; when inserting it, allow it to penetrate to the bottom of the layer as quickly as possible under its own weight. If done slowly, the top part of the layer will be compacted first, making it more difficult for the entrapped air in the lower part to escape to the surface.

Leave the poker in the concrete for about 10 seconds. Withdraw it slowly – the main thing is to see that the hole made by the poker is closed up, otherwise you will be left with a hole in the finished concrete. If this does happen, and it may be difficult to prevent if the concrete is very stiff, put the poker back in near enough to the hole for the next spell of vibration to close it up.

For the final insertion, withdraw the poker even more slowly and wiggle it about to ensure that the hole closes up properly.

Generally, the poker should be put back in not more than about 500 mm away from its last position. With the smaller diameter pokers closer insertions will be needed.

Avoid touching the form face with the poker. Not only will the form face be damaged – 'poker burn' – but a mark will be left on the finished concrete surface. To be on the safe side, keep the vibrator about 75–100 mm from the formwork.

Avoid touching the reinforcement with the poker. Provided that all the concrete is still fresh, vibrating the reinforcement should not do any harm and could improve the bond. The danger lies in the vibrations in the reinforcement being transmitted into parts of the section where the concrete may have stiffened, in which case the bond may be affected.

Avoid using the poker to make the concrete flow. Avoid sticking the poker into the top of a heap; although heaps should be avoided in placing they are sometimes unavoidable or caused by mistake. To flatten a heap, insert the poker around the perimeter. Do this carefully to avoid segregation. Remember that compaction starts after the heap has been flattened.

Make sure that the poker extends about 100 mm into any previous layer – this will knit the layers together and any laitance on top of the lower layer will be mixed with the bottom of the top one.

Put the whole length of the poker head into the concrete – this is essential to keep the bearings cool. Avoid leaving the poker running when it is not in the concrete, otherwise there is a risk of bearings overheating, and avoid sharp bends in flexible drives.

Remember that where finish is important, a little bit of extra vibration can reduce the number of blowholes.

Finally, make sure the drive motor will not vibrate itself off the staging – do not move it by pulling the flexible drive – and make sure the poker is cleaned after use.

Q72: What are the effects of low and freezing temperatures on concrete?

A: Low and freezing temperatures have two effects on concrete, both of which can be harmful and have to be guarded against.

Firstly, if freshly placed concrete cools below freezing point, the expansion of the water as it freezes will cause permanent damage to the concrete, making it useless. Even after concrete has hardened it can still be permanently damaged by frost action when it is young and has not developed much strength.

However, for all practical purposes it has been found that, provided the concrete is allowed to achieve a st. ength of about 5 N/mm^2, it can then largely resist the expansive forces caused by the water in the concrete freezing. For most mixes, this critical strength is achieved after about 48 hours at or above 5 deg. C.

Secondly, after concrete has reached a strength of about 5 N/mm^2, low temperatures will slow down the strength development. The strength of a typical 25 N/mm^2 concrete kept at 2 deg. C for seven days is less than half that of similar concrete kept continuously at 20 deg. C and remains lower for several weeks.

The two main objectives during cold weather are therefore to keep the concrete warm for the first 48 hours after placing so that it can achieve a strength of about 5 N/mm^2, and to ensure that the strength is permitted to develop even though at a lower rate than at high temperatures.

Provided that these two objectives can be satisfied, concreting can be done during cold and even freezing weather conditions.

External paving is particularly vulnerable to the effect of low air temperatures because the concrete is laid on cold ground and its surface area is large in proportion to its volume.

Q73: What checks should be made to formwork before the concreting is started.

A: Provided that a sound formwork method has been devised and that the work has been done in accordance with the planned intentions of the persons responsible for the work, a successful casting should result.

In the interests of accuracy and safety, however, a careful and thorough inspection should always be made by the supervisor as soon as the work is finished and before concreting starts. This inspection should include, where applicable, answers to the following questions.

Are bolts and wedges secure against loosening due to vibration? Has the right number of ties been used and are they in the correct places? Are all the ties properly tightened? Are all inserts, void formers and cast-in fixings in the right position and secure? Have the stop ends been properly secured? Have all the joints been sealed to stop grout loss – especially where the formwork is against a kicker?

Is the formwork correctly aligned and level? Are all the props plumb and at the right-spacing? Are the props and struts properly tightened up and locked? Can the formwork be struck without damaging the concrete? Has the release agent been applied and is it the right one?

Is the reinforcement correct and does it have the right cover? Are there enough spacers? Are the forms clean and free from rubbish or odd bits of timber or metal? (Tie-wire droppings will cause a stain on the face of the concrete.)

Is there proper access for concreting compaction? Can necessary inserts or box outs be done when concreting? Is all the ancillary equipment available, such as vibrators, lighting, skips and hand tools? Is the curing equipment and covers ready, especially in winter? Have all the necessary guard rails and toe boards been provided?

On completion of the initial checks by the tradesmen and supervisors concerned, the work will normally be inspected by the Clerk of Works or the Resident Engineer, before concreting is allowed to begin.

The above checks, combined with a general check on the security and tightness of forms, can save accident and injury or even loss of life.

Q74: What is the purpose of air-entrainment and what improvements does it make to the properties of fresh concrete?

A: After compaction, normal concrete will usually contain about one per cent of air, this unwanted entrapped air being unevenly distributed and consisting of bubbles of irregular shape and size.

Intentional air-entrainment introduces a controlled amount of air (normally about five per cent by volume) in the form of millions of small bubbles of uniform size and uniformly distributed throughout the concrete mix.

These minute bubbles act as small ball-bearings in fresh concrete and greatly improve the workability. For example, if an air-entraining admixture is added to a normal mix with a slump of 50 mm, the slump would increase to something over 150 mm.

However, this move workable concrete would lose about 20 per cent of its strength because every one per cent of air, whether accidentally entrapped or deliberately entrained, produces a four per cent loss in strength.

However, if the water content of this higher workability concrete is reduced to bring the slump back to 50 mm, most of the strength loss will be regained. Entrained air will also improve the cohesion of harsh mixes and reduce segregation and bleeding.

Q75: How important is it that steel to be used for reinforced concrete is completely free of rust? What effects will rust have on the concrete and how can problems be avoided?

A: The strength and performance of reinforced concrete depends on a good bond being achieved between the steel and the concrete, therefore the steel must be in a good condition when the concrete is placed around it.

All reinforcement needs to be kept clean from excessive rust, grease, oil, mud, mould, oil, loose mill-scale, loose concrete and ice.

Steel should not be left exposed for any length of time once it is fixed, otherwise rain will wash off some rust onto the formwork which will then leave a permanent stain on the concrete once the formwork is struck.

Starter bars from the tops of columns and walls are a frequent source of rust staining on concrete below. So, if they are going to be exposed for more than about two weeks, cover them with plastic sleeves or paint them with a cement grout wash.

Mortar droppings or grout droppings do not need removing from reinforcement providing they are firmly adhering.

The effect of rust on the bond between steel and concrete is often a controversial issue on site, and sometimes rust is removed unnecessarily at great expense.

In fact, a little rust is not harmful, but loose mill-scale and excess flaky rust not firmly adhering should be removed. Normal handling will remove excess rust and usually removes mill-scale – the same effect can also be achieved by dropping bars, or cages, to the ground.

Similarly, if there is any concern about starter bars which have been projecting for some time from existing concrete, a firm tap will knock off any excess.

Steel which has been stored outside for a long time may have rusted to the extent that the diameter has been reduced. This does not often happen, but if there is any doubt then check the diameter with a gauge or, more accurately, by weighing a length of about 300 mm.

Q76: *Under what circumstances are retarding admixtures used? What are these admixtures made up from and how much generally should be used?*

A: Retarders slow down the setting and early stiffening of the concrete so that it stays workable for a longer time than it otherwise would.

The main active ingredients in these materials (which are usually liquids) are either hydroxcarboxylic acids and their salts, or unrefined lignosulphonates containing sugars. They act by forming a film around the cement grains, thus slowing down the initial reaction between the cement and the water.

The length of time during which a concrete remains workable depends on its temperature, workability and water/cement ratio. Retarders may be useful in warm weather, when the temperature is higher than 20–25 deg. C, to prevent early stiffening and loss of workability, which would otherwise make placing difficult.

When a large pour of concrete will take several hours to complete and must be constructed without cold joints, a retarder helps to keep the concrete workable for longer.

Other times when these may be useful are when slipforms are being used or when a long delay, around half an hour, is likely between mixing and placing.

The dosage for each 50 kg of cement in the mix will be small – 0.1 to 1.0 litres – with the actual amount depending on the length of retardation required which in practice will usually be between two and six hours.

Trial mixes are essential. The seven day and 28 day strengths are not likely to be affected, except by over-dosages, but the strength at 24 and 48 hours may be reduced and so influence formwork striking times.

Always add the retarder, through a dispenser, at the same time in the mixing cycle – retarders added towards the end of mixing can lead to considerably greater retardation than a similar dosage at the beginning.

Q77: *How much can the water content of aggregate affect the final concrete mix? If this does have an adverse effect how can the water content be controlled when the aggregates are stockpiled?*

A: The amount of water in the aggregate is very important because it will affect the total amount of water in the mix. A wet batch of aggregate will make the concrete mix wetter, and too wet a mix makes the concrete weaker.

Although this can be compensated for to some extent by the person responsible for mixing the concrete, it is easier said than done to make these allowances. Obviously the ideal is to get the mix right first time.

It should also be borne in mind that if the water in the mix is not kept constant the workability, as well as the strength, will vary from mix to mix.

Variations in the moisture content arise not only between fresh deliveries but also from changes in the weather and storage time in the stockpile. Although it is difficult – and sometimes impossible – you should aim at keeping the moisture content in the aggregate constant. One way of doing this is by keeping stocks of aggregate as large as possible and letting them stand for at least 16 hours before being used so that excess water has time to drain out.

Gravel aggregates are usually damp or wet when delivered to site but, because the excess water can drain away fairly easily, the moisture content does not vary too much and so does not have a large effect on the concrete mix.

Similarly, crushed rock coarse aggregates, which are usually delivered dry, do not have much effect on the water content of a concrete mix. Only in special circumstances is it necessary to stockpile coarse aggregates for some hours before using them.

It is the sand which usually causes the problems due to changes in the water content. If the sand is regularly received in a wet condition and the loads vary widely in their moisture content, extreme care must be taken.

A sand which has been stockpiled and allowed to drain for about 16 hours will have a moisture content of about 5 per cent. However, sands are usually delivered with moisture contents between seven and 10 per cent and even up to 15 per cent, so you can see that this will have a big effect on the mix.

With sands in particular, and especially where a high standard of control is being exercised, try to have two separate stockpiles so that one can be draining while the other, which has already been drained, is being used.

However, two sand stockpiles are rarely practicable or economical on any but the very big jobs and this is one reason why it is often more difficult to achieve good control on smaller jobs.

In any case, try to avoid using the bottom 300 mm to 600 mm of any stockpile because this is the part which will have gradually become saturated with water, especially in the case of sand.

Leave this layer at the bottom to act as a drainage layer for the rest and keep to the upper part of the pile which will have a more consistant water content. Another point here is that the bottom layer of a stockpile will have often collected dirt and dust washed through from overlying layers and would not be suitable for good concrete in any case.

Q78: *Can you set out some guidelines for the placing and compacting of concrete in walls?*

A: Establish in advance from the reinforcement and other drawings that there are not likely to be problems in placing concrete or in getting the pokers in. If reinforcement cannot be rearranged, decide just how the concrete will be placed and compacted and, having decided, tell the concreting gang so that they each know exactly what is to be done and how it is to be done.

With a good cohesive mix and freedom from obstruction, concrete can be dropped from the top of the formwork. However, it must not come into contact with the form face – baffle boards at the top are useful for this.

It is essential to be able to see the concrete being both placed and compacted: in thin sections, some lighting is necessary.

If the height of pour exceeds 3 m, make sure that the flexible hose or power line is long enough for the poker to get to the bottom.

Place as uniformly level as possible, avoiding heaps and inclined layers. If skips are being used, control the discharge – do not drop a full load all at once, it will only segregate. The skip should be moved horizontally along the line of the wall – this is not easy and needs care.

Pay particular attention to the placing and compaction of the first layer of concrete on the horizontal construction joint or kicker – it should not be thicker than 300 mm.

Allow for the time it takes to move the poker horizontally from one insertion point to the next. With through bolts and other obstructions, the poker head may have to be withdrawn to the top of the formwork before being lowered again for the next insertion. For a 6 m length of wall with insertion points at 400 mm centres, at least three pokers will probably be needed.

For thin (300 mm) wall, it may be best to have a continuous banker board along the top on which the concrete can be placed before being shovelled into the form.

At stop-ends and vertical construction joints, good compaction is essential. One way is to have the poker about 300 mm from the joint or stop-end and feed the concrete carefully and slowly to it. Another is to move the concrete in a tongue towards the joint – in this case, vibrate the concrete after moving it.

Q79: *Could you please explain why it is necessary to compact concrete? I know it loses strength if not compacted properly, but do not know the 'science' behind this fact.*

A: After concrete has been mixed, transported and placed, it contains entrapped air in the form of voids. The objects of compaction is to get rid of as much unwanted entrapped air as possible – down to less than 1 per cent is the aim.

The amount of entrapped air is related to the workability; concrete with a 75 mm slump contains about 5 per cent air, while concrete of 25 mm slump contains about 20 per cent. This is why a low-slump concrete requires more compactive effort.

It is important to remove this entrapped air for the following reasons:
— Voids reduce the strength of the concrete. For every 1 per cent of entrapped air, the strength falls by about 5 to 6 per cent. So a

concrete with, for example, 3 per cent voids will be about 15 to 20 per cent weaker than it should be.
— Voids increase the permeability, which in turn reduces the durability. If the concrete is not dense and impermeable, it will not be watertight, it will be less able to withstand mildly aggressive liquids, and any exposed surfaces will weather badly.
— Voids reduce the contact between the concrete and the reinforcement and other embedded metals; the required bond will then not be achieved.
— Voids produce visual blemishes.

Q80: *Can you give guidance on construction joints, i.e. where fresh concrete has to be placed on or against concrete which has already hardened?*

A: Whether or not a good bond is required at a construction joint, the placing and compaction of fresh concrete on or against a joint needs particular care and attention.

Poorly compacted or honeycombed concrete at the bottom of a lift in a wall or column leaves both a weak and an unsightly joint.

First, any dirt or dust must be removed from the surface of the concrete as these would act as a separating layer. Similarly, any sawdust, pieces of wood, nails and bits of tie wire must also be removed. This can best be done by blowing out all the dirt and rubbish with a compressed-air hose. If compressed air is not available, it will have to be brushed out thoroughly.

This cleaning should be done before the formwork is erected, but if there is still some debris left after erection remove it by taking out one of the stop ends.

The use of mortars or grouts, or wetting the face of a joint, on prepared concrete surfaces is not recommended for the following reasons.

● Tests have shown that the bond between the hardened and fresh concrete is not significantly increased.

● The restricted access to a horizontal joint at the bottom of a lift for which the formwork has been erected makes it difficult to make sure the grout or mortar has been uniformly applied. In any case, it needs to be scrubbed into the surface to be effective.

● It is virtually impossible to apply mortar or grout to a vertical joint – especially when the formwork is in place.

● There is a danger the grout or mortar will dry out before the concrete is placed. Any drying out would simply mean that you have put back the laitance which you may have already carefully removed.

• The appearance of the joint may be spoiled by a line of different colours.

Q81: *Is it normal practice for drivers of ready-mixed concrete trucks to add water to the mix when on site?*

A: Concrete mixed at a depot, either in a central mixer or in a truck mixer, should arrive on site with the ordered workability. No extra water should need to be added.

Some suppliers using dry batching add the water when the truck arrives on site and it is then the driver's responsibility to add only the amount of water which he has been told to – and this should be on the delivery ticket.

All drivers of truck mixers have instructions that no extra water is to be added to the mixer unless specifically required and signed for by the purchaser.

When the site asks and signs for additional water to make the concrete more workable, the supplier cannot be held responsible for the concrete mixing a strength specification.

Do not allow unauthorised people to have extra water added. Concrete that is not within the tolerances of the ordered workability should be rejected.

The important thing is to have a responsible person supervising delivery. It is not unknown for drivers to add water near the end of delivery to 'clean out' the drum, and so speed up the turn-round time at the depot.

Q82: *Can jacks be used to move precast concrete units on site?*

A: The use of jacks to move units is not common, but there are some instances where this method is suitable.

Whenever jacks are used they should be of adequate strength and capacity to raise safely and hold the load. Steel or hardwood wedges should be used to provide an additional safeguard when a unit is required to remain raised for some time, and whenever practicable adjustable steel props should be used.

When jacking up a unit the foreman should ensure that the jack is sited on a firm level base. If jacking from a floor ensure that the floor is capable of safely supporting the jack and the weight of any load being raised.

The most common use of jacks is in conjunction with adjustable steel props to break the frictional bond between wide slab units and their bearing, so that barring over can be carried out more safely. When carrying out this type of jacking, the person who operates the jack should ensure that the adjustable prop is held vertically.

The unit should not be raised by this means more than is sufficient to break the bond, normally a matter of a few millimetres.

Q83: *When concrete is being poured into formwork what measures should be taken to spot likely problems and, if possible, remedy them before they are allowed to do any damage? If grout runs do appear, how can they be removed?*

A: Someone experienced in the construction of formwork, preferably a tradesman, should always be standing by when the concrete is being placed so that he can keep an eye open for any dangerous situations and deal with them effectively.

To do this, he should have a supply of suitable materials such as props, bolts, etc, to cope with any emergency.

Tell-tale devices and stringlines should be fixed at appropriate positions so that a continuous check can be made on alignment, camber and plumbness while the concrete is being placed.

The vibrations transmitted to the formwork can be considerable and can loosen wedges and fixings; a close watch should therefore be kept on all fastenings to see that they do not work loose. Similarly, wedges should be regularly checked and tightened.

Timber spreaders to hold formwork apart – as used in walls – should be removed as concreting proceeds.

Where unsleeved bars are being used to form holes, ease them before the concrete sets, and remove them as soon as possible afterwards: if the bar is left in overnight it is more difficult to strike the formwork without damaging it.

Imperfectly sealed formwork at a construction joint will allow grout or mortar to run down the face of the completed work. If the grout cannot be wiped off immediately, it should be left until it has become brittle enough to be removed by careful chipping with a piece of hardwood or a bolster. This can usually be done in such a way that the grout run is removed cleanly and the underlying surface is not damaged.

5 Damp/Decay

Q84: *Could you tell me what causes damp and mildew in bedroom wardrobes, on a solid or cavity, with or without pebbledash etc.*

A: Forming a non-vented cupboard, i.e. a wardrobe against an internal skin of an external wall, will produce condensation on the wall, due to the extra insulation afforded by the cupboard.

This, unfortunately, will happen both on cavity or solid walls. To overcome this problem, a false back which is ventilated by a through draught (i.e. vents) should be installed. This will enable the surface temperature of the wall behind the cupboard to be the same as the rest of the room and will eliminate moisture on the cold wall.

Q85: *I have the job of installing a fitted wardrobe in a bedroom that suffers from condensation, three walls are external. Can you tell me the best method of building the wardrobe, showing how to prevent condensation occurring along the back?*

A: The only way to prevent condensation is to provide adequate ventilation. This is the main reason why condensation is such a problem in centrally heated houses.

Set out to provide adequate ventilation in your wardrobes right from the beginning (Fig. 22).

Fit plywood backs, 6 mm is thick enough, leave a space between the ply and the brick wall and fill it with glass fibre, 12 mm is enough.

Through the brickwork and ply, etc., form a duct, closed on the outside with a 225 mm by 225 mm air brick, square hole or louvre,

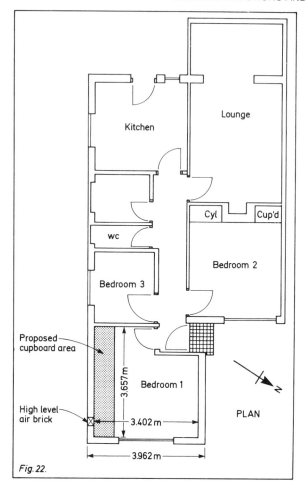

Fig. 22.

and closed on the inside with fine copper or brass wire mesh, fine enough to keep out the creepy-crawlies. Form two of these ducts, one at low level, as low as possible, and the other at high level, as high as possible. Put them as far apart as you can.

Somewhere just above the low-level duct fit a holder switch, etc., for a 25w mains powered electric lamp. Fit a shield around the lamp formed or either perforated zinc or wire mesh and giving about 150 mm space around the lamp. The shield is to prevent clothes, etc., from touching the lamp.

The lamp will consume very little current. The type to use is called "Pygmy". You should keep it on permanently.

Clothes hung in the closet will always be damp — from perspiration — from rain and other things. The lamp will provide the necessary current of air and will dry the clothes and keep the closet quite dry.

Q86: *How do I tell the difference between wet and dry rot?*

A: Timber affected by wet rot will be saturated, dark in colour and any cracking will be in the direction of the grain. Timber that has been destroyed will be dark brown when wet, and break down into slime when touched. Any threads that appear will be yellowish at first, turning to deep brown or black.

The tell-tale signs for dry rot are grey web-like strands of fungus. If the timber is badly ventilated and the surroundings moist, the fungus will spread quickly — working through the timber and cracking the surface across the grain. The affected area of dry rot often spreads much wider than is visible.

Q87: *A dividing wall between the entrance hall and men's toilet in a six-year old social club is showing bad stains on the entrance hall side. The single brick wall is plastered and wallpapered.*

On the toilet side there is a urinal stall against the wall and although it is well fitted and all joints are in good condition, it is believed to be the cause of the trouble. The stains are about the width of the urinal.

The clients do not want the expense of resiting the urinal on an external wall and an effective way of treating the brickwork from the entrance hall side is required.

A: While it may be possible to alleviate the damp stains showing through for a time by applying a surface preparation I feel that only some form of separation of the existing wall with a finishing material will stand the test of time.

The suggestion I would make is to strip off the wallpaper and clean down the wall and then to fix Newtonite bitumen lath over the whole area affected and then replaster. This would give a complete separation from the existing plaster/brickwork and there would be a certain amount of air space between the bitumen lathing and the existing plaster face so that it would allow the probable slight amount of salt moisture to clear itself.

One other form of surface treatment that may help in this matter is the hydro epoxy resin-based emulsion types of paints. They need a clean surface and two coats to ensure a full cover and have to be mixed on site as they are two-pack cans.

Q88*A stone/brick/double-glazed extension to a house is to incorporate a swimming pool and there is concern over the possibility of interstitial condensation occurring.*

The extension will be about 18 m by 6 m and the pool about 8 m by 3 m. The greater part of the outer walls will be of cavity construction — stone on the inside and lightweight insulating block on the outside, with the cavity filled with foam insulation.

Is interstitial condensation likely to arise? It is presumed that it means the possibility of condensation forming on the inside walls and, as a result, spoiling the stonework. It is difficult to understand how this can happen with good insulation from the blocks and the foam insulation. Presumably any dew point must be well to the exterior of the wall.

Moreover, it is assumed that because of the insulation the inside of the stonework is as high as the temperature of the atmosphere above the pool — and therefore hot and sometimes moisture-laden air is not effectively in contact with the cold surface — thereby causing condensation.

A:The very basic cause of condensation, wherever it happens, arises from the fact that warm air can hold more water vapour than cold air. If warm moist air meets a cold surface it is cooled and gives up some of its moisture as condensation.

Air containing a large amount of water vapour has a higher vapour pressure than drier air, and therefore readily disperses towards dry air. Escape may be through windows, doors and gaps, but vapour can also pass through many building materials. If in passing towards the outside it meets cooler surfaces, then it may condense within the structure.

Vapour pressure will drive water vapour through all except completely impermeable materials and there can be conditions within a wall sufficiently cold to cause condensation to occur, giving rise to structural damage. Interstitial condensation may occur even when surface condensation is absent. (Fig. 23).

When there is an impermeable barrier at the inside surface to prevent the passage of vapour, interstitial condensation is not

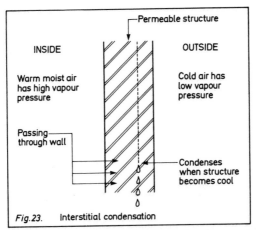

Fig.23.   Interstitial condensation

possible. However, completely impermeable vapour barriers at the inside surface of a wall are not easy to accomplish, but a partial vapour check is better than nothing.

When some form of composite construction is used every effort must be made to keep as much of the structure as possible in a warm condition. If possible insulation materials are better placed as near as possible to the outer face. If insulation is placed near to the inner face it may be desirable to protect it on the warm side by a vapour barrier.

It is possible to design to avoid interstitial condensation, and this involves a certain amount of calculation, references to graphs and tables in addition to the preparation of a diagram.

Such a diagram is shown in Fig. 23A.

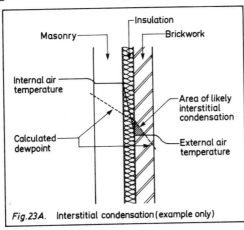

Fig.23A.   Interstitial condensation (example only)

It is obvious why the internal surfaces of the walls be bathing pools are as impervious as possible, and that should they present an absorbant surface interstitial condensation is more than a possibility.

Essentials in the construction in an indoor bathing pool are:

a. Quick removal of water vapour by ventilation, possibly fan-assisted.

b. Room walls and ceiling surface as impervious to water vapour penetration as is possible.

c. Highest possible insulation standards.

Q89: *Different types of damp-proofing to a proposed bungalow with a retaining wall of about 1.2 m, which also forms the rear wall, are shown in Figs. 24 and 25.*

There is a difference of opinion with the local building inspector as to which is the more suitable of the two.

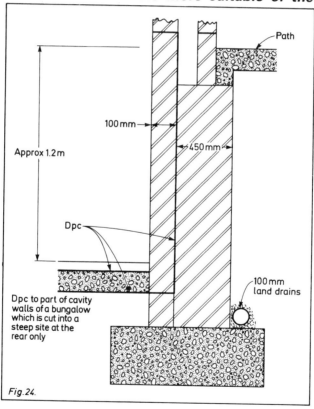

100mm

Approx 1.2m

450mm

Path

Dpc

100mm
land drains

Dpc to part of cavity
walls of a bungalow
which is cut into a
steep site at the
rear only

Fig.24.

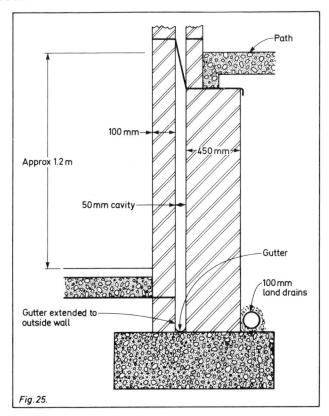

Fig.25.

A:I see several problems with the method in Fig. 25.

(a) The 450 mm wall will always be damp, possibly wet at times and the air in the cavity will become very humid.

(b) This humidity will penetrate into the 100 mm skin and if there is heating in the internal room then evaporation will almost certainly take place into the room.

(c) The cavity in these circumstances will serve little value as an insulant.

(d) Wall ties present a hazard should they have the slightest mortar dropping thereon, or develop slimy growths.

(e) The gutter may readily be partly choked by slimy growths which I would also expect on the faces of the walls in the cavity.

With regard to the method in Fig. 24, I wonder, if the floor and wall are correctly tanked, whether the upper dpc in the floor is required. In this respect there is no information in the query regarding materials to be used.

I would select the method in Fig. 24.

Q90: *Excessive condensation is occurring in the kitchen of a house (Fig. 26) built close to the sea on a beach oversite in 1830.*

External walls are half-brick thick rendered and Sand-texed. These are two windows which are usually kept shut and no ventilators. It is suspected that there is no dpc.

Internally, the walls are rendered and plastered and covered with 3 mm polystyrene and wallpapered.

The floor is solid stone and appears to be the original. It has been lino tiled and has a vinyl covering over this. Condensation occurred between the two layers causing damp spots at the bottom of the outside walls. The vinyl covering was removed and within 12 hours the lino tiles curled and lifted off the floor.

The ceiling is of t & g boarding and an oil stove is used for heating.

A: It would seem from the details given that everything possible in this kitchen is contributing to the condensation problem.

The walls are only half-brick thick, rendered inside and outside, so there is no insulation on these areas.

If there is a dpc, by now it would have perished, so no help here.

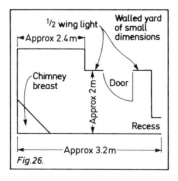

Fig.26.

An oil stove is used for heating, probably the worst type of heating appliance one could choose for creating moisture vapour in the place, and no ventilation.

The floor is solid stone, again there would be no dpc membrane as it was not usual to lay this type of floor with one and again, by now it would have perished.

Now to sort out some items which would help to reduce the condensation.

1.   Remove all the lino tiles and as much of the adhesive as possible and coat over the whole floor with an epoxy pitch type of cold-applied membrane, giving the floor a good round coat so that it does fully cover the floor. If the floor is uneven first lay over with one of the special floor levelling compounds, such as cold-applied epoxy pitch compound and **Aquaseal No. 10**. These are two-part compounds.

Then one could lay over with a proper adhesive thermoplastic or other tiles or sheet material, but the floor coverings must be laid in an adhesive, loose-laid coverings will always give rise to condensation between the floor covering and the solid floor.

2.   Fit a ventilator in one of the windows, this could either be an electrically-operated one or a Ventamattice could be used, these operate by wind pressures and are quite useful, but obviously the electrically operated ones are more effective as they can run at any time.

3.   The thin sheet form of expanded polystyrene is not in my opinion thick enough to give any degree of insulation, if good insulation is needed, and I feel it is. The sheets should be at least 13 mm thick, they could be stuck on with Synthaprufe or similar bitumen-based compound and then papered over.

As an alternative the walls could be battened out with deal, pre-treated timber and then lined with polythene-backed plasterboard and decorated as required. Keep the plasterboard clear of the floor finish.

4.   Introduce electrical heating or use the existing chimney for an inset solid fuel fire or a gas fire as long as it is vented into a flue (a balanced flue could be used), but on no account fit one of the unflued so-called portable gas fires, for they are as bad as oil heaters.

5.   If the matchboard ceiling cannot be insulated from above with an insulating quilt 50 mm thick, then again the ceiling could be lined with expanded polystyrene tiles. Make sure to use the types labelled "Will not support spread of flame," and use at least 13 mm thick tiles.

Q91: *After laying vinyl floor covering over red tiles in the kitchen of a semi-detached house built in 1937, damp patches appeared on single brick walls and after several weeks extended to the hatched area shown in Fig. 27.*

Floor boards were removed at "x" and found as Fig. 27. Since removing damaged plaster with the intention of containing the area, it does not appear to move any further upwards although bricks show dark with moisture. Near the pantry door there is a considerable amount of white powder in certain brick joints.

In the morning the moisture content showing through the paper is high, but it reduces by evening.

The vinyl was removed from the kitchen and moisture from rain was found beneath the covering near the outside door and water had fallen behind the sink unit, which is against the wall. Around the house is concrete sloping towards the house. There is ample air circulating around the base and below the floor boards.

A: In a house built in 1937, where quarry tiles have been used to form the floor finish in a kitchen or similar room, it was not the general rule to place a dpc membrane over the base concrete, the actual tiles being regarded as reasonably waterproof if laid in a

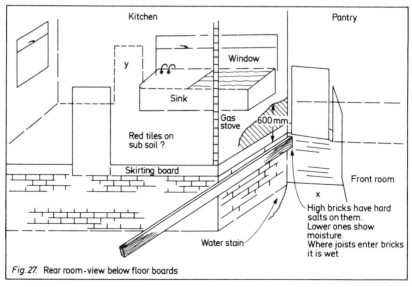

Fig.27. Rear room-view below floor boards

cement mortar. Thus there could well be some moisture rising above floor levels on the inside of these walls.

The fact, too, that "salts" are showing indicates that moisture is present and after a period of over 30 years one would have thought all these salts would now have been dissipated if the walls had gradually dried out. I am rather surprised, too, that the brickwork is wet underneath the wood joists of the suspended floors, this surely points to a breakdown of the dpc in the walls or the lack of one at all. Where suspended floors are formed, the dpc must be underneath the joists.

Again, it is stated that the concrete path slopes towards the house. Is this path above dpc lines or is there so much water that it is soaking through the brickwork and filling up the cavity? Has the cavity been checked at these levels?

Any form of sheet floor coverings placed loosely over quarry tiles or thermoplastic tiles for that matter will set up condensation between the floor and the floor coverings. If it is necessary to cover the tiles, one of the special floor levelling compounds should be used and then the floor could be tiled over, but the tiles must again be laid with a suitable adhesive.

While it may appear that there is ample air circulation under the suspended floor, there is a fair area of solid floor and this does mean that some corners just do not get any air circulation. If this is allied to some rising moisture (is the ground heavy wet clay?) then it can easily mean that certain areas of the walls become damp and activate salts in the mortar and plaster, obviously some bricks, or sand contain more salts than others.

Points to consider, then, are:

1. Check to see if the cavities around this area are clear.

2. Check to see if the dpc if functioning.

3. Make sure that there is an air brick right close to the solid floor at points marked X in Fig. 28.

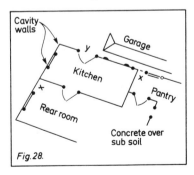

Fig. 28.

4. Remove any salt-affected plaster, dry brush down the walls, treat with two coats of Synthaprufe or Aquaseal (dry dash the second coat over with sand) and then replaster with a cement/sandbased plaster, but do leave the wall to dry out as long as possible. If this job can be carried out in dry weather, so much the better.

5. If possible, ensure that surface water from the concrete path does not run on to the walls.

Q92: *A car park running along one side and across one end of a timber framed t & g clad building 42 m long by 15 m wide, has been successively built up over the years and is now up to or above the dpc between the timber framing and concrete foundation.*

Could you suggest a suitable method of applying a vertical dpc to the cladding? It is appreciated that the car park immediately against the building will have to be excavated away.

I have several rolls of asbestos dpc. Is this suitable for the purpose?

A: Fig. 29 shows what could be expected to be found at present, a plate set on a damp-proof course and overhanging the foundation concrete so that the boarding can form a drip.

Fig. 30 is my suggestion. Plug a batten to the foundation concrete — this batten should be preservative pre-treated — the

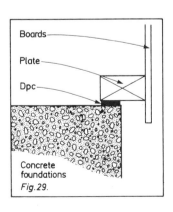

Boards
Plate
Dpc
Concrete
foundations
Fig.29.

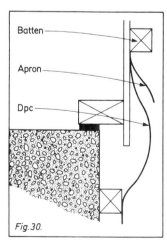

Batten
Apron
Dpc
Fig.30.

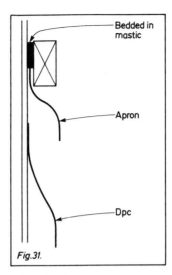

Fig.31.

Labels in figure: Bedded in mastic, Apron, Dpc

damp-proof course should be close copper nailed to this, the asbestos dpc will do fine. This damp-proof course is carried up as far as it will go and then secured to the boarding with open copper nailing.

Fig. 31 is an enlarged detail of the top of Fig. 30. It shows an apron of damp-proof course material. The apron is secured by having a batten fixed over it, and to stop rainwater penetrating behind it is bedded in mastic. The bottom of the apron is not secured.

The new concrete should, of course, be kept below the apron.

Before fixing the damp-proof course you should give the concrete foundation and the boarding and plate three coats of Synthaprufe or something similar. Carry this Synthaprufe up above the top batten.

Q93: *What are the types of beetle which attack timber, how do they cause the damage and how does one deal with infestation?*

A: Figs. 32 and 33 show the kinds of beetle that attack timber, although generally it is their larvae or grubs that do the damage.

The beetles usually lay their eggs in cracks in timber, in open joints, old exit holes, rough sawn surfaces and surfaces where the grain has been torn up by planing.

The eggs hatch in a few days or weeks and a cream-coloured grub — the larva — emerges from each egg. It burrows into the

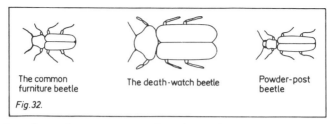

The common furniture beetle

The death-watch beetle

Powder-post beetle

Fig. 32.

wood and continues to tunnel and eat through the timber for one or two years and often for much longer.

When fully grown the larva changes into a pupa for a few weeks and then into a fully developed beetle which gnaws its way out of the timber, leaving the tell-tale exit hole on the surface. Then, the life-cycle begins again.

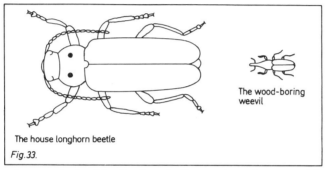

The wood-boring weevil

The house longhorn beetle

Fig. 33.

New 'worm holes' in timber indicate that the wood has been under attack for at least a year, and that some beetles have already left to spread infestation.

Insecticides brushed over the surface and worked well into the cracks and crevices will kill eggs and newly hatched larvae, but the problem is bringing the insecticide into contact with the larvae which have burrowed deep into the timber.

Larvae which escape contact may emerge as adult beetles since, while a surface layer of insecticide may prevent further egg-laying, it may not kill every emerging beetle. However, a single thorough application normally eradicates woodworm in softwoods.

Q94: *I am living in a new bungalow (nine months old) and mildew has appeared in two bedrooms on the walls and also on the furniture. The rooms face east and there are no fireplaces as it has gas central heating. Could you advise on the best way to deal with this problem.*

A: This is a classic problem. The mildew is almost certainly caused by condensation. You have really diagnosed the problem: gas central heating, no fireplaces, (and double glazing?). The price we often pay for keeping warm and conserving energy is all too often condensation because the house is not properly ventilated.

Try to keep the heating at a consistent temperature — it is better to have it on low all day than to suddenly turn it up high twice a day. Leave a fanlight open, or doors ajar and the difference will be quite noticeable.

It is difficult to recommend a remedy for the mildew without knowing the extent of the problem. It may be necessary to re-decorate the walls, and to treat the furniture with proprietary products (when they have dried out) — but do make sure that the condensation has been eliminated first or you will be back to square one.

Q95: *What can cause staining on wallpaper once it has been hung?*

A: There are several possible causes of staining. Moisture from a damp patch will carry salts and impurities to the surface of the paper leaving a brown stain round the edge of the patch. The source of the dampness must be found and rectified and the surface allowed to dry out thoroughly before redecorating.

Slow drying past in cold rooms or surface condensation will encourage mould growth and discolouration of the printing inks. Some form of heating will usually help to avoid this.

Unsealed steel nail heads will cause rust staining. All exposed nails or screw heads should be sealed with oil paint.

Starch past allowed to contaminate the face of the paper will cause staining, as will marks made on the back of the paper with ballpoint pens or indelible pencils — always use a black lead pencil to mark the paper or the wall.

Q96: *Can you indicate how woodworm attacks can be detected?*

A: Much trouble and expense can be saved if woodworm attack is detected in its early stages, for once established in a building, it can spread rapidly.

It is a good idea to inspect timber and furniture every year, preferably during warm summer weather when the beetles are likely to be most active. Look for the typical exit holes and for small piles of powdery sawdust-like material (frass) expelled from the workings.

Pay particular attention to damp or out of the way spots in under-stair cubby-holes; roof spaces; skirting, floor and window boards; woodwork under sinks and baths; and to the backs and undersides of furniture.

Dampness, incipient decay and excessive sapwood all make timber more susceptible to attack.

Q98: *Can any effective measures be taken to prevent woodworm attacks on timber?*

A: Much can be done to discourage beetle infestation simply by sound construction; for example, proper ventilation for all timber.

Timber can be protected against all timber-boring beetles (and at the same time from rot) by treating with a preservative before use. In certain districts where the house longhorn beetle is prevalent this is a Building Regulation.

The best treatment is to have the timber cut to size and then pre-treated by a firm specialising in the process. The wood may be pressure-treated with water-borne salts or treated by vacuum or dip processes with organic solvent-borne preservatives. Timber which has been treated while still green with boron preservative is also protected against wood-boring insect attack.

Pre-treatments are available which will not 'bleed' from the timber or stain plaster, have no persistent smell and can be painted over. Creosote is a useful and inexpensive preservative for sheds and outbuildings — though it is generally unacceptable within dwellings because of its smell and staining properties.

If you have to cut or bore timber after it has been treated, be sure to brush preservative generously on every cut surface.

Treating timber with preservative by spraying, brushing or cold dipping is not as effective as the methods covered above, since only a surface layer of wood is impregnated with preservative and if the timber subsequently cracks or splits, beetles and rot spores can gain access to untreated wood.

Q99: *The difficult problem of condensation and the use of vapour barriers has arisen again. I have a client who has a residential property constructed in solid 200 mm brickwork, with a bedroom on an exposed corner, which suffers from condensation problems.*

Accordingly, he proposes to batten plasterboard to the external walls, incorporating an insulating material between the battens.

I would be grateful if you could advise if it is necessary to incorpoate a vapour barrier and if ventilation to the area behind the studding needs to be considered. Do the same principles apply to vapour barriers, and flat, board and felt roofed constructions?

A: Battens for dry-lining should be pressure impregnated with a preservative and fixed to the wall with non-corrodible nails. Narrow strips of dpc material should separate the battens from the brickwork. A vapour barrier, for example sheet polythene, should be fixed over the battens before fixing the plasterboard.

Foil-backed plasterboard is an acceptable second best . The vapour barrier must be as air-tight as possible — if practicable without perforations to accommodate services or fittings.

There should be no need to ventilate the cavity so created, but if this is insisted on, as only a vapour diffusion outlet is needed and not a through flow of air, ventilation holes should lead to the outside at low level with none at high level.

Unlike a solid brick wall which is never completely waterproof and allows some air diffusion, a roof covering has to be impervious to air and water. Furthermore, the materials from which flat roofs are built are likely to be more sensitive to moist conditions then is brickwork.

It is essential that a boarded and felted flat roof be maintained free of moisture on the cold side of the insulation. To achieve this ventilation to outside air of the space above the insulation is necessary.

The correct position for a vapour barrier is on the warm side of the insulation. Cavities on the warm side of a vapour barrier should not be ventilated to outside; to ensure that the underside is warmed to room temperature, there should be free circulation of internal air up to its level.

Q99: *A local church has called me in to see if I could give them some advice over a very bad case of condensation. The main problem is the roof which is constructed of pre-stressed concrete trusses with two concrete purlins running down each side of the church.*

During this last spell of weather the water has been dripping off these purlins onto the congregation also staining the oak pews rather badly.

There is also a problem with the windows which are formed with concrete mullions. The windows are double glazed; the plasterwork beneath the windows is badly stained. The roof space is completely open, there are no opening windows at high level only at head height.

The heat is by five gas radiant heaters fixed to the lower purlins. Would fitting air vents at a high level help? Would covering the concrete roof purlins with timber or polystyrene help? Also what would cure the condensation on the window mullions?

A: Gas heaters themselves burn giving out moisture into the air, therefore you may be fortunate enough to cure the condensation by natural ventilation. Are the radiators ventilated both in and out? If not, they will cause condensation.

The best way of dealing with condensation on the purlins in the roof space would be either of the following methods;

1. Fixing a mechanical extractor fan at one gable end, but the noise aspect of this should be considered. If the purlins are clad with polystyrene or timber, the condensation will form on either the rafters or the underside of the roof covering.

2. By providing non-mechanical air vents to both gable ends to allow a through passage of air at high level. Unfortunately you will have a heat loss, but you will not have drips!

To rectify the condensation on the windows, it is recommended that a 50 mm air gap between the concrete window frame and mullions may be maintained by a timber sub-frame structure and the double glazing to be fitted to this frame keeping the air gap constant so that you do not create cold spots for the condensation to form on the windows.

Q100: *Would you advise me of the best method of inserting a dpc in an old building with solid walls approximately 450 mm thick. There seem to be various methods all claiming to fit the bill.*

A: All the methods of damp-proof coursing that you mention have their own merits, one is as good as another. It all comes down to costs and the person who actually does the work.

Since you do not state the material of the walls, choose the most suitable and go ahead. There is no greater comeback from a company which has an Agrément Certificate, it merely means that the product attains a certain standard.

Q101: *The problem concerns a new bungalow with conventional roof structure. The property has double glazing throughout, full gas central-heating and 100 mm Fibreglass insulation laid between ceiling joists in loft space.*

The client has complained of severe condensation in the loft to the extent that damp patches are appearing on the ceilings. Heat must obviously be escaping into the loft space, but how?

A: Condensation within the roof space can be caused by lack of sufficient through-air passage. If there is not sufficient air circulation above the insulated ceiling then the fluctuation of air temperatures and the heat on the roof from the sun causes condensation to form on the coldest point, i.e. the insulated surface.

1/100th of the roof space volume should be given to through ventilation by means of vents. The Swedes, who use timber framed housing on a large scale, allocate 1/5th of the roof space volume to ventilation.

Q102: *I have a cottage on the Isle of Skye which is faced with white Skye marble chips, and I am having a problem with dark patches appearing due to moss. Could you advise me as to a preparation to kill the moss without reacting with the marble?*

A: The best method to kill moss and lichen on stone work and roof without affecting the surface of the material is set out below;

1. Brush surface with stiff bass broom to remove all loose debris.

2. Apply a strong moss killer. This can be obtained from most large builders' merchants or ordered direct from the manufacturers (i.e. Grangers). Apply the solution, with a large garden spray, taking all precautions as per manufacturer's instructions.

3. Leave for a period of three weeks and brush off all dead moss and lichen.

This will leave a sterile surface on which the moss spores cannot germinate.

Q103: *The front elevation and the chimney stack above the roof is constructed of Welsh slate. About 150 mm above the lead flashing, on two surfaces of the chimney white staining has occurred which has begun to stain the concrete roof tiles. The chimney is constructed with flue liners surrounded by at least 120 mm thick slate, the joints which are affected by the white staining have been cut out and repointed, but the substance still finds its way through. The flue is used for a gas fire. The bungalow is built near the coast.*

A: Without a detailed examination of the chimney it is only possible to make general comments about the problem. Most chimney staining is black or, at least, dark in colour and can usually be attributed to the formation of tar-like deposits in the upper part of the flue, due to condensation of flue gases and smoke on the interior surfaces of the chimney when the flue is cold. Your particular problem with white staining is unusual.

One possible explanation is that the white staining may be caused by the lime used in the brickwork's mortar leaking through the joints between the brick courses. You do not mention what kind of mix was used but, if this is the cause of the trouble, it would be reasonable to suppose that the richer the mix in lime the worse the problem is likely to be.

The bungalow is evidently in an exposed position on the coast and therefore the chimney stack is likely to be exposed to driving rain. The two surfaces of the stack where trouble occurs are presumably exposed to the prevailing wind.

It would probably be worthwhile inspecting the stack and, in particular, the capping. It should bridge the gap at the top of the stack making a watertight seal. The terminal (chimney pot) no doubt goes through this capping. Pay special attention to the capping itself. Is it a properly constructed capping of good quality concrete of the pre-formed kind and is it still in good condition? If so, there are two main points to watch. Does the capping fit the top of the stack properly and does it rest securely on the top course of brickwork with a weatherproof bed of mortar? Also, does the terminal fit properly where it passes through the circular hole in the capping and is the joint around the terminal still sound and in good, weatherproof condition? The capping should be slightly domed on its upper surface to drain any rain which falls from it.

Also examine the base of the terminal to see that it is not cracked as this might let in water which could wash out lime in the mortar.

The object of your inspection will be to find out whether or not the chimney is in good, weather-proof condition. If it admits the rain, the white staining is likely to continue if it is due to lime seepage. In extreme cases a suitable cowl over the top of the terminal may prove useful although if the chimney is lined (and if the lining is still in good condition) it is unlikely that water would enter at the top of the terminal in sufficient quantity to cause the trouble.

When you have done everything you can to prevent water getting into the chimney and washing out the lime, you may need to demolish the existing stack and rebuild, if you consider the white staining of the roof tiles too bad to tolerate. In this case you may care to consider one of the ready-made stacks available.

Q104: *What is the best method of removing moss and ivy from stone bridges?*

A: Moss grows in damp situations but the presence of ivy indicates that the joints and pointing have eroded. Two different treatments are necessary.

For moss, remove as much as possible with blade scrapers and wire brushes, dilute Gloquat C to the maker's specification and apply with sprayer on a course setting as a flood coat, from top down in 100 mm bands.

Leave for one to two weeks then brush off dead growth with bristle brush.

Then spray Nurosol 20 diluted to maker's specification: after absorption by the residue of the growth, spray on a second coat.

For ivy, cut off main stem(s) near ground level—the plant will eventually die but will take two years to do so. To hasten destruction, cut a frill girdle on the stem base and coat with a paste made from ammonium sulphate crystals (obtainable from Boots Agricultural Supplies). The top growth should be cut and removed in sections, care being taken to remove from joints with minimum of damage.

Q105: *Can you help me to solve a problem involving dampness on the inside wall of a chimney breast. My* *customer has dampness on his bedroom wall. I have had a cursory look from outside and the tiles, soakers and flashings appear to be satifactory. After rain dampness appears on the wall which suggests that rain is coming in rather than being drawn through the brickwork.*

A: Without examining the damp chimney breast concerned there is no definitive answer. However, you have examined the building from the outside and, presumably, the chimney breast within the room. Since you say that the tiles, soakers and flashings look satisfactory, you believe that the trouble is more likely to be due to rain getting into the building — particularly the chimney breast — than to some other cause.

Usually dampness or discolouration appearing on a chimney breast is due to condensation within the flue which leads to a deposit of tar-like substances on the flue's lining. This sometimes works through the brickwork and causes dark staining. However, your case seems to be different and I think you are probably correct in believing that the dampness is worse after rain and is therefore likely to be coming in from the outside.

Dampness appearing on chimney breasts is most often found on houses between 60 and 100 years old. If the damp patch appears only after heavy rain, I think you should look at the stack's flashings more carefully. It is possible that the chimney is sited in the wrong position from the point of resisting the weather. Defects in the damp proof course or the flashings may not necessarily be obvious. If this is the cause, to provide a really satisfactory remedy it may be necessary in some instances to dismantle the stack.

Generally, however, dampness is due to the presence of salts in the plasterwork where the patch appears in the house. If the chimney breast is papered chemical analysis of a piece of the wallpaper at the seat of the trouble may disclose that the trouble is due to deliquescent salts, particularly chlorides. In modern houses chimney liners prevent the transfer of dampness from within the flue to the outside of the chimney breast.

I think you should inquire from the householder whether the dampness is really worse after heavy rain. If it is, then you should examine the roof, the state of the tiles and the flashings very carefully indeed. But if the householder agrees that the discolouration is not worse after heavy rain, then you should suspect that the trouble is due to condensation within the flue — especially if a solid fuel appliance is being used. In such a case the remedy may be to line the chimney.

Q106: *Please state methods which can be employed to prevent rainwater penetration at threshold level.*

A: 1) Fit a water bar into the top step and use a rebated bottom rail on the door.

2) Fit an aluminium threshold which has a compressible pvc insert in the top of it, the door being cut at an angle so that the pvc insert is pressed tightly against the bottom of the door.

3) Incorporate a gutter in the top step under the door. This gutter will have a perforated grating over it and a drain-off pipe through the step.

4) A hardwood timber threshold bedded on mastic and screwed down on the top step will form a water bar and as the door closes on top of it there is clearance for the carpet.

Q107: *Can anything be done to save a timber fence once it has been badly affected by rot?*

A: A timber fence has a couple of points which are vulnerable to attack by wet rot. The gravel board can be easily replaced, but the post will begin to rot after a few years just below the ground level and the arris rail will decay where moisture can collect, i.e. in the joint between post and rail.

If a fence has become unstable, remedial action should be taken as soon as possible — strong winds may blow it over and a fence can often be beyond repair if this happens.

The base of the post can be replaced by a concrete spur which is set in concrete and bolted to the post. Some strutting will be required while the spur is being fixed, although the time to fix the spur is before the post has rotted through and become unstable.

A galvanised sheet-steel bracket can be used to replace this joint on the end of the arris rail.

Q108: *A house built around the turn of the century has damp patches on the chimney breast. What is the likely cause and what remedies are available?*

A: If the damp is apparent after rain, then it is probably due to an absent or defective damp-proof course or flashings in the chimney stacks. Examine the dpc, flashing and chimney stack for defects and carry out repairs as necessary.

It may be that the chimney pot and/or its bedding on the stack is defective, allowing penetration of water. If so, replace or re-bed the pot.

If an open fire is used, then the damp may be due to chemical action. For badly affected areas techniques involving covering, relining or replastering are possible.

If a solid fuel, gas or oil-fired boiler is used, the problem may be condensation in an unlined flue. The condensation can be reduced by lining the flue with an impervious liner or flexible metal pipe, depending on the type of appliance.

Q109: *What types of fungus attack timber?*

A: Many types of fungi affect timber, but only three types occur to the extent that they involve and affect the average craftsman.

On new timber the most obvious is the blue or sap-stain fungus which feeds on the starches and sugars contained in the sap (especially softwood). The fungus will only develop when the moisture content is above 20-25 per cent. It does not weaken the timber, but the staining does reduce the value of joining timber and even more so when the joinery is to be polished or varnished.

Damage by sap-stain fungus is often prevented on joinery grades of timber by dipping it in a suitable fungicide soon after conversion but before the initial drying.

The most destructive of all common wood fungi is dry rot; it will spread rapidly in poor ventilated areas where the moisture content is above 20 per cent. The filaments or strands of the fungi can travel through porous plaster and brickwork.

The name 'cellular' fungus is often used to describe wet rot. It will only exist and grow where the timber is wet. Unlike dry rot it will not affect the timber beyond the wet areas, and if the dampness can be prevented the fungus will die.

6 Drainage

Q110: *Excavations for an extension have revealed a circular honeycomb brick soakaway with a dome shaped roof.*
How was this constructed? It is proposed to build a new soakaway in the same way.
How was the term 'pig' for uneven brickwork introduced?

A: The soakaway encountered during excavations had obviously been provided in place of a land drainage system from a septic tank or other form of private sewage treatment plant, where there was insufficient land for land drains to treat the effluent from the tanks.

In order to retain the soil and allow for maximum soakaway, this was constructed of open brickwork, it being a domed roofed tank prior to the use of reinforced concrete. The open brickwork was similar to the construction provided for sleeper walls for ground floor suspended wooden floors (Fig. 34).

The term pig for uneven brickwork comes originally, I believe from the term used in the brick manufacturing industry. Pigs being hand-made bricks fired in a small kiln alongside the main kiln. This small kiln was referred to as a pig perhaps because of its size and shape, and as these hand-made bricks were uneven, the term pig was passed on through the bricklaying trade as referring to uneven brickwork as well as uneven bricks.

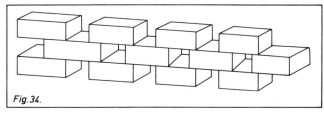

Fig.34.

Q111: *A septic tank which has worked well in treating horse manure and been unopened since its construction in 1931, has not previously handled kitchen or bathroom waste. Now it is intended to divert kitchen waste into it.*
What would be the effect of detergents, etc., in the waste water? Would the bacteria be destroyed and the breaking down process stop, with the tank becoming clogged and inoperative?
The tank is sealed and could not be emptied.

A: I am not very convinced that bacteriological action in a septic tank itself does much good. I feel that the bacteria in the surrounding soil through which the overflow from a septic takn passes has a much more positive effect on cleaning the effluent.

It is true that detergents contained in such discharge may have a detrimental effect on the operation of bacteria, but in normal circumstances, especially where bathroom facilities are also included, the detergent is so watered down that the effect is nominal. The majority of housewives use far more detergent than necessary and it is this surplus which has an effect on bacteriological growth in the tank rather than the use of detergent itself.

The greatest drawback to the treatment of waste from bathrooms and kitchens is the clogging effect of grease and soap, etc., on the soil surrounding the tank. Depending on the type of soil, it is only a matter of time before the soil becomes clogged and ceases to filter the effluent from the tank. The soil is then known as 'sewage sick'. This then normally creates a problem from discharging fresh crude sewage into the soil.

If it is gravel, sand, fissure chalk, etc., there is no problem for the discharge of one house-hold into such a tank.

Whatever happens, if it is intended to use this tank for domestic discharge, arrangements must be made for access to the tank.

Q112: *A new inspector just arrived on the local scene insists on all drains being filled over before he pressure-tests them.*
Previously we had them tested before filling in and then, sometimes, re-tested, according to where the job may have been.
What is said in the Building Regulations on this point?

A: Many builders would like a more universal application of the Building Regulations; but one would like to believe that decisions like the time drainage would be tested should rest with the chief officer of the particular department in which the building inspector is employed and not left to the man on the job.

This kind of situation leads to many problems and should be remedied wherever it is discovered.

What do the regulations say?

A.11 says that a builder must furnish the local authority with: (a) At least 24 hours' written notice before any drain will be haunched or covered in any way and;

(b) A notice, which must also be in writing not more than seven days after the work of laying a drain has been carried out, including any necessary work of haunching or surrounding the drain with concrete and backfilling the trench.

A.12 gives a duly authorised officer of the council the authority to make such test of any drain as may be necessary to establish compliance with the requirements of Part N which sets out what must be done when constructing drainage systems.

There is more about testing drains in N.11 which stipulates that any drain, after the work of laying has been carried out, including any necessary work of haunching or surrounding the drain with concrete and backfilling the trench, be capable of withstanding a suitable test for watertightness.

These regulations seem to indicate that a building inspector may apply a test to the drainage system of a property before any haunching or surrounding with concrete takes place. If he does and defects are noticed then the remedy is normally simple and comparatively inexpensive. If the first testing is left until after haunching or surrounding, or even backfilling, then to remedy defects can be a tedious and expensive operation.

It must not be overlooked that in addition to an early test a drainage system may be tested again just prior to the buildng being occupied. This makes the need for care in backfilling, the stacking of materials and the driving of vehicles over drain trenches just backfilled, so very apparent. If defects are shown in the system when a building is just ready for occupation they may be difficult to locate and entail the excavation of paths or driveways.

There must be a measure of discretion in the timing, number and nature of any tests applied by a building inspector. These are made, not as an aid to the builder, but to enable a local authority to be satisfied that the regulations are being complied with.

If a test is not made by a building inspector prior to haunching or surrounding with concrete, then the builder would be wise to make his own test in order to satisfy himself at that stage that his work is sound.

Q113: *A 100 mm nominal bore field tile drainpipe is being used throughout its length — 100m — as a land irrigation drain and to take all the rainwater and effluent from three houses.*

Now, the local authority has given permission for another house to use the drain.

It is a private drain and my client, one of the three original users, is concerned whether the drain has sufficient capacity for additional water.

The following data from the Institute of Plumbing and Building Research Establishment has been used to assess the load of water the drain would be expected to carry.

For roof drainage the usually recommended rate of rainfall in Britain is 75 mm/hr.

Total roof area of four houses=650 m².

Gradient of drain=1:40.

Coefficient of friction=50.

(This is for glazed pipes; there are no figures for field drain pipes.)

Pipe diameter=100 mm. (This is too large: field drain pipes never turn out regular in diameter after kilning and the inevitable staggering of the joints when laying and filling in will reduce considerably the actual diameter of the drain.)

I arrived at a discharge rate that calls for a (glazed pipe) size of 113 mm.

What about the effluent and field irrigation water?

My client complained to the local authority and council officials have said the drain has surplus capacity to take another 185m² of roof water. This they said, was more than sufficient for the discharge of effluent from the four septic takns. No mention of land irrigation water is made.

The council used a figure of 37.75 mm/hr., which is only half the recommended figure. The authority was not aware that more than one house was using the drain.

Section M1 of the Building Standards (Scotland) Regulations 1974, states that 'every house shall have an adequate drainage system'.

In my view, this new house will not have one and the other three will be deprived of an adequate system.

A: Before going into the problems of pipe-carrying capacity, it is important to consider the legal situation.

It is stated **'it is a private drain'**. The Public Health Act (does not extend to Scotland, but they do have a similar Act) defines a **drain** as being '. . . a drain used for the drainage of one building or of any buildings or yards appurtenant to buildings within the same curtilage.' Curtilage can be taken as being an area attached to dwelling house. All pipework within the querist's boundary is legally drains.

The same section defines a **sewer** as '. . . not including a drain as defined (above) but, save as aforesaid, includes all sewers and drains used for the drainage of buildings and yards appurtenant to buildings'.

Confusing maybe, but to try and put the above in simple terms — any 'pipe' which is not a drain as already defined must be a sewer. The question now is to decide whether the sewer (e.g., the main run of pipework that takes the discharge from all the three houses mentioned in the query) is a **public** sewer or a **private** sewer.

A **public** sewer is one vested in or in other words; 'is the property of' the local authority whether they constructed it or someone else did the work privately.

The relevant section is not a simple one and too lengthy to spell out here.

A **private** sewer is one which is not a public sewer — is privately owned and maintained and I am wondering if the querist means (legally) that the pipework he is referring to is a private sewer and the word 'drain' is only being used in the general sense, being that all such pipes are involved in drainage.

The question of the absolute right of an individual (or even a local authority) to insist on connecting additional property to an existing private sewer without first obtaining permission from the owner(s) concerned is just 'not on'. If the sewer is 'public', then it is a very different matter.

The legislation is lengthy and complex and I would recommend that advice be sought from someone who is an authority on Scottish drainage law. A local authority in the area will know the answer, but I feel that, if I am correct in assuming that the 'drain' is privately owned, the local authority has no legal right to demand that this fourth house be connected to someone else's drainage system without the owner(s) permission and there is the right of refusal.

Just because the owners (the 'three original users') are enjoying the use of what appears to be an effective drainage system which is functioning without complaint and accepted by the local authority as an adequate drainage system, is no reason for the authority to go ahead and grant approval for another house to make use of this sewer.

If the sewer is a public one then the whole matter becomes the responsibility of the local authority — for its maintenance, problems if things go wrong, and if the drainage is proven not to be adequate, etc.

To summarise so far, based on the facts as presented to me in the question, I would suggest that the querist challenges the right of permission being granted by a third party. Remember that the local authority may approve a drainage scheme as far as they are concerned, but obtaining actual permission from the owner(s) of a private sewer may be left to the applicant.

Regarding carrying capacity there are so many imponderables that any attempt to calculate with any acceptable degree of accuracy would be a wasted exercise. I can confirm that my accepted figure (for calculation purposes) of rainfall for roof drainage in the UK is 75 mm, although opinions do vary and 50 mm and 40 mm are sometimes quoted. For general surface water drainage, a figure lower than 75 mm is acceptable.

I cannot help but wonder how the authority could be so definite in stating another 185 m^2 of roof water could be accepted into a land irrigation drain when other considerations are so variable and with a situation that could change from almost hour to hour depending upon weather conditions, to say nothing about the variations from season to season.

The assumption that only one house was using this 'drain' makes the matter even more ludicrous.

The authority may be right in considering that a 100 mm pipe is suitable for the four houses in this instance (they know the ground and areas presumably; I, of course, do not) and under normal circumstances, but one could well imagine the possibility of some abnormal conditions arising.

A 100 mm pipe should be capable of taking the foul and surface water discharge from four average size properties — I am assuming the use of proper 'drain' pipes, correctly jointed and laid,. Such a 100 mm pipe will carry a discharge of about 11 litre/sec when laid at a fall of 1 in 40.

But the sewer mentioned here is anything but the 'proper drain' described above and proof that the pipe will carry the discharge is no proof that it can be disposed of at all times.

Q114: *Local authorities often ask for percolation tests to be carried out to soils for the purpose of irrigation when septic tanks are to be constructed or provided in connection with building projects, in order to comply with the requirements of the Building Regulations. How should these tests be carried out and calculations made to satisfy these requirements?*

A: Taking the word 'irrigation' to mean disposal of effluent to underground strata and confining my answer solely to the percolation test and the amount of land required for a given situation, I would suggest the following:

1. Dig a square hole 0.3 m by 0.3 m, to a depth of 0.6 m and then fill it with water, which should seep away overnight.

2. Re-fill the hole the following day to a minimum depth of 0.25 m and check the time (in seconds) for the water to soak away completely.

3. Divide the time observed by the depth of the water (in mm) used in (2) above to obtain the average time required for the water level to drop 1 mm. The test should be repeated at least three times and the average result taken.

4. For each second it has taken for the water level to drop 1 mm, allow 0.5m^2 area of land per person for the 'irrigation' area.

Q115: *How should sanitary appliances be discharged to the drain?*

A: In the case of the 'two pipe' system, soil appliances are discharged to the soil pipe or in the case of ground floor appliances directly to the drain, while waste appliances discharge to the waste pipe which is itself disconnected from the drain by means of a gully trap.

In 'one pipe' and 'single stack' systems together with the various modified systems, all appliances of whatever classification are connected directly to the soil pipe or the drain.

Q116: *What is the difference between combined and separate systems of drainage?*

A: A separate system of drainage is one in which separate sewers are provided to receive foul water and surface water; the two types of discharge are kept separate, and foul water drains may not be connected to surface water sewers and vice-versa.

The reason for the separation of the two types of discharge is not only to assist in controlling the size of foul water sewers, but also to ease the problems of sewage treatment particularly during storms.

In the combined system all foul water and surface water is discharged into one foul water sewer.

Q117: *Could you please tell me what a Buchan Trap is, and give a simple illustration of one? A clue to the question is that it is used in connection with a cesspool associated with a large and lavishly designed Victorian house built about 1890. I have consulted a number of reference books without success.*

A: A **Buchan Trap** (Fig. 35) is an intercepting trap with a horizontal inlet having also a vertical socket on the inlet side of the trap for the connection of an access pipe. It is also obtainable with means of access on the outlet side of the trap.

The term is a Scottish one and has been rarely used in England and Wales, where the more familiar term is an 'interceptor', of which there are many types.

As it is still recommended practice to insert an interceptor (or disconnecting trap) in a run of drains leading to a cesspool, the original work of 1890 could be described as above average standard.

Fig.35. Buchan 100 and 150 mm

Q118: *We have had an extension built at the rear of our premises, for which Planning Permission and Building Regulation approval was obtained.*

In the course of the work it was found that a foul sewer crossed the site of the extension and eventually the local authority which is agent for the sewer authority gave us a licence to build over the sewer. The sewer cannot be all that old as it is of salt glazed pipes with Hepseal joints. There are no manholes or other markers to indicate the presence of the sewer on our land.

The cost of work due to deep foundations and reinforced concrete ground beams has increased over original estimates. We feel that the local authority should have drawn our attention to the presence of the sewer at the planning or Building Regulation application stage — this would have enabled us to make a decision on whether to proceed.

We would be pleased to hear your views.

A: There should be in the deeds of your property a wayleave allowing the drain to pass through. However, check with your solicitor that a wayleave is held by the council to enable it to have access to the drain. If it does not have one, it requires one.

The District Surveyor employed by the council is responsible for drains and he inspects the drawings when they are deposited with the council.

The drawings that have been placed with the council by contractors and then adopted after completion of a project, in most cases, have variation which do not allow for accurate plotting.

If you are asking whether the local authority is responsible for the extra costs you have incurred, the answer is probably no. Generally it is the responsibility of whoever does the original drawings to note these things. If you wish to pursue this matter it would be advisable to take appropriate professional legal advice.

Q119: *Why and how are drains ventilated?*

A: Efficient ventilation of a drainage system is essential to prevent the build-up of foul air and to maintain equilibrium of pressure within the drain.

Ventilation in drains occurs due to natural convection currents. Provision for this is by means of a vent pipe placed at the head of a vent pipe placed at the head or highest point of the drain, replacement air being supplied from a ventilated sewer.

Except in special circumstances, the use of an intercepting trap on a drain should be avoided, but, if one is necessary in the disconnecting chamber at the boundary of the premises, this effectively disconnects the drain from the sewer.

To provide for ventilation a fresh air inlet with mica flap should be fixed either directly from the chamber in the case of stoneware drains, or in cast iron systems from the socket on the inlet side of the intercepting trap.

Q120: *Is it true that excessive, or even any, use of proprietary household lavatory cleaners (liquid and powder) can upset the balance and process of a septic tank, causing secretion of foul odours into the air?*

A: In very large quantities such cleaners may upset the balance of the septic tank, but this is rather unlikely.

There are a number of reasons why these odours may be secreted. Possibly, the tank may need emptying. Most tanks are designed to be emptied every six to 12 months.

If the tank has been emptied, it may have been drained too much, some sludge should be left in the bottom to keep the anaerobic digestion process in the tank on the go.

The other possibility is that this is a new system which has not yet been established — particularly if it was started from empty. A system is normally started with a tank full of water.

Q121: *What methods are commonly used to test drains at the time of laying?*

A: There are three basic methods of testing — with water, air or smoke. These are used to test the drainage system before the pipes are covered with earth.

In the water test a stopper plug is fitted to the end of the drainage pipe at the lower manhole to form a seal, and the next manhole higher up is filled with water to the top. The water level is observed over a period and, obviously, if it is maintained then the length of pipes and manhole are watertight, if not, a leak exists.

In order to test the pipe and not the manhole a temporary bend and a vertical pipe can be fitted. Swift falling means that there is a serious leak that may necessitate relaying of the drain but if the falling is only slight it denotes a small leak which can probably be repaired.

The smoke test is not as searching as the water test, but it does locate the position of a leak rather better. Stopper plugs are fitted to each end of a drain length, smoke being pumped through a nozzle in one stopper and the pressure maintained. Escaping smoke will show the position of any leaks.

For the air test stopper plugs are fitted at each end of drain length and pressure is applied by air pumped through the nozzle inlet at the stopper. Pressure is maintained and measured on a pressure gauge. Loss of pressure indicates leakages.

Q122: *Could you please explain the revision of CP (BS 5572) related to a four branch boss which advertisements state eliminates parallel branch connections?*

4-Boss branch.

4. Exploits revision of CP (BS 5572), and eliminates paralle branch connections.

5. Bosses can accept waste entries up to 50 mm.

6. Available in all-socketed or spigot/socket versions.

My local authority technical officers/building inspectors have always stated 'No connections to the soil pipe for 200 mm below wc connections", whereas these advertisements show bosses within this 200 mm.

A: The inquirer's local authority technical officers/building inspectors were right up to 1978 when CP 304 was replaced by the current Code of Practice 5572, which now permits connections at

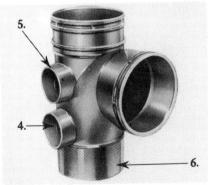

Fig. 36.

right angles to the soil connection, sub section 8.3.2.6 to which the accompanying illustration refers.

The new Code of Practice is quite clear on this and we can only presume some local authorities have not got round to digesting its implications.

Q123: *What are the requirements for a uPVC foul drain in a trench beneath a building with a suspended floor? (Building Regulation requirements for trenches adjacent to foundations, avoidance of damage by differential movement and provision of inspection pits and rodding points are understood).*

A: With uPVC (or any) drains passing under buildings, the foundation of any load bearing walls will require to be taken down below the invert level of the drain trench.

A pre-cast concrete lintel will have to be placed over the drain run, allowing at least 225 mm clearance above the crown of the pipe to allow the brickwork to pass over. uPVC pipe will still require shingle bed and surround. If in doubt, consult your local uPVC pipework supplier.

Q124: *I want to buy a plot of land with outline planning permission for the erection of one dwelling. The plot is on a small housing development which was completed some years ago. Searches have revealed that the roads have been adopted by the local council but the sewers have not.*

If I purchase the plot, what is the position regarding my drainage? Am I permitted to connect to those sewers without seeking authority or should I seek out the developers or ask the permission of my 'new' immediate neighbours.

A: You are very wise to be cautious regarding the purchase of the plot. You have discovered that the sewers are not 'public' sewers and are therefore 'private sewers'. There are many questions and pitfalls. Are the sewers under the roads or do they pass through another persons land before connecting to the private sewer?

Crudely put, the sewer is owned by the persons who use it, and directly or indirectly paid for it and are responsbible for the cost of its repair and upkeep. Permission to connect could entail the agreement of all these people, and not just immediate neighbours.

However, begin with the present owner of the land. Before proceeding any further it is important that his deeds contain the right to make a connection to the sewers and that this right can be transferred to you.

You do not say whether the land is an original plot which has been empty since the site was developed, in which case the deeds ought to make provision for drainage, or whether the land is a piece of the garden of an existing dwelling. The deeds in this instance may also provide for drainage, but not include for drainage arising from a division of the site.

This is a difficult problem, but first seek to obtain from the owner, information regarding the rights he possesses and the rights he proposes to transfer to you — then show this information to a solicitor before moving any further in the purchase of the plot. It is most imperative that a solicitor is consulted before any commitment is made to purchase.

Q125: *I would like to know if there is a pipe available (flexible if possible) for inserting inside a 100 mm earthenware drain, which serves a kitchen sink and washing machine only.*

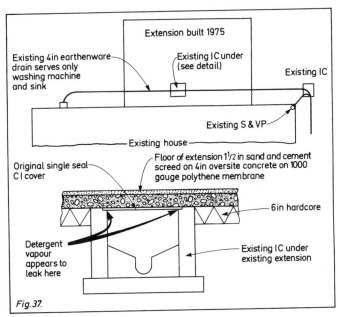

Fig. 37.

When the extension was built over the inspection chamber a double seal bolt-down cover was not used. It was considered that the concrete floor and membrane would be a sufficient seal.

However, some hours after the washing machine discharge, a detergent and soap smell is noticeable in the extension, probably indicating a defective seal to the cast iron cover and frame.

To avoid breaking up the floor to locate the inspection chamber and fit a double seal cover, a flexible pipe of not more than 75 mm outside diameter would appear to be the answer.

A: The present situation seems to indicate that the hot waste from the washing machine is entering the drain and where it passes through the manhole it is able to evaporate here. There could indeed be a slight blockage in the drain which is causing the water to backup and lie in the manhole.

Inserting a flexible pipe of external diameter 75mm would not be satisfactory as this would cause a contravention of Regulation N10(2) of the Building Regulations 1976 which requires the internal diameter of such a drain to be 75 mm. In any case this does not seem to be the answer.

It would appear that the system needs venting at the outlet point of the washing machine by the use of a back inlet gulley. This would open the hot waste from the washing machine to the air thus allowing vapour to be given off at this point. Also it would be advisable to rod the drains run first to clear any blockage (Fig. 38).

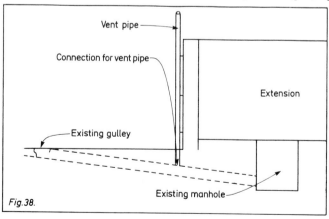

Vent pipe

Connection for vent pipe

Extension

Existing gulley

Existing manhole

Fig.38.

7 Floors

Q126: *What method should be used to stiffen joists?*

A: A floor needs strutting if the span exceeds about 1.5 m. Short ends of joists can be nailed between the bridging joists to form solid strutting, the lines of struts being equally spaced across the floor at intervals of not more than 1.5 m.

The struts are cut in tight between the joists and nailed. Shrinkage can be a problem, and a squeaky floor can often be traced to solid strutting.

With herring-bone strutting the more the joists shrink the tighter the struts will become. Timber about 50 by 32 mm in section should be used and the struts should be kept away from the edges of the joists by about 15 mm to allow for any shrinkage in the joists.

If this is not done the struts may damage both floor and ceiling, the points of the struts sliding across the face of the joist as it shrinks.

Struts should be fixed soon after the joists have been built in to prevent any great movement of the floor timbers.

Q127: *Several rows of wooden blocks have come out of level with the rest of the floor in a kitchen. Why should this have happened and are there any remedies other than replacing the whole floor?*

A: First you should check for signs of dampness or fungal attack and also look to see whether the blocks have come away from the adhesive or blocks and adhesive have come away from the floor screed.

The usual cause of blocks lifting as you describe is an increase in moisture content of the blocks themselves, causing them to swell.

Are the blocks which have lifted perhaps near the kitchen sink, washing machine or other appliance which uses water?

The increased moisture content forces blocks up from their bedding. This may arise because the blocks have been laid in a very dry condition where the humidity is subsequently high.

You should dry out the blocks and re-lay them after the source of the dampness has been taken care of. Where humidity conditions are high, the blocks should be conditioned to a higher humidity content before re-laying. It is also a good idea to provide a compression joint at the perimeter.

Q128: *A village hall is in need of repair. It is an old building comprising of timber roof with felt, timber walls which have been lined inside, and a suspended floor of t and g boarding. It has been supported underneath by some extra 4 by 2 joists. I would like to place a new type of floor on the existing one.*

It has been suggested that I use a ply or chipboard (floor grade) screwed and sealed. Would this be suitable or can you suggest any other ways in which it can be done?

A: If the existing floor is structurally strong enough then leave the old boarding and cover it. The best covering is plywood of sufficient thickness, say 10 or 12 mm, screwed down.

This does not present a good wearing surface, so the best covering to that is probably a good substantial linoleum, such as a 3.2 or 2.5 mm thick, toughened linoleum which stands wear, high loading, stiletto heels etc.

Q129: *A local authority has asked for figures to prove the adequacy of 225 by 75 mm floor ceiling joists at 400 mm centres over a span of 5.4 m specified by the architect. The width of the room is 7 m.*

A: The Building Regulations make a special concession to buildings, not exceeding three storeys in height in 'deemed-to-satisfy' requirements in relation to floor joists, provided that the quality of timber conforms to CP 112 part 2. The quality of the timber must not be lower than grade 40 for imported Douglas fir, or for redwood, whitewood (red and white deal) hemlock, etc., not lower than grade 50.

The dead load is the self-weight of the structure including the floor boards, joists and ceilings, floor finishes and any permanent loads such as partitions carried by the floor. It is presumed that the last two are not significant in this case. The imposed load is the load applied by usage, people, furniture, etc.

In Schedule 6, Table 1 of the regulations gives the maximum permitted span of joists of various sizes at spacings of 400, 450 and 600 mm respectively in three sets of columns when the dead load (excluding weight of joists) is not more than 25, 50 and 125 kg respectively. This, therefore, may in the present case be presumed to represent the weight of ceiling and floor boards only. Assuming 9 mm plasterboard ceiling at 9 kg/m^2 and 22 mm floor boards at 11 kg/m^2 total load$=9+11=20$ kg (well under the 25 kg allowed).

From the tables under the first set of columns 225 by 75 mm joists spaced at 400 mm crs can be used over a span of 5.49 m which is just over the span specified. The joist size quoted should therefore be adequate for the job provided that authorities accept it as a suitable grade (lowest but one for redwood).

An alternative to accepting the deemed-to-satisfy provisions is to calculate the actual joist size to resist bending and deflection. To satisfy the Building Regulations these must conform to CP 112 where applicable. The bending moment equation is

$$\frac{WL}{8} = \frac{fbd^2}{6}$$

When W $=$ total load dead and imposed in Newtons (1 N $=$ 10 Kg approx.)

L $=$ span in mm.

f $=$ safe fibre stress which for 50 grade redwood (CP 112) 6.6 N/mm^2.

b $=$ Breadth of joist in mm.

d $=$ depth of joist in mm.

In terms of joist size which is the only unknown bd^2 $=$

$\dfrac{6WL}{8f}$ W is made up as follows — Load/m run (expressed in kg).

$$\text{Joist} = \frac{225 \times 75 \times 500}{10^5} = 8.43 \text{ kg}$$

$$\text{Plasterboard} = \frac{9 \times 400}{1000} \qquad = 3.6 \text{ kg}$$

Flooring $= \dfrac{11 \times 400}{1000}$ $= 4.4$ kg

Imposed
load $= 1.44$ kN/m^2

$= 144$ kg/m$^2 = \dfrac{144 \times 400}{1000}$ $= 57.6$ kg

Total load/m run $= 7.43$ kg $= 743$ N

Total load on one joist $= 743 \times 5.483$ N $= W$

$L = 5483$ mm

By substitution bd$^2 = \dfrac{6 \times 743 \times 5.485 \times 5485}{8 \times 6.6} = 2.55 \times 10^5$

Let d $= 225$ then b $= \dfrac{2.55 \times 10^5}{225^2} = 50.4$ mm. The 0.4 mm can be ignored so 225 by 50 joist would do for bending.

Next check for deflection. CP 112 requires max deflection as 0.003 of span.

Deflection equation $=$ for uniformly loaded

beam is $D = \dfrac{5}{384} \dfrac{WL^3}{EI}$

Where D $=$ deflection E $=$ modulous of elasticity $= 8300$ N/mm^2

and I (for rectangular section beam) $= \dfrac{bd^3}{12}$

By substitution $0.033I = \dfrac{5 \times 12 \, WL^3}{8300 \, bd^3}$

Thus bd$^3 = \dfrac{5 \times 12 \, WL^2}{8300 \times 0.003}$

Taking the depth of the joist as 225

$b = \dfrac{5 \times 12 \times 743 \times 5.485 \times 5485^2 \text{ mm}}{225^3 \times 8300 \times 0.003} = 68$ mm. The nearest commercial size to this is 225 by 75.

Q130: *Could you please give the correct method of fixing 2.4 m by 0.6 m chipboard floor boarding? Should it be glued (as well as nailed) to the joists? Can anything be put*

between the boards and the joists to reduce noise transfer?
What nails should be used?

A: The flooring should be laid across the joists with staggered headings and nailed with 50 mm or 63 mm lost head nails punched in the usual way at about 222 mm centres on heading joints and 300 mm elsewhere.

Tongued and grooved joints can be glued with PVA glue, keeping them clean, but a small gap should be left around the walls to allow for moisture movement.

Airborne sounds are likely to pass through the floor up and down but impact sounds are likely to occur with persons making contact with the floor.

If a thick carpet is used then this sound will commonly be muffled, but if additional insulation is needed then this is best provided by a floating floor.

The naked floor joists are covered by resilient quilting forming an effective overall blanket. The actual floor sheeting is then either nailed to battens resting on the quilting over the joists or made up and nailed to battens first, before laying; the battens being arranged to come midway between the joists.

The battens must not be nailed through the quilting into the joists. The skirting should be bevelled back at the bottom edge so that only a knife edge makes contact with the floor.

Airborne sounds are checked only by density or inertia and a sound barrier is most conveniently provided by a 50 or 75 mm layer of dry sand resting on the plaster or plasterboard ceiling which should be firmly nailed.

Q131: *I have a Beech block floor which was laid approximately 35 years ago on a lime and cement screed containing 'Lillingtons Metallic Liquid', which I presume was for damp-proofing.*

The blocks are now working loose and on taking some up I found that the surface of the screed has come away and after a check I found that the screed is very damp.

Would it be possible to remove all the blocks (50 m²) and replace with a screeding compound which would have to be about 25 mm thick and include some means of damp-proofing?

A: You are correct in assuming that the metallic liquid was used as a water repellant agent. It is possible to remove the wood blocks and apply a damp-proofing screed and the following method is suggested. After taking up the wood blocks, you will need to remove the architraves and skirtings and apply three coats of either Synthaprufe Liquid Waterproofing Blacking or Aquaseal Liquid Black over the floor area and to lap the damp proof course on the wall (dpc is usually found at original floor level or lap up wall, minimum of 150 mm) ensuring good application in the corners, junctions etc.

Allow two days to dry thoroughly. Apply screed of not less than 25 mm to the floor with Ordinary Portland Cement (not sulphate resistant) and sharp washed sand in the ratio of 1:3.

Allow seven days to dry before walking on it. Refix architraves and skirtings. If you wish to re-use the blocks, then ensure that the floor is level (you could use Sealoflor levelling compound) and bed the blocks in with hot bitumen.

Q132: *When I first laid ceramic tile floors it was done between screeds, in strips about 2 m wide with 3:1 mix; the soaked tiles were laid on this.*

Today whole floors are screeded off with semi dry mix and the tiles laid over the top. Which is easier, and what is the right way to carry out this work?

A: There are three or four different methods of tiling, according to the British Ceramic Tile Council.

The standard or direct method is to use cement-sand mix/normal mortar i.e. 3:1 up to 20 mm thick, which can be used with a separating layer if there is likely to be movement, but it is only suitable for light traffic areas.

Semi dry mix: greater thickness is used and the mortar is dryer. This method needs to be carried out by experts because if too dry there will be a lack of compaction in the bed and it will collapse.

With adhesives, tiles are usually laid flat.

The British Ceramic Tile Council, Federation House, Stoke-on-Trent, has published a series of technical specifications on ceramic floor tiling including: tiles laid in cement-sand mortar, laid by the semi-dry mix method, and laid in cement-based adhesives.

Q133: *Could you please supply information on a method of cleaning marble floors and stone walls without sand blasting or other mechanical means.*

A: Marble floors are normally polished and the normal cleaning method is to wash with tepid soapy water and rinse down with clean water. If stubborn marks are encountered scrubbing with a bristle brush may be necessary. If required a light application of non-slip liquid wax polish can be applied.

Any mechanical process such as sandblasting or wire brushing will probably damage the polished marble surface and dirt will be attracted with cleaning becoming progressively more onerous.

Because you mention stone walls in conjunction with marble floors, it is assumed that the cleaning is to be carried out internally. Scrubbing with plain water is the safest and best proven method, a fine spray being best for internal work. The stone should not be oversoaked or saturated. Excess water may find its way through joints to timber and in inclement weather the stone may take a long time to dry out. You do not name the type of stone and it is therefore worth mentioning that cleaning with water is least effective on sandstone.

Chemical cleaning is not recommended but if used should be carried out only by expert professional operators.

Q134: *I laid 448 floor tiles, quarry type, 150 mm×150 mm colour oatmeal, frost proof. After they had set I cleaned them with 50 per cent linseed raw oil and white spirits.*

The problem is that they appear to be patch dried. I believe the reason is because they are sheltered by the walls of the house and the low brick wall of the patio on which they are laid and therefore there is nothing that can be done about them drying the same shade all over. But I would like your opinion on this.

Fig. 39 shows how the patio is sited and the reason as to why they are holding damp in my opinion.

A: Your problem would appear to be due to moisture rising up through the ground and drying off quickly within the area of sunlight, and remaining damp on the areas shaded from natural sunlight.

Remedy

Take up tiles and bed. Apply 3 coats of liquid damp-proof membrane. Allow to dry and relay tiles on sand/cement bed.

Disadvantages

1. Liable to deteriorate with extremes of weather i.e. frost.

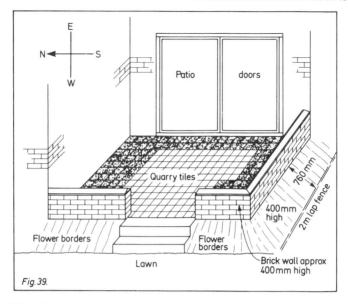

Fig. 39.

2. Will still show dampness of colour shading after wet weather until fully dried out.

3. Cost.

All products not impervious to weather will show shading to some degree when they have been laid in shaded areas exposed to the elements.

Q135: *Will chipboard floors be adversely affected by water? How should they be protected?*

A: Chipboard floors must be protected from water. Once wet, chipboard is seriously weakened. A seal for all grades of chipboard floors, including those of moisture resistant quality for bathrooms, should be specified. The floor under the bath panel is a particularly vulnerable area.

Wetted chipboard does not fully recover strength when dry, so dry storage on site is vital.

Floor tiles (e.g. vinyl) or other jointed finishes may not give adequate moisture protection, BS 5669 requires 'tanking' using plastics sheet.

Q136: *Would you please suggest the best way to clean chipboard floors?*

A: Scrubbing with soap or detergent and a very modest amount of water is usually successful, although stubborn local accumulations of plaster and paint may need to be dealt with by 'Brillo pads' or decorator's knives.

A quick coat of varnish applied immediately after the floor is laid will make the later cleaning much easier.

Wax covered chipboard used to be available, which was readily able to be cleaned, but this is no longer manufactured.

Q137: Concerning suspended timber ground floors, what regulations must be followed regarding fire and damp prevention?

A: All suspended timber ground floors must be constructed in such a way as to prevent the passage of mosture from the ground to the upper surface of the floor.

A damp proof course must be inserted at not less than 150 mm above ground level. No timbers are allowed by Building Regulations to be built below the dpc.

As for fire, if a fireplace is to be built a concrete hearth of not less than 125 mm thickness must be provided. The hearth should extend not less than 500 mm in front of the chimney breast and must extend beyond the inner face of the brickwork jamb, not less than 150 mm on each side.

This means that no timber must be closer than these measurements to the fire opening.

Air bricks built into the external walls of the building allow a continual flow of air to ventilate the under-floor area, thus preventing dampness which can lead to dry rot or other forms of decay.

Q138 How are hardboards conditioned and fixed?

A: The moisture content of the board will be related to the relative humidity of the air where the hardboard is fixed. This will mean that in new buildings and for situations where there is moisture and not much heat the boards will need to be conditioned to an equilibrium moisture content.

For standard and tempered hardboard this will mean brushing about one litre of water into the mesh side of each sheet and then stacking them flat, back to back, allowing time for the water to be absorbed into them. Standard hardboard should be allowed to condition for 48 hrs, and tempered hardboard, because of its oil content, for 72 hrs.

When hardboard of any type is to be used in well-heated buildings, the boards should be air conditioned for a period of 72 hrs to allow them to complete any moisture movement before they are fixed.

Boards conditioned with water should be fixed as soon as the conditioning period is up — any movement will then be shrinkage and the surfaces will remain flat.

Fixing should normally be done from the centre of one end, working outwards and downwards to obtain a flat surface.

Q139: *Gaps have begun to appear between timber floorboards and some of the edges are curling upward. What could have caused this and what remedies are suggested?*

A: This type of deformation is usually because the boards have not dried out properly before being fixed. Shrinkage occurs which the nails are not able to hold. This leads to gaps and then curling, particularly where the boards are not tongued and grooved.

Nail down the loose boards and check the existing nailing. The boards can then be planed or sanded to an overall flat surface.

8 Insulation

Q140: *As a surveyor I have been asked to advise on the best method of sound-proofing the cavity party wall of a modern terraced house.*

A: Now that the houses are built it is a little bit late to think of sound-proofing. The only time to consider sound-proofing is at the design stage. Now all that you can hope to achieve is an amount of sound reduction and absorption.

The heavier the walls are, then usually the greater is the amount of sound insulation. The sound insulation of a cavity wall increases as the number of points at which the walls are rigidly held decreases. Sound strikes a wall surface and sets up a vibration in it and then has to cross the cavity into the other leaf; the more the connections between the leaves the easier it can pass across.

If the houses share a concrete raft with the dividing wall built directly onto it then sound can travel directly from one house into the other through it. The use of a heavy underfelt and carpet will reduce this noise. Where the floor is of timber construction there should be as little timber touching the wall as possible (Sketch A, Fig. 40).

Insulating materials such as glass fibre quilting, vermiculite crystals, etc. can be placed between the joists. This can also be done under bedroom floors and in the roof space.

Plastic foam injected into the cavity adheres to the wall and fills it completely. Although basically it is for heat insulation it will absorb a certain amount of noise. This material is also fire-resistant.

Our ancestors probably had the right idea in using heavy draped curtains or hanging carpets on the wall. Curtains hung from the ceiling to the floor without coming into contact with the wall could have quite a noise reducing effect.

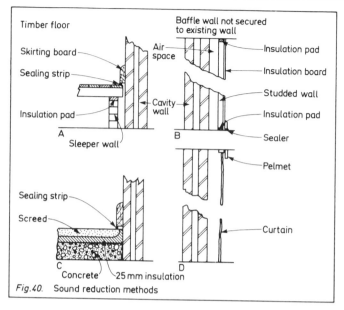

Fig.40. Sound reduction methods

Q141: *Sound-proofing is to be carried out to a first floor flat over a ground floor flat in a Cotswold property with 610 mm solid exterior walls in local stone.*

The floors between are at present 25 mm hardwood, elm and oak square edged, on 125 mm by 100 mm hardwood joists, with lath and plaster ceiling beneath.

Advice is required on the most economical way of tackling the job.

A: A lot depends on the kind of sound that has to be stopped, and in which direction it is travelling.

If noise produced on the ground floor is causing annoying to the people on the first floor then the best thing to do is for the people on the upper floor to go and live somewhere else. This statement is not intended to be funny, annoyance from noise is a very serious thing, far too serious for joking.

If the noise produced on the upper floor is from a loudplaying radio or similar, then again it would be better for the people on the ground floor to move house.

Most annoyance is caused to the people on the ground floor by people on the upper floor walking about, moving furniture, and such; or, quite often, by playing a piano. This annoyance can be reduced very considerably, and, at the same time, it will reduce annoyance from the other sounds, but not to an extent to warrant much expense. 'Impact' noises will be reduced to an extent which would probably justify the expense; but 'air-borne' noise will not be reduced by very much.

The treatment to the floor described will, if conscientiously carried out, reduce impact noises by around 50 to 60 decibels. Now this is quite a lot. A reduction of three decibels halves the power of the noise, but, due to the way our hearing is made, it requires a reduction of 10 decibels to give an apparent reduction in the intensity of the sound of half.

This 50 per cent reduction is cumulative. Say we start with a noise with a perceived intensity of 100; reduce it by 10 decibels and the perceived intensity is now 50; reduce it by a further 10 decibels and the perceived intensity is now 25; a further 10 decibels leaves 13; a further 10 leaves 6; and a further 10 leaves 3. But it still leaves some and it is not unknown for people of a highly strung disposition to 'strain' their ears and claim that the annoyance is still considerable.

Do not promise your clients anything. You can tell them that the work proposed should produce a good reduction, but do not go beyond that.

Fig. 41 shows what is required.

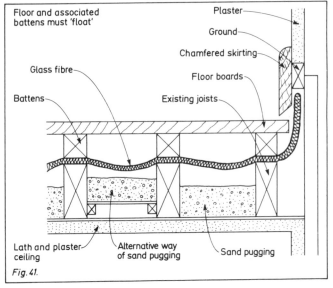

Floor and associated battens must 'float'

Plaster

Ground

Chamfered skirting

Glass fibre

Floor boards

Battens

Existing joists

Lath and plaster ceiling

Alternative way of sand pugging

Sand pugging

Fig. 41.

You first take up the floor boards then 'pug' the ceiling. This is no more than putting 75 mm of dry sand on top of the plaster ceiling. The lath and plaster ceiling should carry this if the laths are adequately nailed. If in any doubt plant a fillet on the side of the joist and put a sheet of compressed asbestos-cement across to carry the sand. The sand should be dry of course, a little dampness will not matter much as it will dry out fairly quickly.

Then drape glass fibre sheet over the joists as shown and let it hang loosely. Put it paper face downwards. Do not omit to turn it up between the floor boards and the wall as shown, and do this all the way round the floor. The floor must nowhere come into contact with the wall. At doorways where, obviously, you cannot turn the glass fibre up like this you will have to use a cork strip as insulation.

The next step is to loosely tack 50 by 50 mm battens to the existing joists on top of the glass fibre. 'Loose' is the operative word.

Now refix the floor boards on top of the battens using nails or screws which will not penetrate the battens into the joists, as you fix the floor boards take out the fixings of the battens. You now have a 'floating' floor whose only contact with its supports is via the glass fibre.

I would repeat the very important part—when the floor is complete there must be absolutely no contact between the floor battens and the joists; no nails, screws, or other fixings may penetrate thte glass fibre. And the floor boards are fixed to the floor battens only—nothing else. This injunction is very strict, if you break it in the smallest degree it will provide a channel which will let the annoyance through almost undiminished.

The heavy elm oak floor boards are excellent in this kind of situation and should be retained, or, if they are spoiled in the taking up, replace them with similar heavy timbers.

If you will set out to make the floor 'float' then you will achieve the objective. The floor cannot float far since it is retained by the glass fibre turned up around the edges. Note that a small gap, at least 1 mm must be left between the bottom of the skirting and the floor boards. The same point must be observed at other points around the room where similar conditions may apply. Any radiators and similar should be fixed to the wall clear of the floor.

Q142: *A client has asked for a chipboard floor to be laid on the ceiling joists in part of the roof space so as to provide a storage platform. The joists are 100 mm deep, with 80 mm* *glass fibre insulation between them laid on the plasterboard ceiling, and are adequate for the limited load to be carried.*

However, I am concerned that because of the insulation there will be virtually no circulation of air between the joists and I would like your opinion as to whether the condition so created will encourage the development of dry rot or other forms of decay.

A: Assuming that the roof is watertight, the only way in which trouble can come is through condensation. For this to take place the temperature of humid air must be lowered below its dew point.

In the summer the air in the roof space is likely to be considerably warmer than in the rest of the house and well above its dew point. As the roof covering is likely to be hotter still, no condensation will take place.

In the winter, however, the roof is going to be colder than the air within which will have gained some heat and perhaps moisture from the rooms below, so that condensation may occur on the underside—perhaps to drop on the the ceiling.

Whether or not this takes place will depend on a number of factors such as heating used, degree of insulation in ceiling and roof etc., but if it does the cure is to ventilate the roof space to the

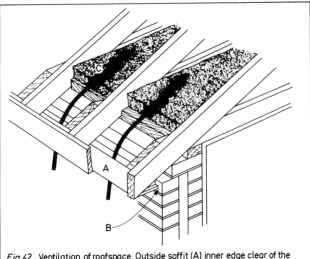

Fig. 42. Ventilation of roofspace. Outside soffit (A) inner edge clear of the wall, leaving slot (B) for ventilation. (Without this ventilation holes are necessary) Insulation must not block air flow at its outer edge (C) but needs to cover the whole width of the ceiling

outside air (Fig. 42). This air coming in at a lower temperature must have a lower dew point even if warmed afterwards.

If there is at present no condensation within the roof space, then flooring the ceiling joists with chipboard will seal the insulated cavities between the joists, and by improving the insulation make the roof space even colder and reduce, not increase, the risk of damp.

Q143: *I have had an inquiry of some sound insulation and fire protection work to be carried out in a local hotel. The customer wishes to provide sound proofing with half hour fire protection between proposed self-contained flatlets.*

The existing walls are to act as the partition walls and are constructed of 12 mm plasterboard on both sides of 100 mm studwork. Could you advise on suitable products for this purpose besides the more commonly used Fibreglass insulation wool.

A: You are very limited as to what is acceptable to the Fire Brigade. They have a list of materials that they will accept together with thickness of same. Their requirements are sometimes different from those of the Building Inspectorates.

The Fire Brigades' requirements are generally of the following:
a) Plasterboard and Fibreglass or plasterboard and Rockwool;
b) Supalux or Masterboard, filled and painted;
c) Lightweight blocks and plaster.

Q144: *How does one soundproof 100 by 50 mm stud partition which has skimmed plasterboard on either side.*

A: Barring violent activity by a party on either side of the partition the only requirement is likely to be insulation for airborne sound.

However, airborne sounds striking the plasterboard wall surface are likely to set up vibrations in the boarding which will then pass through the timber framing and reproduce them in the sheeting on the other side.

This can be avoided at some extra cost by having a double row of studding, a separate set to the plasterboard on each side—the two sets being staggered so that they do not make contact and so that the sheeting to one is, say, 12 mm away from the other set.

Fixing at ceiling , floor and walls will then be to 50 by 50 mm battens, one set to each side nailed to the structure through strips of felt to avoid solid contact with the structure.

A layer of resilient quilting, as dense as possible zig-zagged through and nailed to the backs of alternate studs will give a slight increase in insulation.

The other alternative is to provide a brick nogged partition; the gap in the studding being completely filled with brickwork.

Q145: *Can Polystyrene beads be 'poured' into the cavity loose without adhesive (as in the Shell system), to comply with insulation regulations?*

A: Polystyrene beads cannot be poured into the cavity under the Building Regulations, but need to be blown in using a drilling pattern specified under the relevant British Board of Agrement Certificate. There are various systems including loose beads, but recommend the use of an NCIA contractor.

Q146: *Could you please advise on the following:*
The correct method of calculating in respect of Building Regulations F6(2); should the total 'R' value be calculated for the entire structure by taking the values for each of the elements, then dividing by thte total external wall area to get the unit 'R' and getting the reciprocal 'U', or should one work in 'U' values throughout?

A: Regulation F3 requires the external wall of a dwelling to have a maximum U-value of 0.6 W/m^2 deg C. In such walls 12 per cent of the area of perimeter walling may be single glazing. (F6(1)). F6(2) allows a greater area of windows if double or triple glazing is used.

The important measurements are those for perimeter walling. These walls are measured internally, between finished floor and ceiling levels. All openings in the wall are included in the overall dimensions. Perimeter walling also includes separating walls in semi-detached and terraced housing.

It is unlikely that the front, back and side walls of a dwelling will have different U-values so the calculations are straightforward.

The lintel, jamb or sill used in conjunction with an opening can be considered either as part of the wall, or as part of the opening. If considered part of the wall the maximum U-value must not exceed 0.6, but there are now a variety of components available to enable this standard to be achieved.

If the wall is of a 'standard' 0.6 construction within one of the deemed-to-satisfy specifications, the area of single glazing allowed is 12 per cent of the perimeter walling, increased to 24 per cent double-glazed or 36 per cent triple glazed. There can, of course, be a mixture of single, double, and triple-glazing.

Pilkington Flat Glass has published an almost indispensable brochure called *Windows Area and the Building Regulations*. It contains a number of charts which enable one to rapidly obtain appropriate glazing areas for external walls having U-values from 0.6 down to 0.1.

Q147: *My problem is a floor of 35 m² area and consisting of 150 mm stone, 50 mm of sand blinding polythene dpc and 100 mm of concrete that has to be covered with 150 mm by 150 mm by 15 mm quarries or 6 mm by 6 mm by 5 mm Johnstone fireflash tiles. The thickness from top of concrete to finished floor height is 75 mm.*

For thermal insulation of floor would it be possible to lay 12.5 mm polystyrene sheet over subfloor prior to screeding for quarries or tiles or as an alternative could granular vermiculite incorpoated in the floor screed mix do, and at what ratio to sand/cement?

A: Normal practice in countries that suffer from extremes of temperature is to insulate the ground floor slab by concrete blinding, then lay a 50 to 75 mm polystyrene insulation slab followed by a concrte oversite, the insulation being taken up all sides of the concrete slab, thus giving a fully insulated floor.

If you are intending to lay 12.5 mm polystyrene on a concrete slab, you will require to level off the top of the concrete to a smooth finish or you will break the insulation when applying the additional weight of the finished floor construction on top. An insulation of approximately 12.5 mm would only give a minimal increase to any thermal properties.

Most lightweight screeds which entrap air (thus giving light weight) should give better thermal properties than 12.5 mm polystyrene. These tend to be laid by specialists and to achieve best results, contact your local screeding contractors.

Q148: *We are having a steel portal frame extension built to house our joinery shop and plan to build the walls of blockwork with a rendered finish. What is the cheapest way* *to get a U value of 0.6 W/m² deg. C as required by Part FF of the Building Regulations? (There is a small firm making dense concrete blocks close by.)*

A: Without checking delivered prices in your area it is hard to say for sure, but as it is an industrial building and you are planning to render in any case, the cheapest solution overall might well be a solid wall of 200 mm thick low-density (475 kg/m³) aerated blocks such a Thermalite Turbo, Celcon Solar or Durox Supablock. With a dense 20 mm render this should meet the 0.6 U value requirement without any additional insulation.

With an outer leaf of dense blocks from your local supplier it would be necessary to use at least 130 mm of low-density block for the inner leaf with a clear cavity, or additional insulation: either would probably be more expensive.

Q149: *Can you please explain to me what is meant by the term 'K Value'.*

A: A K Value is a measurement of the heat conductivity of an insulating material. It is measured in watts per m² area by metre thickness per degrees C temperature. Not all types of insulation material perform in the same way. The smaller the K Value the greater degree of insulation from the material.

Vermiculite granules have a K Value of 0.065 while glass fibre has a value of 0.04. This means that for a given thickness of insulation material, you would need about 1½ times more vermiculite as glass fibre to insulate to the same degree of heat saving.

Q150: *I have just carried out a complete insulation job on a customers house. This includes cavity fill insulation and double glazing, as well as 100 mm of insulation in the roof space. The customer now complains that some of the rooms in the house are colder than the others and I cannot get to the bottom of the problem.*

A: It sound as if the whole-house thermostat for the central heating system is situated in a room or an area which has a greater degree of insulation (heat loss) than other parts of the house. This is causing the imbalance in the room temperatures. The answer would be to improve th insulation in the colder rooms or simply to fit individual valve thermostats to the radiators which would balance the system. Although this will increase the amount of fuel needed to heat the house it will still be less than before the insulation work was carried out.

Q151: *Can you please explain to me how insulating a property affects the speed of temperature change in different rooms. I have looked at a number of jobs where insulation has been installed and they all heat up and cool down at different rates. Could this be due to the structure or the method of insulation?*

A: The speed of temperature change within a building depends on where within the structure the insulation is placed. For example a room with solid brick or concrete block walls stores a lot of heat but takes a long time to heat up and also to cool down. It acts just like a large storage radiator. While the walls are heating up the room may feel uncomfortable.

However, if insulation is placed on the inside of the wall the room will heat up a lot faster, but it will not store any heat in the brickwork. It will not stay warm either once the heat source is removed. Often it is beneficial for a room to heat up quickly but unless there is heat storage to that room it may suffer condensation when the heat is switched off. If a solid wall is insulated on the outside, it will still heat up slowly and once thoroughly warm will stay warm for a long time, even days.

Cavity walls, filled with insulation, heat up quicker than solid walls and cool down slowly. Slow cooling rooms are less at risk from condensation, and if they cool slowly overnight need less heat next day to restore the room temperature to the pre-set comfort levels.

Q152: *What is the minimum number of air changes permitted in a house for it to be safe for the occupants? I have read about air tight houses but these cannot be allowed or health would surely suffer.*

A: The minimum number of air changes in a building is one complete change every two hours or ½ every hour. Less than this would be dangerous to health as it would allow a build-up of radon gasses an carbon dioxide which would kill. Also it would create a great deal of condensation. Air tight houses have forced air ventilation giving about 1 complete air change per hour, but the fresh air is heated first.

Q153: *What causes air to circulate through a house, creating draughts?*

A: Air is forced around a house by the differences in air pressure between the inside and outside through any place that air can pass through such as air bricks, gaps in doors etc. These pressure differences are created by wind or by what is described simply as the chimney stack effect (Fig. 43). This is where the warm air in a room rises and replaced by cold air entering the house. The presssure here is created by a temperature difference such as in a chimney. Cold air is denser than warm air hence the circulation of air. The cold air is more noticeable as a draught because it is more uncomfortable.

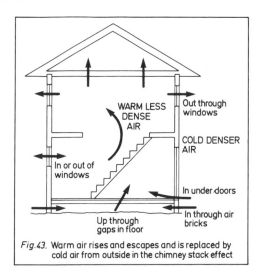

Fig.43. Warm air rises and escapes and is replaced by cold air from outside in the chimney stack effect

Q154: *How much heat loss is there through a roof space in say a year? The roof in question has an area of 45 m².*

A: You do not state whether the roof is with or without sarking felt. On the basis that sarking felt is fitted about 5,000 kWh of electricity or 260 therms of gas can be expected to be lost in a roof of your size during a typical heating eason. Without sarking felt this could increase by half as much again. Although once insulation is fitted the effect of heat loss via the sarking felt would be negligible.

Q155: *What degree of savings could be expected in heat loss in a roof with an area of 45 m² with 80 mm of glass fibre insulation?*

A: Laying 80 mm of glass fibre should result in savings of about 4,000 kWh of electrical heating or 205 therms with gas, provided the temperature levels remain the same as before insulation was installalled ie. the central heating is turned down accordingly. If the heat output of the heating system remain the same the comfort level will increase but the savings could be reduced to nothing (Fig. 44).

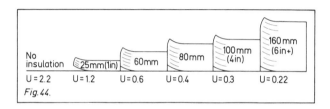

Fig. 44.

Q156: *Can you please outline the different types of insulation available for use in the roof space?*

A: There are five basic types of insulation materials suitable for use in a roof space. The commonest is glass fibre or mineral wool quilt supplied in rolls and in widths to suit common joist spacing. Both types are very easy to work with and simple to lay. They are resistant to dampness but can sometimes cause skin irritations when laying.

The remainder can be classified as loose fills. These include cellulose fibre made from waste paper and treated with a fire retardant. It is usually cheaper than other forms of insulation but can become soggy if it gets wet, so must be fitted into a completely dry roof space. Polystyrene beads are easy to use and clean but being extra lightweight have a tendency to blow about in the roof space in draughts. Exfoliated vermiculite or 'Micafil' is made from natural clay blown up like popcorn. It is a bit dusty when laying but otherwise safer than most other forms of loose fill but its major snag is that to achieve the same heat savings you need almost double the thickness of material, (130 mm of vermiculite to 80 mm of glass fibre quilt). Finally there is glass or mineral wool fibre as a loose fill. This is generally applied pumped into the roof space by a specialist company. It is safe to use, unaffected by damp but can be a lung and skin irritant.

Q157: *How much heat is lost through the walls of a typical three-bedroomed semi which has no wall or cavity insulation?*

A: The heat loss during the winter heating season could be around 10,000 kWh of electricity or 500 therms of gas, depending obviously on the standard of heating in the house. Cavity filling would reduce this loss to around 3,000 kWh of electricity.

Q158: *What sort of materials are suitable for use as an insulator on water tanks in roof spaces? Is it suitable to use waste insulation left over after the joists have been filled?*

A: Almost every insulation material is suitable around water tanks. It can be the flexible type of mineral or glass fibre mat or quilt or the rigid type such as sheets of polystyrene. Even loose fill insulants can be used provided a container is built around the tank to hold the material. About 50 mm thickness is all that is required in normal situations but if a roof is highly insulated then there is a greater risk of freezing in the pipes and tank so up to 10 mm may have to be considered.

Q159: *I have heard that by insulating a roof it is possible to create an overheating of the electrical wires and cables and cause a fire. Is this the case and if so what should be done to avoid a dangerous situation?*

A: Regulations for wiring rule that where cable is within or next to thermal insulation, its current capacity should be reduced by 0.5 or 0.6 of the original allowed capacity. This is simply to avoid overheating. If the wiring is old there is a greater possibility of fire from overheating than if the cable is fairly new. Also junction boxes should be covered and you should avoid damaging cables by walking over them. Lighting cable usually is generous for its load, but if rewiring is needed it should be carried out before insulation is placed.

An alternative way of ensuring that an overheating does not occur is to change light bulbs for the new low energy consuming type which use about ¼ of the current.

Q160 : *I know that double glazing helps reduce heat loss but could you tell me how much it actually saves?*

A: Normal double glazing will cut down heat loss through windows by about 35 percent of wood windows. If however, timber windows are changed for aluminium or steel which are not thermally broken then the new metal frames will cancel out much of the saving from the double glazing. Triple glazing now common in most Scandinavian countries offers a saving over single glazing in the order of 55 per cent in heat loss. Double glazing without some form of trickle ventilation fitted to the windows will suffer from condensation.

Q161 : *I have just fitted secondary double glazing to the windows of a house and now condensation is forming in the cavity between the two panes. What causes this and how can it be overcome?*

A: The condensation is caused by moisture vapour leaking into the gap between the two panes from th room. Once within the cavity the vapour condenses on the colder outer pane and is trapped there.

If the cavity has a couble of fairly large holes for ventilation to the outside, it will stay clear most of the time, but even if condensation does occur it will clear in time. Remember, water vapour can penetrate into an area even if air can not. Without ventilation the vapour will stay in the cavity and just keep accumulating.

With secondary double glazing some condensation is to be expected. If there is none it is probably due to the fact that there is too much air leaking through both windows and that an incoming draught is keeping the cavity dry. On the way in the incoming air is warmed and keeps the cavity dry. This however, reduces the thermal effects of the double glazing.

Silica gel placed in the cavity will absorb a small amount of condensation and also removes mist from the glass. It needs replacing when saturated though but they can be dried out and re-used effectively. Silica gel or sometimes crystals can be obtained from most chemists.

Q162: *Is it cost effective to insulate the floor of an existing house?*

A: The simple and most straightforward answer to this question is no. In most houses it is simply not worthwhile. It would involve a new floor finish and the fuel saving made would not repay the investment in anything less than 30 years. It would be easier just to lay thick paper over the existing floor and fit good thick carpet wall-to-wall.

Q163: *I have heard that the plate connectors of roof trusses might be affected as a result of insulating the roof space. Is this correct? If so would other metal fixings in the roof be at risk?*

A: It is true that in a roof space which has been highly insulated all metal fastenings are vulnerable as there is a greater risk of condensation in the roof space after insulation. Nail plate connectors are at risk even if they are galvanised, as where they are pressed out after galvanising, leaving bare steel surfaces.

Wrought iron corbels to wall plates of floors and ceilings may be at risk if the wall suffers from interstitial condensation and stays wet for long periods of time.

Corrosion may also be caused by some of the chemicals used in the insulating materials particularly some fire retardants used with cellulose fibre insulation.

Q164: *Are there any health risks associated with most common types of insulation materials?*

A: None of the common forms of quilt or loosefill insulants has yet shown up as being a risk to health although a dust mask should be used when installing to prevent dust getting into the lungs. Cavity foam using formaldehyde or slab insulant made with the same chemical can give off gasses of formaldehyde which can cause sickness and nose bleeds.

9 Electrical

Q165: *How do I go about obtaining electrical supply on a building site, and how do I estimate the demand loads?*

A: The most convenient and generallly the most economic supply is from the Area Electricity Board's network.

The board can usually provide a supply, but this may not always be possible at short notice. Ideally, they should be advised of the project as early as possible—preferably when the site plans are first discussed.

An application for supply should be made to the Construction Industry Liaison Engineer who is appointed within an area board to advise builders and to provide technical information on construction sites.

The builder must pay the board for providing and dismantling a supply used for construction purposes only. Money may be saved by arranging for the permanent supply from the outset.

A simple estimate for construction site supply is based on a loading of 10 watts per m^2 of the total floor area of the building to be erected.

Q166: *Not too long ago it used to be standard practice to earth electrical circuits and appliances to cold-water pipes. Is this still permissible?*

A: It is certainly not recommended practice. Plastic pipes, which are insulators, are often used in new works these days, and existing metal cold-water installations may be extended or repaired in plastic pipe.

In instances where plastic piping is used, you should be warned that this does not provide an earth unless a metal insert has been provided for earthing purposes.

Q167: *Could you give some guidance on procedures for dealing with underground electrical cables as this is a constant cause of worry?*

A: The first thing to do before starting any job is to check with the Area Electricity Generating Board's engineer and if necessary the local office of the Central Electricity Generating Board to determine the location of any cables in and around the site.

Underground cables are usually laid between half and one metre deep but changes in ground level during construction can mean the 'as laid' depth is no longer correct.

Mechanical excavation should be stopped before cable depth is reached and heavy vehicles should not be allowed to pass over cables unless they have been buried very deep.

Underground cables exposed during excavation work should be propped and the area barred. They should be assumed 'live' and not repositioned or removed until certified 'dead'.

Accidental damage (not necessarily causing power failure) to a cable exposed during excavation should be reported to the Area Electricity Board and the area barred until the cable is declared safe.

Q168: *What kind of area lighting should be used on a site, and will this be sufficient to illuminate craft operations?*

A: Area lighting is used to illuminate the site for safe movement and for outside work, such as concreting, drainlaying and brickwork.

For general lighting use floodlights giving a broad beam distribution mounted so that the patches of light overlap to give reasonably even overall illumination. Narrow beam floodlights may be used to boost the illumination over a local working area, or to light more remote parts of the site.

Floodlights using a 500 W tungsten filament lamp should be mounted at least six metres above ground. More powerful lamps should be mounted at greater heights to limit glare.

Poles and high masts must be securely stayed against strong winds and access to luminaires must be readily available. 240 volt operation is generally acceptable for fixed floodlighting mounted well above ground level, provided that installation practice follows CP 1017 with equipment to BS 4363.

Portable lighting should be used for craft work, such as joinery or plastering, which requires higher illumination. This can be achieved by floodlights, by clusters of PAR (pressed glass aluminised reflector) lamps or by fluorescent luminaires.

As recommended in CP 1017, reduced voltage (110 volt supply from transformer with earthed centre-tap on secondary winding) should be used for portable and easily accessible lighting.

In damp and confined spaces such as wet areas, deep excavation, tunnels headings, tanks and chimneys, lamps should be operated at 25 volts. Better still, use self-contained battery operated cap or hand lamps to avoid danger from entanglement with the cable.

Q169 : What precautions should be taken when work is being carried out in close proximity to overhead cables?

A: Overhead cables are usually uninsulated and are, therefore, a serious hazard. At high voltages, arcing across to nearby objects can occur, so nothing should be allowed to contact or approach close to an overhead line.

The best precautions with overhead cables are to arrange for them to be re-routed by the Area Electricity Board to a safe distance clear of all construction work, or made 'dead' and certified as such by the Board, or protected by a system of barrier fences and timber goalposts so that no part of any mobile crane, earth moving equipment etc. can approach the live cable. Clearance distance should be agreed with the Area Electricity Board.

If work must start before the Board's advice is available, a safe working rule is that nothing or nobody should encroach within 6 m of any overhead conductor.

Q170 : What does site lighting usually consist of?

A: Site lighting usually consists of area lighting (using area floodlights and beam floodlights), dispersive lighting over working areas, ladder and walkway lighting, and local lighting at the working area.

All site lighting should be such that it causes the minimum disturbance to those outside the site.

Q171 : What arrangements should be made for the distribution of electricity on site when mains voltage is being utilised?

A: Distribution units complying with BS 4363 are recommended; the incoming mains supply should terminate in a supply incoming unit (SIU) containing the Electricity Board's fuses and main switch.

A main distribution unit (MDU) for the control and distribution of the electricity on the site is also required.

A combined supply incoming and distribution unit (SIDU) is available for use on sites where it is possible to locate the units together. The units should be housed in a lockable waterproof cubicle.

The layout of cables on site should be carefully planned an those likely to be in position for a long time (for example, supply to a fixed crane) should be well buried and laid on a route where they are not likely to be disturbed by earthmoving or other site vehicles.

The cables should be set at least 600 mm below final ground level and be protected by tiles. At roads and access ways the cables must be encased in clay or pitch fibre pipes which must be evenly supported.

When the trench is filled in, the cable route should be indicated at each end, and wherever practicable, by surface markers at regular intervals.

Cables should not lie on the ground but if this is necessary for short periods they should be encased with reinforced hosepipe.

Where overhead cables are used (for example, fixed flood lighting) the cable should be supported on hangers, from an independent wire suspended between poles sited around the edge of the site, with spurs to supply the various lights, machines and work under construction. Avoid running cables in positions where fouling by cranes or earthmoving machinery is likely.

The minimum clear height for overhead cables should be: a) in positions inaccessible to vehicles—5.200 m, and b) in positions accessible to vehicles or where a cable crosses the road—5.800 m. Where possible they should be indicated by timber 'goal post' markers.

Q172: *On the arrangements for the distribution of electricity on site when mains voltage is being used, could you elaborate on reduced voltage distribution?*

A: Portable lighting, and hand-held tools should be supplied at 110 volts single or three phase, obtainable from a centre tapped double-wound transformer, giving 55 or 65 volts to earth respectively.

It is usually recommended that this voltage be used for all movable plant up to 5 kVA. The use of this voltage greatly reduces the possibility of shock and electrocution.

Long trailing flexible cables should be avoided by planning the installation so as to bring the outlet units near to the working area.

The distribution units used should comply with BS 4363. Different combinations of the units allow different types of supply systems to be formed as required.

Plugs, socket outlets and cable couplers for AC and DC supplies should comply with BS 4343—when these are used electrical apparatus cannot be plugged into sockets of the wrong voltage.

It is recommended that cables and couplers for different voltages should be recognisable by different colours; 25 V violet, 50 V white, 110 V yellow, 240 V blue and 415 V red.

All accessories and wiring should comply with the current edition of the *Regulations for the Electrical Equipment of Buildings* (obtainable from the Institution of Electrical Engineers); including the specific requirement of Section H, 'Temporary Installations and Installations on Construction Sites'.

Only an electrician should carry out the installation and any repairs, alterations and additions.

Q173: *I am presently renewing some mains supply water pipe to a house with plastic pipe. Will this have any affect on the earthing for the property?*

A: It was common practice that domestic earthing of the electrical supply would be via the water mains. As the pipes run generally long distances underground this provided a suitable and easy method of earthing. However, the water boards have never regarded themselves as having an obligation to supply a ready-made earthing system only the supply of water so recently they have been changing mains supply pipes from iron to plastic.

This has resulted in many houses not having sufficient pipework underground for an adequate earth. With the advent of plastic water pipes inside houses the practice of earthing to water pipes has been outlawed on the ground that it may not be effective in times of need. The only certain way is to fix an earthing rod in the ground—normally a copper rod 1 m into the ground. Or cross-bond the system by using the metal outer sheathing of the electrical supply cable as an earth. If in doubt get the local electrical supply company to come and check out the property.

As an additional word of warning, when working on water mains it is best to isolate the piece of pipe you are working on for say repairing a leak or jointing with an electrical by-pass cable, similar to a set of jump leads for a car. These should be connected either side of the area you are working on, just in case there is a fault in the property and the pipe is taking electrical current which has earthed out. This will save you from suffering a certain electrical shock which could be fatal especially if the ground is wet.

Q174: Could you please explain what is meant by the term 'double insulation'? I have seen this on a number of electrical power tools.

A: Simply it is a method of providing a covering of insulating material in addition to the insulation normally provided, so that in the event of a breakdown of the normal insulation a live current is not transmitted through to the tool causing the operator to suffer a shock.

Q175: What are the normal sizes of cable used for example in a house for lighting and power?

A: In the case of normal house sub-circuits it is acceptable to use a 1 mm^2 pvc insulated cable for the 5 A lighting circuits while for a 30 A ring circuit the minimum size is 2.5 mm^2 cable. The IEE Wiring Regulations give a chart for calculating other sizes of cable and these can be obtained from HM Stationery Offices.

Q176: I understand that it is a bad practice to fuse the neutral cable in a circuit. Could you explain why this is so?

A: In the normal domestic supply situation the neutral cable is earthed at the transformer substation. As a result on the development of a leak to earth, there is a low resistance path through earth for the leakage current, so that the total current flowing will be sufficient to blow the fuse. It is therefore essential that the neutral cable remain intact, as any break would nulify the system and the fuse would not blow, making it possible for someone to receive an electric shock.

Q177: Could you please illustrate the two methods of wiring for a lighting system? I always use the method which uses the extra terminal in the ceiling rose but I have been asked to wire up a house using the joint box method and I am not too clear what this involves.

A: Both systems are acceptable for domestic lighting circuits it is a matter of choice and cost which is used. The joint box method is where the sub-circuit live and neutral wires are each taken to terminals in the joint box and then passed on down to the lighting points and switches. Other terminals in the box are used for joints in the wires between switches and lighting points.

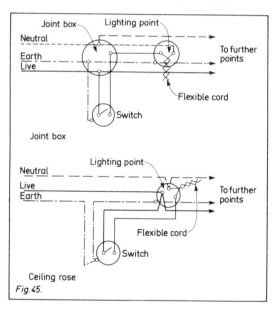

Fig. 45.

The other method simply uses the extra terminal in the ceiling rose to carry the live conductor through, the other terminals being connected to switch wires and neutral. The terminal connected to the live must be so arranged that it cannot be touched when the ceiling rose is removed (Fig. 45).

Q178: I have often seen in shops and factories an overhead busbar trunking system, but could you explain what it is and how it works?

A: Busbar systems are, as you say, used a lot in shops and factories where there are lines of machines, cash tills or desks, but where these may be moved from time to time. It allows a greater degree of flexibility than traditional wiring systems using socket outlets. The usual arrangement comprises rectangular section trunking containing copper or aluminium busbars. At intervals of about every metre a tapping off point is fitted. This can sometimes include a fuse to protect the sub-circuits. Connections can be made with pvc insulated cables in conduit armoured pvc sheathed cables or by mineral-insulated cables.

Q179: *Can you please illustrate how a one-way and two-way lighting control is wired?*

A: A one-way control (Fig. 46) is the commonest system of controlling a light in a room. It uses a single pole switch which must always be connected to the live pole of th supply, never the neutral. Although a single-pole switch wired up to the neutral will switch off and on the light it leaves one terminal of the lighting point permanently live, and could result in a shock if the ceiling rose is removed, say for the replacement of a pull cord.

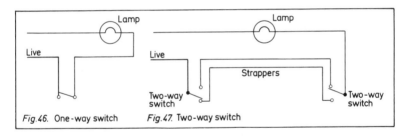

Fig.46. One-way switch   *Fig.47.* Two-way switch

Two-way connections (Fig. 47) involve the use of 'strappers' to allow the light to be switched on and off at two independent points.

Q180: *Is it possible to control one light from more than two switches and if so how is this achieved?*

A: In situations where it is necessary to operate a light from more than two switches it is possible using what is described as intermediate control (Fig. 48). The intermediate switches which have four terminals are connected between two-way switches as illustrated below.

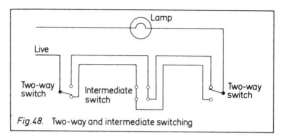

Fig.48. Two-way and intermediate switching

Q181: How do starter switches in fluorescent lights work?

A: Basically there are two types of starter switches for fluorescent lights. One is the thermal type which comprises two contacts and a heater and the other is the glow type which contains two contacts in a gas. In both types one of the contacts is on a bimetal strip which bends with appreciable change in temperature. On switching on the circuit with the thermal type, current flows across the closed starter switch contacts and the lamp electrodes are heated. After a brief time, the heat within the starter is high enough to cause the bimetal strip to bend and to break the circuit. This gives a high-voltage pulse which starts the discharge. While the lamp is illuminated the heater keeps the starter switch contacts apart.

In the glow starter type the contacts are apart on switching on and a glow discharge occurs between them. The heat produced causes the bimetal strip to bend and the two contacts to touch. Current then flows and the lamp electrodes heated to operating temperature. When the bimetal strip cools, it bends, breaks the circuit and causes the pulse necessary to start the discharge.

Q182: I have the job of providing a cooker control unit, can you help by giving me an idea of the load of a modern domestic cooker?

A: Rated loads of modern domestic electric cookers vary widely from 3 to well over 100 kW. Average loading broken down are 2.5 kW for the oven, 2.75 kW for the grill and radiant rings at about 2.75 kW each.

Q183: Is it ever permissible for bare wires to be used in a wiring system?

A: Under the IEE Wiring Regulations bare wires may be used in buildings only for the following purposes: 1) as earth-continuity conductors, earth leads and bending leads, 2) conductors of extra-low voltage wiring, 3) protected busbar installations (Fig. 49) and 4) collector wires for travelling cranes or trolleys.

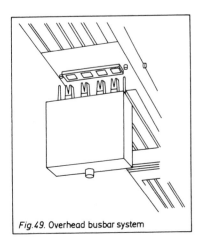

Fig.49. Overhead busbar system

Q184: *Could you please advise me on how to wire up a domestic door bell circuit?*

A: For houses and entrances to commercial or industrial buildings entrance bells are usually operated at extra-low voltage—not over 50 V between conductors and 30 V between conductors and earth. Mostly the supply is derived from a 240 V ac mains via a double-wound transformer. The wiring to the primary side of the transformer must be in accordance with IEE Wiring Regulations while the wiring to th bell pushes and the bell itself is usually in 0.75 mm^2 pvc insulated wiring. This can be run on the surfaces of walls and ceilings. It should not be run inside conduit which contains normal 240 V mains supply cable as the heat generated may cause a short circuit.

Q185: *Advice is sought on what causes an alarm bell to ring continuously after the bell push has been pressed, as opposed to a conventional bell which stops as soon as the finger is removed.*

A: Quite simply the alarm bell is a conventional door bell structure (Fig. 50) consisting of a trembler bell with a spring supported trigger with the addition of a set of contact operated by an electromagnet.

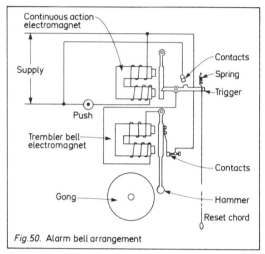

Fig.50. Alarm bell arrangement

The armature of the alarm bell electromagnet contains a catch on which rests the pivoted trigger containing one of the two contacts. When the push is pressed the armature moves forward and the trigger drops. This causes the two contacts to join and connects the bell to the supply. The bell continues to ring like a conventional trembler door bell until a resetting cord is pulled to restore the trigger to its original position.

Q186: *In a completed electric circuit how can I check to seek if the polarity is correct?*

A: If the installation is connected to the mains supply then the check on fuses and single pole devices can be carried out using a neon glow tester. In testing at lighting switch positions, lamps are removed and the tester, having a return connection to the neutral or earth-continuity conductor, is applied to the switch terminals. In testing at socket-outlets, a useful tester can be made from a plug connected to a lamp-holder and bulb with the wires running between live and earth. This is simply inserted into the sockets, if the bulb lights the system is OK. If the system is not connected to mains supply yet either a tester incorporating an ohmmeter or a bell and battery can be used.

Q187: *Could you please explain the purpose of a polarity test?*

A: Simply if a lighting switch is connected in the neutral conductor instead of the live conductor, one terminal in the ceiling rose will remain permanently live whether the switch is on or off. This can cause a shock to someone changing a bulb or replacing a pull cord.

If the terminals of a socket outlet are connected wrongly, metalwork of any appliance supplied from the outlet could become live and cause an electrical shock.

Q188: *Can you explain what is meant by the term protective multiple earthing?*

A: This is a method of connection with earth in which the earthing load is connected to th consumer's earthing terminal which, in turn is connected to the neutral conductor of the supply (Fig. 51). This is used where local earthing conditions are so poor that other forms of earth-leakage protection would not be satisfactory. In such a system all protected metalwork is connected by earth-continuity conductors to the neutral service conductor at the supply intake.

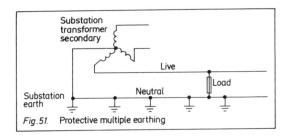

Fig. 51. Protective multiple earthing

10 Plumbing

Q189: *What is the difference between hard and soft soldering?*

A: 1. Soft solders being an alloy of lead, tin and antimony in varying ratios depending on the grade. The melting point being around 183 deg C. Grades D and J can be used for wiping joints on lead pipes. Grades A, F, G and K can be used for the soldering of copper, brass, zinc, mild and stainless steels using a suitable flux. Soft solder should only be used where there is no great stress on the joint/joints.

2. Hard soldering, also referred to as silver brazing alloy or silver solder is an alloy of copper, zinc, cadmium and silver (minimum 49 per cent silver) in varying ratios an the melting point being 620 deg C – 640 deg C. It can be used on mild steels, nickel alloys, tungsten, tungsten carbides, copper, copper alloys and stainless steels using a suitable flux.

3. The main difference between them being the make up, and much higher melting point of the hard solder resulting in a much stronger joint.

Q190: *A banging noise persists in the water supply pipes of a private house. Why should this occur and is there any remedy?*

A: This noise transmitted through pipes in water supply systems is commonly known as water hammer. It is caused when water flowing at a high velocity is abruptly stopped – resulting in an excess pressure build up.

There are a number of possible causes: small diameter pipes operating at high pressure with large and quick closing outlets;

long lengths of pipe without bends which would restrict the velocity; spring loaded taps; plug taps; unsuitable balltaps; soft washers and worn spindles to taps.

Only screw down taps and self closing taps of the non-concussive type should be used on water systems. The flow of water should be controlled by the stop tap.

Balltaps should be checked to ensure that they are suitable. Hard washers may need to be exchanged for soft, or vice versa; a branch connection to be preferred to a straight connection, and in persistent cases an equilibrium balltap may be the answer.

Q191: *Noises occur at about minute intervals when the underfloor pipes of a central heating system cool at night and start heating up in the morning.*

Is there any way of making the pipework run silently? The radiators have often been ventilated.

A: When heating pipes heat up or cool down, expansion and contraction take place. If, therefore, the pipes are solidly fixed so that this movement cannot freely take place, noise will occur as the pipes force their way through brackets and saddles or, in an extreme case, fittings and pipes may actually bend.

The pipe fixings should, therefore, be checked to see that the pipe is free to move. This is especially the case where comparatively long runs of straight pipe are involved. Brackets and saddles should be slackened off so that the pipes are not tightly gripped.

Q192: *What would be the cause of copper tube breaking down—particularly 15mm—three to five years after installation?*

A number of small holes appear and the only cure is to renew the whole installation.

A: Corrosion such as small holes appearing in copper pipes does indeed point to something radically wrong after such a short period of service.

Generally all waters do tend to form a protective scale on the surfaces of the pipes and fittings, but it could well be that the water in querist's area is the cause of his troubles. Only a sort out with the water supply authority can ensure if this is the cause. If it is the authority should have already received complaints.

Another cauase could be dezincification due to the fact that the fittings are pressed out from brass and this contains zinc. In acidic or in alkaline waters of high chloride content the zinc is gradually dissolved out and will eventually corrode the copper tube.

The answer in these cases is to try to introduce lime where the water is acidic or to fit water treatment materials for hard water. Other than that it does mean using either copper or gunmetal fittings in conjunction with copper tube or change to a stainless steel system.

The problem is of course much more complicated than the above few lines can show, so I suggest that querist follows the points indicated below to get a better balanced view of what has to be done to remedy or eradicate this problem.

1. Check with the water authority for the chemical composition of the water supplied.

2. Check that no galvanised fittings have been placed along the pipe runs or in tanks, etc.

3. Check if at all possible to see if any of the copper tube was imported. If so it may not be to the standards laid down for use in this country and tubes with deposits of grease or carbon can upset the formation of a protective scale.

4. If the water is very acidic it may be possible to dose the cold water tank with lime so that a film of scale is formed as protection against corrosion.

5. Water is classified as hard, over pH7, or soft, below pH7, the mean pH7 is a water which will cause the least problems, particularly when it is heated as this is when water is at its most corrosive.

Only on-the-spot inquiries can really solve this problem, but the above points should give a guide to follow and a line of enquiries to chase to prevent this corrosion from taking place again.

Q193: *A three-bedroom terrace house is to be renovated and information is required on a method of fitting a shower, toilet and washbasin over a staircase, or as a different solution, breaking through a back bedroom into a newly-built double extension to form a full bathroom with a shower.*

A: It is impossible to answer this question without at least a full survey of the house, better still, much better would be a drawing and a personal inspection.

A small bungalow which has a very small bathroom, a bare 2 m each way, can contain a bath, a shower, a lavatory basin, a wc pan, a towel drier, a hot air heater and a lot of little gadgets.

So an enormous amount of room is not required. For each of the toilet fittings a space of about 750 mm by 750 mm is required as standing room, but the same bit of standing room can be shared among all the fittings since only one person at a time is likely to be using the room.

Take a bathroom over a staircase first. A plan and section would be the first thing to have. The plan would show the floor space of course, and should also show the position of the services—cold water supply, hot water supply if this is to come from outside the room (water can be heated inside the bathroom), electricity supply, and, very important, the drains. The section would show the headroom on the staircase, this is very important.

Then a visit to a sanitary-ware merchant to see what fittings are available. A catalogue would be a great help. Fittings made for very small rooms are available, but are most likely obtained from a specialist merchant.

Low-level wc pans project further from the back wall than high-level ones, intermediate to these two is th close-coupled suite.

Lavatory basins come in quite small sizes, narrow and/or with a short projection. They are also made to fit in a corner.

Baths, too, come in a range of sizes. I know of a bath called a "sitz," it is about 700 mm each way, i.e. about 700 mm deep at the deep end, halfway along the bottom of the bath is raised to a form a seat.

A sight of a catalogue or catalogues will give you a good idea of what is available and what will fit into the bathroom.

The important things are the services. Getting water to the fittings, and getting the wastes away. And bathrooms require good ventilation, especially if they contain gas heaters.

Much the same remarks apply to the alternative scheme. Headroom is not likely to be a problem. Ventilation can be difficult unless the bathroom is on an external wall. So can drains.

A wc must not open on to an habitable room. If the bathroom door opens into, say, a bedroom, when the wc must be a separate compartment with a door closing it off from the bathroom, and both wc and bathroom must be ventilated. Ventilation does not necessarily mean a window; it can be a vent in the ceiling connected to the outside air, but it must be adequate.

The local authority will require drawings showing what is proposed.

Q194: *Advice is required on the installation of three shower units in a cricket pavilion.*

The building is timber with a flat roof and a men's toilet will be converted into the shower room. The floor area is 3.3 m by 3 m and the ceiling height is 2.8 m.

Both gas and electricity are easily available and it is intended to extend the hot water into the kitchen if it is practicable. The showers would be used only during the summer on two and sometimes three days a week. Fig. 52 refers.

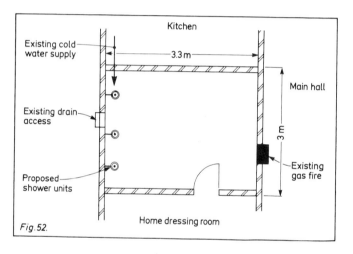

Fig. 52.

A: The main factors to be considered are:

1. A large quantity of hot water will be required over a relatively short period at infrequent intervals.

2. In order to avoid personal attention it is desirable that the heating system should be automatic.

A gas boiler with an output of not less than 30,000 Btu/hr will be required to supply a 300 litre indirect cylinder situated within the building. If the cold water supply is 'hard' an indirectly heated system should be installed.

A 450 litre cold water tank and a 90 litre expansion tank (the latter is required if the system is indirect) will have to be fitted at a height of about 1.5 m above the flat roof. These tanks will have to be enclosed in a timber structure so that they can be insulated. The cylinder should also be insultated with a 75 mm jacket.

Three thermostatically-controlled shower units will be required and it is important that the cold inlet is fed from the cold water tank in order that hot and cold water pressures are about equal.

A tapping from the hot water cylinder can be arranged to supply a hot tap in the kitchen.

The 450 litre tank and the expansion tank (if used) will be supplied from the existing cold water main. Suitable overflows being provided to each tank.

The most economical temperature for the hot water should be found by trial. Start with the boiler thermostat set at 140 deg. F and gradually raise the setting until it is found that there is sufficient hot water available for all the showers during one usage period.

Q195: *Are entirely separate h and c feeds advisable for a shower with the hot feed to the shower taken directly from the cylinder draw-off and the cold connected to the feed pipe out of the cold storage tank to the hot water cylinder?*

A: It is very difficult to maintain a constant shower temperature unless the mixer is thermostatically controlled. Even with such control it is necessary that there should not be too wide a difference in pressure between hot and cold supplies.

Where a shower is interconnected into a system supplying other outlets there is likely to be a change of pressure depending upon the number of outlets in use. As suggested, this will be minimised if the hot supply is taken from the cylinder draw-off and the cold supply from the cold feed to the cylinder; providing, of course, that they are of sufficient capacity to provide the required water flow in all conditions.

For example, the cold feed will be required to supply both the hot outlet and the cold supply to the shower. If the cold water tank has not sufficient height or the cold feed pipe is too small there may be insufficient pressure at the shower.

Q196: *A plumbing installation to improve a bungalow has been failed by a water company inspector.*

A brass stopcock must be replaced by one made of gunmetal and the cold supply from the water tank to the electric water heater must be in copper not plastic.

I had heard that the regulations were changed recently and if the work was started before then some of the rules might not apply. Where can a copy of the regulations been seen?

I am further told that the plastic water pipe from the company's connection in the garden should be encased in another pipe.

A: I am not in possession of a copy of the relevant water byelaws issued by the water undertaking supplying your area and can only refer to the model water byelaws upon which all undertakers' byelaws are based and add a few comments of my own. I will take the points you have raised one by one:

1. **Use of brass stopcock as opposed to gunmetal.** Brass and gunmetal are different alloys with gunmetal acknowledged as being far superior to brass. Use of the latter may be the possible cause of trouble in the future due to the possibility of de-zincification, resulting in the brass becoming "porous".

The model water byelaws require stopvalves to "be made of a suitable and corrosion-resisting material" and gunmetal may be the best material to use under the circumstances existing in your district. Local knowledge of the ground conditions is necessary to decide whether brass would survive or that gunmetal is essential.

The water inspector should be in possession of the necessary facts and advise accordingly—what suits one site may not necessarily suit another. It is a pity that the water inspector was not consulted before the job was started; knowledge of his requirements could have saved money and inconvenience!

2. **Cold water feed to water heater.** Although this is a "cold" feed pipe, it does become quite warm (possibly hot) from the bottom upwards as the heater warms up. Therefore, plastic pipe will soften under these conditions and should not be used. Copper pipe is certainly a very good choice for this purpose and I would endorse the inspector's requirements.

3. **Bylaws.** Regarding local byelaws, they could have been amended in the light of the undertaker's experience, or due to change of water undertaking—there has been some measure of reorganisation. It is usual practice (but not positive) to continue with the byelaws or regulations in force when the job was lawfully commenced. The word "lawfully" is very important in this context.

This point can only be answered by the local water undertaking, because changes could have been made with perhaps a very important alteration to take immediate effect.

4. **Obtaining a copy of the local byelaws.** Normally on request from the relevant water undertaking with perhaps a small charge

being made. If a copy is not available for purchase, or you may not wish to purchase, then a copy can be seen at the offices of the water undertaking. They may seem difficult to understand and, if the wording can be understood, the problem of interpretation is another matter entirely.

It is advisable to accept the interpretation of the water undertaking, even though it is not unknown for inspectors to argue among themselves about such matters, or for one inspector to accept something that another inspector would reject. This may be thought deplorable, but I am afraid it is something we all must live with. Positive and final interpretation can only be decided by the courts.

5. **Service pipe to be "encased" in extra pipe.** Once again, local knowledge of the ground, the relevant circumstances, the requirements or policy of the local water undertaking, local byelaws, etc., need to be known. There are different types of plastic used for water pipes in any case.

The model water byelaws contain many points relevant to this query, such as pipes to be protected from damage (a spade can cut through a buried polythene pipe) and contamination of the water to be guarded against (gas can permeate through a certain type of plastic pipe). Some engineers consider it good practice to "encase" certain service pipes within another pipe for various reasons, whether the inspector requires it or not.

Q197 *A soil pipe is situated on the outside wall of a house which is to be extended and the plan is to construct a new soil pipe inside the house.*

The roof is hipped and the pipe is to be placed in the corner (Fig. 53). There used to be a small chimney stack in this position before it was removed and slated over. The breast inside still remains and will have to be removed.

How should the detail between pipe, coping and slates be constructed?

A: My first reaction to this query is, "why bring the vent pipe through the hip in any case?"

The fact that there used to be a small chimney stack in this corner which has been removed and slated over indicates that there should be no major timber alteration problems, as the necessary trimming will have been carried out in the first place.

However, it will be necessary to clear some lesser important pieces out of the way to bring a vent pipe through in the position shown in Fig. 53.

Regarding the weathering between vent pipe and the roof, which, in this position involves a hip tile(s) and slates, the shape of the weathering piece would have to be a very complicated shape indeed, but not beyond the capabilities of a plumber who possesses expertise in lead-welding. The lead slate would have to be fabricated to suit the exact position and shape as found on the job. A "nasty little job" would be one way of describing it.

I believe the best answer lies in piercing the roof in another position away from the hip and using a "standard" lead slate in the traditional way and avoid the hip completely.

Querist need not worry about inserting bends in the vent pipe portion of the stack, but the soil pipe portion (up to and including the highest branch connection) should be free of bends and offsets except the essential bend at the foot of the stack.

My advice is to insert the necessary bends in the vent pipe—perhaps in the roof space—to swing the pipe direction away from the awkward corner and then back to the vertical again between two roof rafters in a position that will be regarded as "safe", ie. 1 m above the head of any window within a horizontal distance of 3 m.

Fig. 54 shows the fixing of the lead slate and, although tiles are indicated, the same detail applies similarly to slates.

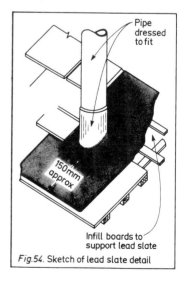

Fig.54. Sketch of lead slate detail

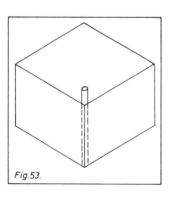

Fig.53.

Although I have continually mentioned lead and acknowledgement is due to the Lead Development Association for allowing me to reproduce the sketch, other sheet materials could be used for this slate, but my preference would be sheet lead.

The size required for the base of the slate may vary a little according to the size of the slate with which it is to be used in order to give adequate cover. The upstand of the lead slate is made a minimum of 100 mm high at the back. Sufficient number of slates is removed, the lead slate is put in position with the back dressed down and the front left turned up so that the slates can be replaced.

The slate is finally dressed down to a close fit to the slates and the upstand to a close fit with the pipe.

Q198: *In installing cold water supply systems, what precautions should be taken against the possibility of freezing due to frost damage?*

A: Water regulations generally require underground service pipes to be laid at a minimum depth of 760 mm as a precaution against frost. The service pipes should also enter the building at a minimum depth of 760 mm and be carried through to an internal wall at least 600 mm away from the inner face of any external wall.

The service pipe should run directly up to the cistern and be kept at least 2 m from the eaves.

Cistern overflow pipes should be arranged to prevent the inflow of cold air. This can be achieved by terminating the pipe about 50 mm below the water line.

Drain valves must be provided so that all parts of the installation may be drained and cisterns must be either well insulated or placed inside an insulated cistern room.

Q199: *How should a vent pipe be terminated?*

A: A vent pipe should discharge into the open air at a point that will not permit any foul air discharged from it to enter a building.

A suitable discharge point is considered to be at least 90 mm above any opening window within a horizontal distance of 3 m. The open end of the vent should be protected by a durable guard cage.

11 Plastering

Q200: *How should a background be prepared for plastering?*

A: Joints should be raked out on all types of brickwork and blockwork and the surface should then be dry brushed. Prior to plastering the whole surface should be dampened.

Concrete surfaces must be clean, dust free and keyed. Keying may be by hacking, spatterdashing, or by applying a patent liquid adhesive. The surface should be dampened.

Q201: *Why does plaster stick to Gyproc plasterboard on ceilings without falling down, as plaster on walls has more key to it?*

A: The form of paper used to cover plasterboard is not just any paper—it is the result of many years of research and development.

Gyproc has a certain setting time designed so that the Gypsum skimming coat, which in setting forms crystals which penetrate the paper covering of the Gyproc plasterboard to give maximum penetration and strength.

Nothing like this can take place when skimming brickwork as the key in this case is a mechanical one formed by the joints being raked out.

Q202: *Advice is required on the correct sequence for plastering. I say it should be: plasterboard ceilings; render and float walls; scrim to joints and ceiling angles; skim ceilings and walls.*

Over the past 15 years there has been a tendency for plasterers to board and scrim the ceiling first with the angle scrim going down the brickwork.

I believe this is done to avoid scaffolding twice and there have been arguments on every job.

A: Nowadays I don't expect there is any sequence in the way in which a building is plastered out. Each plasterer, or team of plasterers, will have different ideas on how the work will be carried out, and by the quickest possible means.

The best way I have found is to erect a skeleton scaffold to enable the boarding to be done.

The skeleton scaffold is erected in this way:

Three bearer planks are placed to the height and spacing required, the space dependent on the width of the room. On this planks, or bearers, four planks are placed at right angles; these are then used by the operatives to stand on so that they can fix the plasterboard to the ceiling joists. To move to fix the next adjacent boards they have only to slide the "platform" planks along the bearers to where required and carry on boarding. This is carried out until the ceiling has been completely boarded.

If the room is large the bearer planks will have to be dismantled and errected more than once.

When the boarding of the ceiling is completed the skeleton scaffolding is then dismantled and removed so that the rendering and floating of the walls can be carried out.

When the walls are completed a proper scaffold is erected so that the ceiling can be done.

First—all board joints are scrimmed, then the ceiling/wall angles, and finally the whole ceiling can be skimmed over and finished off.

When the ceiling is completed the scaffolding is dismantled and removed so that the operatives can carry on skimming the floated walls.

Q203: *Rooms are to be replastered in an old house built with rubble masonry without a dpc.*

The old internal lime plaster had become saturated by penetrating damp, due to material being piled up outside the external walls to a height of 1.2 m (see Fig. 55) and rising damp. The house stands on water-retaining soil and the water table is about 300 mm lower than ground floor level and the ground floor is lower than the surrounding ground.

After the piled up material was removed and the internal plaster hacked off, the walls dried out considerably, although relative humidity remains high. Only the bottom few millimetres now appear damp.

A: This sort of wall does need an internal lining that is actually separated from the inside of the stones as it is virtually impossiblee to guarantee that a plaster with a waterproofer incorporated in it will be laid on soundly enough to ensure that there are no weak spots or no cracks after the material has dried out.

Furthermore this sort of mix will be very dense and could lead to more problems with humidity unless either a sheeting of expanded polystyrene was placed between the waterproofed plaster and the finishing plaster, or plasterboard dry lining was fixed over the waterproofed plaster.

Bitumen lathing seems to be the answer even if it means that the rough stonework has to be levelled over at places with a mortar. The lathing could then be fixed with hardened masonry nails and the usual plastering carried out.

To help the walls to keep in better condition and to ventilate the space between the wall and the lathing, I suggest that inserting 50 mm land drain pipes set an angle sloping towards the ground if a few of these were placed at the bottom and top of the walls it could clear the moisture that rises up from the floor level.

If the new concrete floor has not yet been laid, sheet polythene should be used and turned up at the sides so that it is fitted behind the lath.

With a ground water table so near to the surface, I suggest that if the site is a sloping one land drains be laid to take away water from

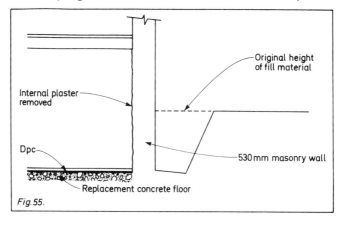

Fig. 55.

Original height of fill material

Internal plaster removed

Dpc

530 mm masonry wall

Replacement concrete floor

the house. This would help considerably in keeping the whole place a lot drier than it is at present.

Q204: *Can you recommend a method for dealing with blackened new, undecorated plaster following a fire in a chip pan.*

A: Having recently had several experiences of trying to clean smoked and sooted plaster walls and ceilings caused by chip pan or modern upholstery fires (these tend to give very similar soot and smoke depositions), I doubt very much if it will be possible to remove the whole of the smoke and soot, particularly on what is virtually bare plaster, so it does come down to a matter of providing a seal and one that not only seals, but penetrates as well.

One product that has been tried out and found to be very satisfactory is Blue Circle stabilising solution, I know this material has not been formulated for this purpose, but it does bind back as well as seal.

Care has to be taken using this liquid and gloves and goggles are recommended, especially so if ceilings have to be treated.

Q205: *What is splatterdash?*

A: Splatterdash is ordinary portland cement and sharp clean sand mixed to a thick slurry in the ratio of 1:2.

Q206: *The architect involved in the modernisation of two cottages our firm is carrying out has asked that Carlite plaster should not be used, if no extra cost is involved.*

The old brickwork is one brick solid. Can you recommend a suitable plaster for this work? The new plaster is to contain a waterproofing agent.

The architect seems to think that in this instance Carlite finish will cause too much condensation and that a more porous plaster is required. It is to be two-coat work.

A: I do not see how an architect can say that by using Carlite plaster for a solid wall it will cause more condensation that any other type of plaster. He also "specifies" that a waterproofer must be used.

It is to be presumed that the waterproofer in the mix is to halt dampness or water from entering through the wall from the outside, does he realise that the same waterproofer is also going to halt any of the humidity in the room from being absorbed by the wall plaster thereby causing condensation to trickle down the wall and eventually causing discolouration of the finished surface?

The best method here is to apply three coats of Synthaprufe to the internal wall surface, each coat being applied when the one before has dried thoroughly. While the last coat is still tacky it should be 'blinded' with a course gritty sand an left for 24 hr to dry out.

The next day take a soft broom over the surface to remove the loose sand. Then apply a floating coat of Carlite bonding plaster, not thicker than 12 mm where possible, bring this to a true and plane surface with a straight-edge, or Darby, then use a scratch-float to form a key for the finishing coat. This can be applied when the floating coat has gone in (set).

I do not know if querist is going to paint the plastered surface when it has dried out completely. If he is then it should be pointed out that to paint such wall with a gloss paint will do it no good as far as causing condensation is concerned.

Another way to "waterproof" the internal wall is to fix Newtonite lath first, then render on a floating coat, ruling off, finishing this off with a finishing plaster in the normal way.

A sand/cement, sand/lime/cement backing is termed as solid plastering and is more suspect as the cause of condensation. If there are no vents in the wall, then there would be no harm in fixing at least two into the wall, that is internal and external, of course.

Q207: *What is bricklath?*

A: This is a pliable metal lathing consisting of square-mesh lath with small pieces of burnt clay at every intersection of the crossed wires.

The burnt clay is similar to common brick and will supply a reasonable amount of suction when being rendered. It is made in sheets of varying sizes from about 2 m by 600 mm and must be fixed across the joists with galvanised nails or staples at 100 mm intervals.

Q208: *What is fibrous plasterwork?*

A: This is plasterwork which contains reinforcement and which has been produced as a cast from a mould. The plaster is usually plaster of Paris, although harder plasters, such as Keene's cement or special class A's, may be used in certain cases.

The reinforcement is usually two layers of jute canvas at a maximum of 300 mm centres. Synthetic fibres may be used instead of canvas, and metal sections or heavier timber instead of wood lath.

Other materials may be used by the plasterer to produce casts, however. Those to be used externally need to be cast from a cement and aggregate mix and reinforced with a rust-proof metal mesh and metal sections. The aggregate is usually sand, but stone dust is used when producing reconstructed stone.

Q209: *How are cracks made good in moulded work?*

A: In fibrous plasterwork they are cut out and dusted, damped to control the suction, and stopped with plaster of Paris as for new work.

In plain mouldings, the new plaster is ruled in with a joint rule or a piece of busk for straight or curved work respectively.

In enriched work, cracks are filled as the plaster becomes cheesey and modelled in with the appropriate small tools.

In old in situ work cracks are cut out, preferably undercut, and dusted to remove all loose material. Although the crack may be damped to control suction, it can also be treated with PVA solution.

This, mixed with three to four parts water and painted on in two coats, allowing each to dry, has the added advantage of penetrating friable, sandy undercoats and stabilising them, as well as improving adhesion and controlling the suction.

Q210: *What operations are involved in fixing fibrous plaster casts on site?*

A: Remove any lifting-out sticks or false brackets from the cast and trim from the strike-offs any selvedge that will prevent the cast from seating properly on its fixings.

Check the cast for correct size, check pick ups, cut to mitres and joints.

When fixings are to be made across the width of a cast from below, mark across the face the position of the wood-lath reinforcement.

Lift the cast into position and hold it there by hand, struts, hangers, cleats or blocks.

Fix the cast to the fixings, straightening and lining through when necessary.

Q211: *Would you please recommend vinyls suitable for either hot or cold pours for decorative plasterwork.*

A: There are several vinyls suitable for cold pours and hot pours. The best is said to be Rhodorsil which is a silicone rubber and produces a clean cast, though it cannot be remelted and used again. It is supplied by Jacobson Chemicals of Churt, Surrey.

Wacker silicone is one of a variety of vinyls and is cheaper. It is supplied by Micro Products of Ickenham.

For hot pours there are a number of vinyls, one of which is Gelflex, supplied by Proplastics of Horley, Surrey.

All the manufacturers produce very good leaflets on the use of their products.

Q212: *What are the causes of plaster setting too fast?*

A: When the material sets too fast to allow for normal working, the cause may be one of several. The plaster may have been too hot or fresh, the mixing water dirty, or the plaster stored under damp conditions.

With plaster and sand mixes, dirty sand will cause an accelerated set. Dirty tools, appliances, mixing boards, buckets, etc., will cause the plaster to set quickly in small quantities, with the result that the mix is lumpy or knotty.

Q213: *I have to carry out a job using fibrous plaster casts, but they will need to be stored on site for some time. Could you explain how best to store these items?*

A: Fibrous plaster casts should always be stored face-to-face and back-to-back and are better fixed together face-to-face in pairs. Any warping—caused by shape and structure—in each new wet cast will then be exactly cancelled out by the other pair, and the face of the cast will not be marked by another's rough back. Cornices are best boxed together and tied with scrim, while flat casts are best cleated.

Q214: *Could you explain what causes cracking in solid plastering?*

A: If the cracks are large then it is almost certain that they are caused by structural movement not as a result of bad plastering. Structural movement causes the background to split and this in turn is transmitted to the plaster surface. If the building is fairly new they may be due to settlement or excessive vibration from other work being carried out in the building.

The only way to remedy such cracks is to cut them right back to the background on either side of the crack and if possible undercut. The exposed area should be brushed dry and free from loose particles, dampened and coated with an emulsion type wood adhesive (pva). Then simply finished in the usual way.

If the cracks are smaller this is more likely to be caused by poor application, strong dense mixes used over weaker backgrounds and backings and shrinkage. These must be cut out, dampened and finished in the usual way.

Q215: *On some recently completed plasterwork there are some white frothy deposits. What are they and how can they be removed?*

A: It sound very much like you are describing efflorescence. This is probably caused through salt being present in either the background or the backing coat. It may also be caused through excessive dampness due to either a faulty dampproof course or the lack of one. Usually it will disappear when the structure dries out, but may return when the dampness does. If time allows, the area should be left until the salts expend their energies.

Q216: *Can you explain to me what causes a rapid set during a job when previous mixes were satisfactory?*

A: When plaster sets faster than normal there are a number of possible causes. Each should be eliminated in turn to identify the real reason. First the plaster could have been too hot or fresh, second that the mixing water was dirty or thirdly the plaster stored under damp conditions. With plaster and sand mixes, dirty sand will cause the plaster to set faster than normal as will dirty tools, mixing boards and buckets etc.

Q217 : Can you please explain what causes plaster to set too slowly?

A: When plaster sets too slowly or is 'dead' it is usually caused by the plaster being stored too long or bags being left open and not used in rotation. Plasters that can be affected in this way normally have a date of manufacture on the bag and it should be used within three months of this date. All plasters should be stored in the dry, off the floor in a ventilated area.

Q218 : Could you tell me how a lightweight screed is applied?

A: It is applied in exactly the same way as an ordinary Portland cement/sand screed, though it is usually much thicker—up to 100 mm is normal. Once it has been laid and flattened, it should be covered with a conventional screed to a thickness of 19 mm to protect the weaker lightweight screed. Mixes for a lightweight screed are 1:6 OPC/vermiculite and for the protecting screed 1:3 OPC/sand.

Q219 : I have a small job which requires the walls to be dry lined. Could you tell me how I should treat the joints between the boards?

A: The methods adopted really depend on whether the boards are square edged or tapered. If square edged the boards should be butted and the joint covered over while the tapered boards are made flush by taping the joints and plastering over.

First the joints are filled with Gyproc joint filler, then a continuous band of jointing tape is applied over the filler, then a new layer of filler applied over the tape. Any surplus must be cleaned off before any set has taken place. Once it has set refill if necessary or sand off the surface flush.

Q220 : Could you explain the correct method of storing plasterboards?

A: What ever size of plasterboard is being used the method of storing is the same. They should be laid flat, on top of each other, to form a stack not higher than 1 m. They must have a level, dry base with timber battens placed at 400 mm spacings. If there are any possibilities of dampness in the storage area then the boards must be protected against it. A sheet of polythene on the floor and around the boards might be the answer.

Q221: *What is the effect of fire on Gypsum plaster?*

A: Although Gypsum plasters are defined under British Standards as non-combustible and will indeed reduce the spread of fire extreme heat will cause a breakdown of adhesion between the background and the backing coat of plaster. This is thought to be greater when the backing coat contains, sand, lightweight aggregates such as vermiculite and perlite provide greater adhesion.

Q222: *What is builders lime and how is it produced?*

A: In plastering work it is pure lime which is used. It is known under a number of names including, white lime, mountain lime, high-calcium lime and chalk lime. It is sold in the form of calcium hydroxide (slaked or hydrated lime) which is an off-white powder.

Limestone or chalk is heated to drive off the carbon dioxide (quicklime). This slaked to hydrated lime by the addition of water. As the water combines chemically with the quicklime, the latter breaks down into a fine, dry powder. These limes will not set in contact with water and are known as non-hydraulic limes. For the plasterer they are prepared and stored wet in the form of lime putty which can be used in sand/cement mixes as a plasticiser.

Limes produced from limestone or chalk containing clay will set in contact with water and are known as hydraulic or semi-hydraulic.

12 Windows

Q223: *A feature of a house completed last year was a purpose-made hardwood window frame to the front elevation, the elevation which takes 90 per cent of the weather.*

A local joinery manufacturer sent out men to measure up and discuss the construction of this frame, which is purely to give light and has no opening sashes. In due course it was delivered and glazed by a local glazier.

Thereafter the frame leaked very badly and it was found that it had been constructed in such a way that the glass had been fitted from the inside as the frame had been rebated in this fashion. The result was that the rain ran down the glass, down the rebate and into the interior of the house.

The manufacturer claimed that this was perfectly normal construction for a frame of this type. The frame has been reglazed at my expense, the glazier using a special mastic compound and this has cured the trouble for the time being, but this trouble may raise again.

Is it good practice to construct the frame in this manner?

A: It is customary for the face side of a window in a domestic building to be on the inside. The glazing beads or putty is therefore on the outside, the side from which the glass is inserted.

If it is desired to make the outside the face side, as it may well be in this case, then the procedure must be reversed. If the window is visible at close quarters from the outside, I would think that this is what the maker had in mind. The frame being in hardwood, could have been naturally finished with polyurethane varnish, etc., and so it would be preferable to glaze from the inside.

External doors are glazed from the inside, the outside being the face, and so are shop windows.

I feel it would be most unfair to criticise workmanship without having seen the job, but it would seem to me that the window could have been glazed originally under unfavourable conditions, perhaps when the frame was damp or with faulty material. I am convinced that now that the glazing has been repeated it should give satisfactory service. It is hoped that the horizontal members of the window frame, particularly the sill, have been made to a suitable section to convey the rain away from the putty line.

Also, do not confuse condensation with incoming moisture which could be present in quantity in a new building.

Q224: *Delivery of windows for an extension to a house was delayed during construction and to allow the job to continue frames were made 12 mm larger than the expected windows.*

When they arrived the windows were fitted with sealant up the sides.

Now, the wet comes in and soaks the Carlite plaster in some places. More sealant outside has improved it. If the same was done inside and the reveals were rendered with a waterproof cement and plastered, would this clear up the remainder or is there a more satisfactory way? The building is very exposed to high winds and rain.

The walls were erected with concrete blocks inside and out, the cavity filled with mineral wool insulation and the walls outside rendered with waterproof cement.

A: There is nothing against fitting the windows after the walls have been erected, in fact most high class buildings with hardwood windows always used to be built like this, but there must be inbuilt into the brick or blockwork a vertical dpc and also one at the head or lintel line.

This is usually fitted by adding a closure to the cavity walling to the window openings. If this was done in this instance it should have been possible to allow the vertical dpc membrane to stand proud of the blockwork openings, thus the material would have provided a barrier to damp penetration.

I wonder if this is the root cause of your problems with dampness showing in several places?

While a lot of mastic sealants are quite good at sealing joints, where the joints are wide they do tend to slip and it is possible that at some small places the mastic has drooped and left a small hole and this is where the water has been able to penetrate.

Furthermore Carlite is a light-weight gypsum-based plaster and such plaster bases do tend to show up any slight dampness and generally make the amount of dampness look much worse than it really is.

I presume that the windows are placed back from the face of the external rendering. If this is the case and the joints are wide round the windows, fixing or wedging in between the frames and blocks with strips of expanded metal and lath and then a mastic should help to make the outside joints watertight.

This, of course, will not help if a vertical dpc has been omitted, for in that case it would be necessary to provide an internal one by fixing bitumen dpc, followed by expanded metal lath to provide a key for the plaster.

Certainly a cement/sand mix will provide a better material for not showing the spread of dampness than will the gypsum-based plaster, but again if there are internal reveals, one could place slates as a vertical dpc bedding them on with a cement mortar. This should prevent any further signs of dampness, and it may well be that attention to both the external and internal reveals will be necessary to make the job satisfactory.

I note that the walls were rendered in waterproofed cement. Much has been said and written about using hard renderings and the general opinion now is that renderings should not be too rich a mix as this only tends to create crazing and cracking of the finish and thus allows some water penetration to the brick or blockwork behind.

This moisture cannot evaporate readily, thus creating problems, whereas a softer rendering mix, while absorbing some moisture, will not so readily crack and craze and will allow the moisture to evaporate quickly, particularly if the rendering has not had too fine a trowelled finish.

Q225: *A few months ago I installed aluminium windows fitted with double glazed sealed units. They are generally very satisfactory and are closely sealed at opening sashes and do not have any condensation 'weep' holes even though there is a condensation tray fitted to the sill.*

In frosty weather there is condensation on the aluminium, but not on the glass, particularly in a bedroom facing north and in a kitchen facing north. Are there any suitable remedies or materials which can be fixed to the aluminium to eliminate the condensation?

A: The reason for the condensation is simply that there is not enough air changes in the room. It is assumed that these windows are replacement windows; the draughts that used to come through the old windows—although causing heat loss—allowed for ventilation. The reason the condensation is on the aluminium is that this is the coolest surface.

The solution does not lie with any type of product, the best thing is to ensure that the rooms are properly ventilated.

Q226: *In a property built in the 1930's the glass in a number of steel window frames is cracked and most of the frames are rusty to a greater or lesser degree.*

Some of the frames have also distorted quite badly. Is it the rusting which has caused these other problems, and if so what remedies can be effected?

A: The main cause of the cracked glass is almost certainly the rusting of the steel framework which was insufficiently protected prior to use. As the rusting takes place it expands the frame, consequently exerting pressure on the glass causing it to crack.

The rusting has probably come about either through the ingress of rainwater down the back edge of external glazing putties or by condensation seeping down and between window pane and frame.

Where the frames are badly rusted the most economic solution would be to replace them altogether. If they are not too severe then remove the putty, glass and excess rust, treat the steel with rust inhibitor and primer and reglaze the window.

Loose putty in other frames where the glass is still intact can be raked or chipped out and any rust treated. It should be noted however that this usually offers only a temporary solution.

Q227: *Could you give some guidance on building steel windows a) directly into brickwork, b) into prepared openings and c) into wooden subframes?*

A: Steel windows built directly into brickwork should be positioned so that a fully weatherproof seal is maintained between the window/wall junctions. The back of the long leg of the frame section rests against the vertical dpc, in line with the inner face of the outer leaf. The fixing lugs hold the dpc in position and prevent it being disturbed during construction.

A 3 mm wide margin between the rising brickwork and frame is recommended on the outside to enable the mastic fillet to form a seal with the dpc—as well as with the window and wall.

It is recognised that, in many cases, the external leaf will butt up to the frame but the mastic fillet should, in all cases, cover adjacent surfaces by about 5 mm to ensure effective adhesion. The compatibility of the mastic and the dpc should be checked with the respective manufacturers.

Steel windows built into prepared openings can generally follow the recommended practice for building directly in. Openings should be only 6 mm greater than the work size defined in both the manufacturers' literature and BS 990. Oversize openings can lead to weathering and fixing difficulties.

The vertical dpc should project 15 mm into the opening to rest behind the long leg of the frame section. Fixing lugs can be set into sand courses left in the brickwork and finally set in mortar or, alternatively, be screwed to the inner leaf.

Steel windows set in wooden sub-frames are recommended where cold bridging/condensation problems are likely to occur. With this method a conventional vertical dpc is not required—the sub-frame itself is used to close the cavity. A watertight seal can be obtained by compressing a self-adhesive flexible polyurethane foam strip between the outer leaf of the wall and the wooden sub-frame. A mastic fillet is necessary externally.

The wooden sub-frame is fixed with galvanised mild steel lugs and rustproof steel screws. Slotted holes in the lugs allow for fixing the sub-frame plumb, square and uniformly tight. The steel window frame is bedded into the wooden sub-frame with a non-curing sealant and fixed with rustproof steel screws.

Q228: *I am about to replace some vertical sliding windows. Could you tell me if these are made to a standard design and size so that replacements might be available 'off-the-shelf' or will I have to find a joinery shop to make replacements?*

A: Like all standard types of casement windows, double hung and vertical sliding windows in timber are the subject of a British Standard specification and therefore are available in a wide range of standard sizes and designs. With the increased interest in renovating houses rather than demolishing them more and more merchants and joinery shops offer a ready made selection of sliding sashes. Two patterns are available. Traditional with weights and cords or the more modern type with spiral balances.

Q229: *Could you please tell me how to fix double hung sash windows into brick openings?*

A: Windows using spiral balances are normally fixed as the wall is built up, as in a conventional timber window. Replacement windows can be easily fixed into existig openings using frame cramps screwed to the back of the pulley stile. Box frames with weights only have a thin back lining so the only method of fixing is to use folding wedges to hold the window in position. The joint

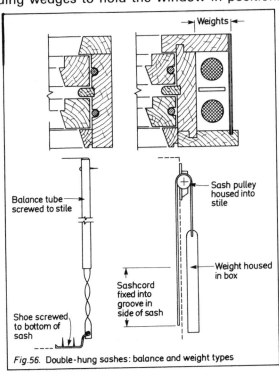

Fig.56. Double-hung sashes: balance and weight types

between the brickwork and window frame should be pointed after fixing to prevent the entry of moisture (**Fig. 56**).

Q230: *The paint on the windows of a property I am renovating is starting to crack and flake off, and they were only painted nine months ago. Can you tell me why?*

A: I am assuming that the windows are timber and if this is the case then the answer could be that the previous surface was not prepared properly and the paint is not adhering properly. Failing this 70 per cent of all paint failures on the exterior of houses is due to ultra-violet light affecting the wood surface. I suggest you try a micro-porous paint which incorporates special filters to prevent the harmful sun rays reaching the wood surface.

Q231: *Is it worth trying to repair the bottom rail of a sash once it has decayed? I feel it would be better to replace the entire sash and more cost effective too.*

A: It would depend on the degree of the decay. If only the tenon is affected with the joint breaking open then it would be better to repair rather than replace. If the window is quite old and has a lot of character then it is better to repair than replace as the original mouldings may not be easy to reproduce.

If the rot and decay has reached up into the stile, then it would be cost effective under normal circumstances with fairly modern windows simply to replace the sash with a new one. If older, remember that the frame might have settled a little over the years and the opening no longer square. This should be carefully measured before a replacement sash is made. A piece of plywood or hardboard used as a template will assist in the making of a replacement. A temporary repair can be made with an angle bracket screwed across the joint but in time the sash will need replacing.

13 Heating/Ventilating

Q232: *Some years ago solid fuel appliances were installed in a three-storey semi-detached house with all fireplaces and flues in the gable end wall. After a very short period, all the chimney breasts showed signs of corrosion and the smell in each room became unbearable.*

At that time, the walls were plastered with lime mortar and finished with lime skimming. All plaster was hacked off and the walls rendered with cement mortar, finished with Sirapite. This proved successful for a few years, but the same signs are appearing again.

Consideration is now being given to taking out all appliances and fireplaces and installing a gas central heating system. This would reduce the number of flues to be used to one or two. If a free-standing gas-fired boiler with a balanced flue is chosen it might be possible to use a short flue pipe instead of having to insert a flexible pipe about 12 m long.

If all flues are swept and sealed, would there be a likelihood that with the change of temperature inside and outside the building there would be a possibility of the corrosion that already exists continuing to eat through the mortar joints causing further trouble?

Would this problem be solved if after sweeping, the flues were filled with foam to keep air out of the flues?

A: To effect a cure it is essential to understand the cause of 'corrosion' in chimneys and flues.

When a fuel is burnt, whether it be solid, liquid or gaseous, heat is produced together with various by-products. In general, these by-products constitute the 'smoke' or materials which pass up the flue and are, or should be, discharged to atmosphere.

The composition of bituminous coal is 40–60 per cent fixed carbon, 28–40 per cent volatiles, 4–10 per cent ash, 2–6 per cent moisture and 6–3 per cent sulphur. The basic heat comes from the conversion of the fixed carbon to carbon dioxide. Among the volatiles there is hydrogen, methane, etc., which if also burnt add to the total heat produced. The extent to which the volatiles are burnt depends upon the temperature of the fire and the provision of sufficient oxygen at the right places in the combustion chamber to enable full combustion to take place.

When a fire is operating at a very low combustion rate some of the volatiles will be heated up to gaseous form, but will not be burnt. They will, therefore, be mixed with the carbon dioxide to form the 'smoke' or flue gases.

If the temperature in the chimney is insufficient to keep the volatiles in gaseous form they will condense to liquid on the walls of the chimney. They are usually black tar like substances containing sulphur, the latter being responsible for the unpleasant smell. The tar soaks into brickwork, cement and plaster and is extremely difficult to remove. However, if the production of the tar is stopped and the walls re-rendered it is unlikely that the trouble will continue.

Of course, if the chimney is lined with a metal liner this will prevent the tar reaching the brickwork, etc. Similarly, increasing the combustion temperature will burn the tar before it leaves the appliance and ensuring that the chimney is kept as hot as possible will help to prevent condensation. Exposed chimneys or flues can be insulated to help maintain the internal temperature.

Another solution would be to use a solid fuel with less volatiles. For example, anthracite has the following composition: 80–90 per cent fixed carbon, 5–7 per cent volatiles, 3–8 per cent ash, 2–4 per cent moisture and 6–2 per cent sulphur. Coke has even less volatiles than anthracite while Coalite has about the same.

Q233: *I built an external brick chimney breast and stack on a modernised and extended timber-framed old cottage, as shown in Fig. 57.*

The complete stack is tied into studwork with L cramps, but otherwise it is free-standing. When a strong wind is blowing from direct north or NNE, down draught fills the living room with smoke. Otherwise the flue operates perfectly.

The stack has been raised to 150 mm above the ridges without result and a galvanised swivelling cowl has been tried unsuccessfully.

Is the trouble due to the wind in this northerly direction causing air currents to swirl around the roof faces? There are no other buildings to affect it and the other stack on the house is 100 per cent.

Would further raising of the stack eliminate the trouble and would the strength of the stack allow a further 610 mm to 900 mm to be added, bearing in mind the timber-frame support?

A: I can understand a NNE wind proving troublesome as it would seem to be passing over a large roof area and in so doing being diverted, thus causing some down draught as there could be slight loss of air pressure during periods of gusts of wind.

Solving such problems is very much a matter of trial and error, the trouble is that this method does involve time and materials so in the first instance I suggest using a reasonably simple method of placing a half-round ridge tile across the top of the existing pot.

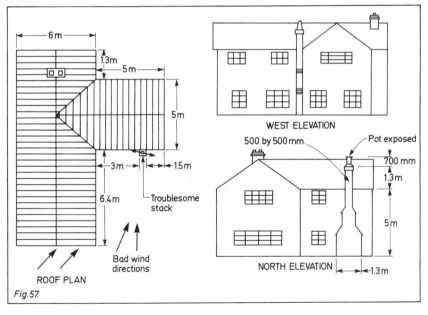

Fig.57

The tile should be bedded on with mortar to make a joint, otherwise it may rattle, and then tying it firmly down to and over the rim of the pot with binding wire, crossed over the half-round ridge tile to prevent it moving.

I suggest that the tile is slightly angled so that lengthways the tile presents a 'block' to the NNE direction (as indicated by the arrowed line across the stack on the roof plan).

If this does not succeed then one other type of chimney terminal that I have tried out successfully in several cases is the Marcone. This can be obtained in several heights and is constructed on the Venturi system whereby air is diverted upwards on the outer surfaces which in turn tends to create an upwards draught which in many cases has stopped down draughts.

Q234: *It is proposed to install a Rayburn open fire in an inglenook.*

Designed for a chimney recess, the fire is free-standing and a 300 mm by 180 mm rectangular flue pipe to match can be obtained up to 2.4 m in length from the manufacturer.

As Fig. 58 shows, there is a large flue void of the old cottage inglenook type and the problem is to provide a small-section flue between the fire and the point at which the existing flue reduces to dimensions small enough to effectively maintain a draught. The ceiling of the inglenook is, at present, plasterboard.

The masonry of the chimney flue internally is rough, as would be expected in property two centuries old. The cottage is occupied and fully decorated so drastic rebuilding of the flue cannot be contemplated.

A: The Rayburn open fire will be satisfactory.

The chimney should be divided into two sections by fitting a galvanised iron register plate at the 'ceiling' of the inglenook. The plate should be cut to receive the 300 mm by 180 mm manufacturer's flue section.

Above the plate a flexible steel flue not less than 175 mm in diameter should extend say 3 m up the chimney.

It will not be possible, without extensive building work, to seal the flexible pipe at the top but, having met this problem in my own house, I have found the suggested arrangement works satisfactorily without being sealed.

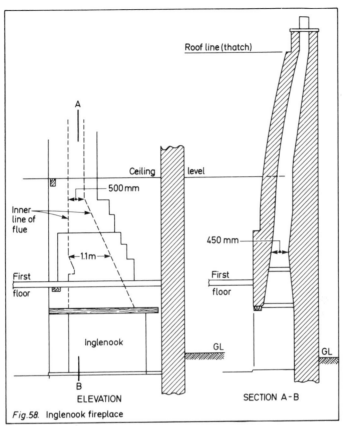

Fig.58. Inglenook fireplace

Some arrangement must be made so that the chimney can be swept. This can be achieved by providing a small brick chamber above the register plate which has a soot door through the wall of the chimney to the outside of the house. The bottom of the chamber receives the 300 mm by 180 mm flue pipe while the rising flexible flue enters the top of the chamber.

An entry slide should be provided in the register plate so that cleaning can be effected if necessary. A 50 mm layer of glass fibre insulation on the register plate to reduce heat losses.

Q235: *Renovating an old house has included bricking up existing fireplaces and installing central heating.*

The owner wishes to retain a fire in one of the rooms and in removing the old fireplace it has been found that the

joists run under the fireplace and are charred.
Advice is required on the precautions to be taken in installing a new fireplace.

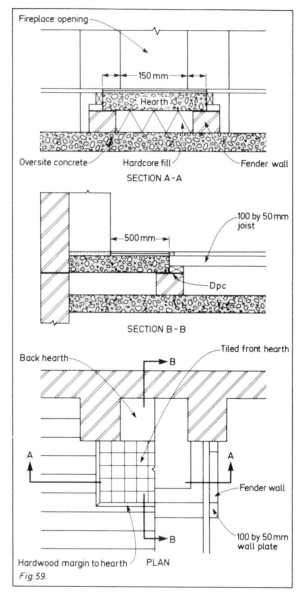

Fig. 59.

A: The situation as described is dangerous and constitutes a high fire risk. The joists should be cut out and the hearth and floor around reconstructed to comply with the requirements of the Building Regulations.

The concrete hearth should be not less than 125 mm thick, extend within the fireplace recess to the back and jambs, project not less than 500 mm in front of the jambs, and extend not less than 150 mm on each side of the fireplace. Fig. 59 shows a plan and sectional elevations illustrating typical construction.

Fig. 60 shows a sectional isometric view to further illustrate the construction.

As the job is a conversion of old property, I would advise querist to check the entry to the flue above the fireplace opening, and if there is an old chimney bar there and a rather large space above the fireplace, to cut out and replace this with a shaped lintel or a throat unit (Fig. 61).

It might also be wise to insert a flue lining, especially if a gas fire or boiler is to be used. Flexible flue liners are available for this purpose.

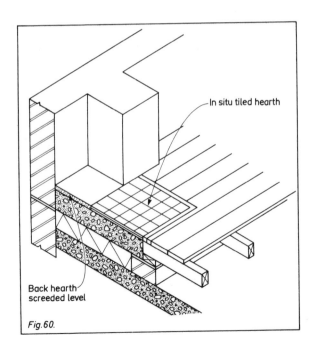

In situ tiled hearth

Back hearth screeded level

Fig. 60.

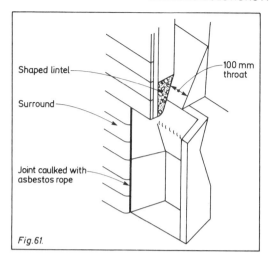

Shaped lintel

100 mm throat

Surround

Joint caulked with asbestos rope

Fig.61.

Q236: *Warm air fan heaters are to be installed in a chapel vestry. There is no insulation in the roof space.*

What size of heater(s) will be required and where would they be obtained?

Where would they best be placed?

If the roof space—10 m by 5 m—was insulated with 50 mm glass fibre, what difference would this make?

A: Churches, chapels and halls where meetings take place at intervals demand forms of heating which will provide a quick build-up of heat. Electric warm air fan heaters or infra-red heaters do this sort of job efficiently and cleanly. They do not need much attention once they have been fitted properly and are of the right size and type for the job in hand.

If this warm air type of heater is selected then it would seem that one at either end of the hall fixed at around 3 m above floor level would be suitable, the most appropriate size would be 4 kW, but they should be fitted with thermostats to each so that they can be set to a given air temperature.

This type of heater can be adjusted to any angle so that if it is not possible to place the heaters centrally on the end walls, the heater can be swivelled round so that the warm air is directed to cover the whole of the hall.

No mention is made of the type of ceiling. If it is matchboard there is bound to be cracks where the tongues have split or broken, thus the insulation value will be rather poor. A layer of 50 mm quilt will make a lot of difference; it will allow the heaters to warm up the hall more quickly than would otherwise be the case, but as there are so many other factors in the place it is not really possible to give any degree of the actual difference that would be made by using insulating quilt.

Any reputable electrical wholesalers should be able to supply these heaters, but it will mean a complete wiring job to supply the power so it would be advisable to either seek out a firm of electrical sub-contractors and get a price for the whole job, or check with the electricity board and ask them to check on forms of heating, supplies, availability of heaters and a cover price for the complete job.

There is no necessity to accept the electricity board's price, but at least it will give a specification to work to. This sort of service is or should be offered by all the board's areas or districts, without charge.

Q237 : *The smell of gas fumes is constantly present in the living room of a ground floor back extension to a two-storey house where a gas fire has been fitted.*

The chimney pots were removed about five years ago because they started to keel over and the brickwork was lowered and capped with half-round stoneware.

To test the flue, the gas fire was removed and paper was burnt in the grate with the result that more smoke came into the room than went up the chimney. There, apparently, is not enough up-draught. How can this be overcome?

A : Without seeing the situation of the house and the surrounding features such as trees, other buildings, etc., it is difficult to give precise information.

The half-round capping of the chimney will obviously have a directional effect and if the prevailing wind is in alignment this could be the cause of the trouble.

In considering the matter the basic facts of chimney operation should be kept in mind.

Any heating appliance fitted at the bottom of a chimney heats the air which therefore becomes lighter than the air at ambient temperature. The lighter warm air rises up the chimney because it is displaced by the colder heavier air. In an extreme case the warm air rising up the chimney may be cooled by a damp wet chimney so that its temperature falls to ambient temperature. This situation is the equivalent of a more or less complete stoppage of the chimney.

To sum up. The internal area and insulation of a chimney must be related to the size of the appliance being used. A large, badly insulated chimney and a small appliance may cause trouble. Too large a chimney can be overcome by fitting a flexible metal liner.

Q238: *I have a solid fuel burning appliance and frequently smoke blows back down the chimney into the room. What are the possible causes?*

A: The downward wind current blowing on to the top of the chimney is often the cause of flue gases and smoke being blown back down the flue and out into the room.

This type of downdraught can be caused by the chimney being near to high objects such as taller buildings, trees, and higher neighbouring chimneys.

Another cause could be the position of the chimney in relation to the surrounding land. If it is situated in a depression in the ground or standing on sloping ground the wind following the contours may blow down on to it.

Raising the chimney or fitting a taller pot may be the remedy in a few cases, but mainly this condition will require an anti-downdraught cowl fitted to the chimney outlet.

Differential air pressures set up by the wind flow around the building is another possible cause. The air pressure is usually positive on the windward side and negative on the leeward side. Negative air pressure will cause suction of air from a room through ventilators and round ill-fitting doors and windows.

This air being sucked out of the room has to be replaced and may be drawn down the chimney.

Q239: *I have a problem with my boiler flue on which I would like your advice and suggestions for solving.*

An existing brickwork flue serving an oil fired boiler, installed some five years ago, is lined with Kopex stainless steel flexible flue liner terminating with a weather cap. Discoloured water now discharges through the plaster face of the flue in the kitchen causing damage to the decorations. This occurs most frequently immediately after wet weather or extremely humid conditions.

A: It would be worth checking to make sure that the weather cap is completely sealed as water may be coming in there, filtering down through brickwork which, even if the chimney was thoroughly cleaned, will still be stained and ending up discharging through the plaster face. Alternatively it may be caused by water filtering through the external wall of the chimney with the same result.

One other possibility is condensation caused by the boiler on the outside of the lining, travelling first upwards then coming down again mixed with the soot.

Really, a stainless steel insulated chimney should have been instalaled in the first place. The only solution we can suggest is that you seal off the chimney at the top and bottom and run a flue up the outside of the building.

Q240: *What is meant by a comfort zone?*

A: This is a conception used in the design of air conditioning systems. For winter, the most comfortable equivalent temperature in England is 16.8 deg C. This is for people doing light work. In summer, the temperature should be about 2.2 deg C higher, lower for heavy work.

Q241: *Do radiators have to be fitted under windows?*

A: There is no need to fit them if you have double glazing. If you do not, then the under-window radiator does counteract the descending cold air—but at a price; the warm air meets the coldest surface, giving the greatest heat loss initially. In addition a radiator against an outside wall is about five per cent worse off than a radiator against an inside wall.

Q242: *What is a pipe or duct ventilated motor?*

A: This is a motor designed for high-temperature applications, and is, therefore, provided with a ventilation system in which air is conveyed by pipes or ducts.

There are three main kinds. In a self-ventilated motor, cool air is drawn in to take the place of rising warm air. In a forced draught motor, cool air is blown into the machine. In an induced draught motor, cool air is drawn through.

Q243: A few years ago I built a two-roomed single storey extension—one room an extension to the kitchen, the other to the lounge—with a built-up felt roof.

A problem has arisen; the felt and the chip felt between the joist topside and the chipboard has gone spongy, as if the chipboard were damp. The felt on the roof is in perfect condition.

At the client's request there are two layers of 80 mm Cosywrap in between 125 mm joists, and I installed a vapour barrier of 500 g polythene nailed underside of ceiling, followed by 12.5 mm plasterboard and skim.

I have built a great many extensions with a vapour barrier but with only one layer of Cosywrap in the roof space, thus allowing an air space, and have had no complaints.

When I take remedial action would it pay to remove one layer of Cosywrap to make an air space or should I cut out the vapour barrier?

A: You have really put your finger on the problem. The two layers of 80 mm Cosywrap squashed into the space of 125 mm joists will have made quite sure that there is no possible way of ventilating the roofspace. Consequently the sponginess you have observed is in all probability a degradation of the chipboard as a result of regular wetting by condensation moisture.

Cold roofs, that is, roofs which have a deck above the insulation should have a space (above the insulation and below the deck) that can be, and is, ventilated to the outside air.

It is virtually impossible to form an effective vapour barrier at ceiling level; at best the membrane checks the movement of water vapour into the insulation. Nevertheless, removal of the vapour barrier would only make the problem much worse.

Q244: How can I prevent scaling in hot water pipes and boilers?

A: Scaling is caused by hard water. This is not a risk to health but it does have a number of disadvantages. Apart from the depositing of scale in hot water pipes an boilers, scum may be the result in domestic use. In addition, soap does not lather well in hard water.

There are several ways in which water may be softened. The first is the base exchange process, the second the soda lime process, and finally, inhibitors may be used.

Domestic water softeners belong to the first method. The water is passed through a medium called zeolite which converts the calcium, magnesium or potassium salts in the water (it is these which cause the hardness) into sodium salt, which does not. From time to time the zeolite medium requires regenerating by passing strong brine through it, which converts the medium back again to sodium zeolite.

A modern development of this process employs synthetic resins in place of the natural zeolite, so that water of comparable purity to that of distilled water can be obtained for certain industrial processes. This is expensive, however, and unnecessary for domestic water.

Q245: *Can you help me out with regards to the legislation affecting a ventilated lobby? I cannot seem to find any although my council says there is a requirement.*

A: The 'Greater London Council By-Laws, Water-Closets, Urinals, Earth-Closets, Privies and Cesspools' contain the following clause under the section headed 'Water-Closets':

"(2) *Entrance and entrance lobby*—Such water-closet shall not be situated within nor entered from any room used for human habitation, or as a scullery, schoolroom, office, factory, workshop, workplace, or for the manufacture, preparation, storage or sale of food or drink for man, or as a public room, except through the external air or an intervening entrance lobby.

The entrance lobby shall be constructed of solid and suitable materials so as to secure aerial disconnection between such water-closet and any room specified in the foregoing paragraph of this by-law, and such lobby shall be:
a) provided with close-fitting and self-closing doors;
b) adequately lighted and ventilated.

Provided always that a water-closet used exclusively with a bedroom or dressing-room may be entered directly from such room."

The By-laws are made under the Public Health (London) Acts of 1891 and 1936.

Q246: *I wish to block up an existing toilet and put a new one in the existing bathroom. This means that I will need a passage from the kitchen to the bathroom. Could you please advise as to the minimum area of the passage and*

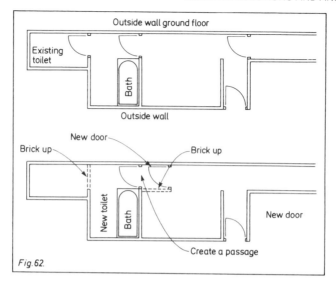

Fig. 62.

what the walls should be made of—will single lightweight blocks do?

A: The existing wc is separated from the kichen by means of the bathroom which acts as a ventilated lobby as required under the Public Health Acts (Fig. 62).

It is assumed that the bathroom is ventilated by either a window with opening lights or by a mechanical extract. Closing off the original wc compartment and transferring the closet to the bathroom requires the provision of a ventilated lobby.

There is no area laid down for this—in fact if the lobby was made about 300 mm deep, sufficient to allow the forming of two air brick vents, size 225 mm square, one at floor level and one at ceiling level to provide ventilation, and the two doors hung so that one opens into the bathroom and one into the kitchen, this should meet all requirements.

The construction of the separating wall between kitchen and ventilated lobby can be of lightweight block or even stud partitioning—the method is immaterial.

Q247: What could be regarded as a minimum reasonable bedroom temperature?

A: The Chartered Institution of Building Services' manual on building services recommends that the bedroom in living accommodation should be designed to give a comfort heat of 18 deg. C (64 deg. F).

Q248: *Could you offer any advice on the prevention of scaling in boilers?*

A: While chemical treatment of boilers is well established there is a growing use of magnetic treatment of water to prevent scale not only in boilers but also in cooling towers etc.

Liff Industries' Turbomag electromagnetic water conditioning system not only prevents scale build-up, but also eliminates existing scale.

It conditions water by means of an externally powered, intensive static magnetic field, combined with the action of a freely revolving, magnetised impeller in the water stream.

The impeller transforms the static magnetic field into a non-homogeneous, rotating magnetic field, the intensity of which varies with the rpm of the impeller.

Solids precipitate to the bottom of the boiler or tower basin in the form of a powdery sediment, inert sludge or muddy substance which are easily removed by regular blow-down or bleed-off procedures. In closed, relatively high velocity systems, precipitated solids remain in suspension and are passed through to drainage.

Q249: *What is a trough cistern?*

A: Trough cisterns are used extensively in schools, factories and similar buildings to provide ever ready flushing arrangements for ranges of wc's during busy periods.

The cistern consists of a continuous trough fixed at a high level above the range of wc pans, each closet being fitted with a siphonic flushing apparatus which delivers a predetermined flush of water to the pan. The volume of the flush is not affected by the water level in the trough and it is possible for the same siphon to be repeatedly flushed, with a pause of only a few seconds between each flush.

Q250: *I have recently installed an immersion heater for a client. I told the client that it would be more economical to*

leave the heater on all the time but he said he thought the best thing would be to switch it on and off as required. Who is right?

A: An immersion heater has its own thermostat, so once switched on it may be left and forgotten, and, withdrawls excepted, hot water will always be available. For most of the time the stored water will be at its hottest.

However, the law of physics dictates that the rate of cooling is proportional to the excess temperature, that is, the amount by which the hot temperature exceeds the cold temperature, which in this instance means the air outside the cylinder.

Therefore, a cylinder which is most of the time at maximum temperature has most of the time the greatest excess, and so the greatest heat loss.

By contrast, an immersion heater which is switched on only when required is rarely at maximum temperature, because hot water is wanted as made, and is drawn off.

The solution could be to install a time clock to do the switching on and off as required.

Q251: *What is the general thinking as to the usual minimum height above roof level for a chimney or flue pipe?*

A: The top of a chimney, not including the pot, must be at least 1 m above the highest point of contact with the roof. If the chimney is within 600 mm of the ridges of a pitched roof then it may be 600 mm high. Where an opening window is within 2.3 m then the top of the chimney is not less than 1 m high.

Q252: *Could you advise me on a problem caused by a wood burning stove? Tar marks are showing at ceiling height and condensation appears to be seeping through the joints of the brickwork, which is not accessible because of the way the roof is constructed. The chimney breast is plastered on the hard. Do you consider that the fitting of a flexi steel pipe or an asbestos pipe would cure the problem?*

A: Without examining the chimney and stack I cannot give you a categorical answer. However from the facts as you have given them, I think you are correct in attributing the tar marks (or staining) to condensation in the flue caused by the use of the woodburning stove.

The trouble will be aggravated when damp wood is used; you should not burn wood with a greater moisture content than 20 per cent. If you do the smoke and gases of combustion are likely to condense on the inside of the flue, especially in the upper part of the chimney.

The stains at ceiling height suggest that dark patches are showing in the room in which the chimney is situated. If this is a ground floor room it is unfortunately likely that the chimney breast passing through any rooms(s) above may also become stained.

Unfortunately, once the damage has occurred there is very little you can do to cure it. You can try raking out the pointing between the bricks as much as possible, where you can get at the brickwork prior to repointing.

You can also remove the plaster on the chimney breast where the staining has occurred, clean up the brickwork as much as possible (perhaps using a wire brush) prior to replastering. This should help for a time but I am afraid the stains will eventually reappear.

Apart from the stains inside the house, it is assumed there may be more on the stack itself—the stack being, in this context, the portion of the chimney above the roof line. Stacks can become badly stained and, short of demolishing them to just below the roof line and rebuilding with fresh materials, there is little to be done.

I think your proposal to put in a chimney lining is a good one. You mention a flexi steel pipe or an asbestos pipe. The latter material is out of favour. In general it is not advisable to use most flexible stainless steel liners for solid fuel chimneys although there is now at least one make on the market for which the manufacturers claim a good performance with solid fuel and even with wood, providing it is dry. I think you should choose a liner with an Agrément Board Certificate if you decide to install one. While the fitting of such a liner should act as a reasonably effective safeguard against the formation of tars in the flue in future, it will not prevent staining from tars already present in the flue structure. They will continue to work their way outwards and more stains are likely to appear.

It seems that the construction of the roof prevents you from getting at the outside of the chimney stack easily. You will have to solve this problem if you have to rebuild the stack. Once this is done, pay careful attention to the way the woodburning stove is operated. As explained, only dry wood should be used. Timber felled, cut into logs and left for at least a year is likely to be nearly dry enough. If it can be stored under cover for two years, so much the better.

Condensation is worse when the flue is cold and there is not a great deal of draught up the chimney. Try burning the fire brightly for, say, twenty minutes or so each day after you have had the chimney thoroughly swept. This should help, by burning off any deposit of tar-like substances which may be starting to build up. It is also important to have the flue swept regularly—preferably twice during the season when the stove is used regularly. Burning only dry wood is the best safeguard against this problem arising and making sure that there is a a good draught up the chimney. Smoke from the chimney terminal should go straight up into the sky.

Q253: *Are there any domestic incinerators on the market which would deal with packagings etc. and at the same time provide some addition to the hot water system?*

A: Domestic incinerators are used at such infrequent and irregular intervals that being able to provide an input to domestic hot water seems unlikely. The following companies might, however, be able to offer something:

Motherwell Bridge Tacol, Green Dragon House, 64-70 High Street, Croydon, Surrey:

Robert Jenkens Systems, Wortley Road, Rotherham, S. Yorkshire; The Incinerator Co., Howard Road, Eaton Socem, St Neots, Huntingdon, Cambridgeshire.

Alternatively you could contact the Institute of Waste Management in Northampton.

Q254: *I have a chimney, built in 1956 and lined with 225 mm pots from the part of the stack that extends beyond the roof.*

During the past year I have debris falling on the throat plate of my Parkway which contains flue lining. On inspection I found five of the seven liners had been eaten away.

My problem is how to remedy the problem without rebuilding. Even on rebuilding I would welcome advice. The stack was built in sand face flettons, square, with a precast capping.

A: I believe this is caused by the combustion gases and smoke rising in the flue condensing on the inside of it, forming a tar-like deposit which, over a period, has corroded your liners.

The trouble seems to have occurred only above the roof line where the stack is exposed to the wind and rain, encouraging a build-up of the tar-like deposit especially in cold weather.

The condition would be aggravated if you have been burning wood with a moisture content in excess of 20 per cent. A slumbering fire would also be likely to contribute to this condition.

Carried out by specialists, an inflatable tube of suitable diameter is inserted down the existing flue from the top; the bottom of the flue is blocked up.

Working from the top, a concrete mix is then poured down the existing chimney around the tube when it has been inflated. In this way the inflated tube acts as 'shuttering'. When the concrete mix has set the tube is deflated and the material blocking the bottom of the flue removed. The deflated tube is then drawn out of the chimney.

This method enables a defective chimney to be relined without having to break into the flue every few feet or so to insert liners.

An alternative method is to use one of the special chimney systems made from stainless steel. It is recommended that you choose a double sleeve system, i.e., a steel tube within a tube having insulating material between each of these tubes. The Selkirk SC chimney system is interesting because the jointing method between each section is designed to ensure that the column of insulation is unbroken between chimney sections.

With such a method you can build yourself a new chimney very quickly and easily. Alternatively, you can reline your existing chimney—probably working from both top and bottom. But you will need to break into the flue at one or more places.

The third method uses the 'Block Chimney' components, not to be confused with clocked chimneys. With such systems, you construct your chimney using prefabricated parts. Some systems use separate liners and shells with insulating materials between. In other systems the liner may be attached to the shell (or outer casing).

Whichever method you use you will need to make provision for sweeping.

Q255: *I would like some advice on a heating system for a barn conversion. I have arrived at three options on which I would like an opinion a) Stiebel Eltron heat pumps for* *domestic use; b) the Medio-Duo or Thermorossi multi fuel boiler; c) economy 7 electric storage heaters. All this bearing in mind that gas is unobtainable.*

A: Before considering heating you might do well to consider the building itself and insulation. You do not mention the material of which the barn is built, nor what you are doing to convert it. If the walls are brick and there is a timber and tile roof, the barn will be very much like many other country buildings.

But if the barn is timber framed with infills of lath and plaster on the inside and weatherboard on the outside, it requires careful thought if it is to be kept warm economically.

You should start by finding out the U values of your building materials and the computing your rate of heat loss. Having done this you can begin to think about the form your heating should take. Our comments on the three you suggest are as follows:

Heat pumps have proved to be efficient and economical in many industrial applications but they have not yet become as extensively used in houses as their merits probably justify. The initial cost of a suitable heat pump has probably caused the slow growth of heat pump penetration in the UK domestic market.

If you do not mind the expense you are wise to consider heat pumps.

The Stiebel Eltron WPW heat pump is now available in single phase operation. There is also the Stiebel Eltron WPW 34 model which is suitable for larger property. This model provides domestic hot water but presumably you would use it for space heating. It is worth considering if your conversion is not larger than 1,000 m^2.

Lennox heat pumps are likely to be of interest if your barn is a big one. The company's 'Quickguide' has some useful charts or sizing graphs.

Myson Copperad supplies Pacific heat pumps and air conditioning equipment. The company's split system acts as a means of heating and air conditioning.

As an alternative multi-fuel boilers can be efficient and should prove reasonably economical. You mention the Medio-Duo and the Thermorossi.

The Medio-Duo is for oil/gas or for wood/solid fuel. Since you say you have no gas available, we assume you are interested in the latter version. These boilers are built to DIN standards in Germany. Other models in the range such as the Medio-tri (for oil, gas or wood/solid fuel) and the Medio-wood. Should you happen to be a farmer you may also be interested in the Medio-straw.

The RT22 Thermorossi range of multi-fuel boilers, by U.A. Engineering has oil, coal and wood burning facility and the results with these three fuels have a practical interest.

Other multi-fuel boilers worth investigating include the Boulter Pathfinder M2 M3 by Boulter Boilers.

The Heatrae Sadia Economy 7 central heating boiler offers the convenience of electricity with what is expected to be real economy. The heater has been developed in co-operation with several Area Boards which provide 'Economy 7' electricity. The model includes additional elements at the top to help boost the heat during the day. Domestic hot water—if you want it in your barn—would be provided from a separate 'Economy 7' unit. The sensors of the controller are located in the system to monitor temperatures and are pre-set to the following:

	House deg.C	Bungalow deg.C
Night store temp.	98	92
Day elements	70	70
Limit temp.	103	97
Return water temp.	40	40

14 Painting

Q256: *Can paint be left in brushes and rollers?*

A: It can, but only for short periods and air must be excluded to prevent the paint from drying. To do this either cover the filling or cylinder completely with paint, or, place in an air tight bag, stand or suspend brushes in water to cover the filling.

Q257: *Before a recently completed small kitchen extension was decorated, the client had a fire in a chip pan and the ceiling and upper walls were blackened.*

Detergents have been tried without success. How could this be cleaned or alternatively decorated to ensure that it will not show.

A: Removal of soot from a chip pan catching fire does not prove too difficult when the surface is sealed or decorated for the paint stops the soot and grease penetrating the surfce of the plaster.

Unfortunately the surface was new undecorated plaster and although the damage was thought to be superficial the soot had indeed penetrated the pores of the plaster.

If the damage is indeed superficial, cleaning and/or sealing the surface may be sufficient, but should the damage be more serious or deep-seated then hacking off the plaster that is affected and re-plastering may be the only answer.

The soot from a chip pan fire is usually excessively greasy or oily due to the incomplete combustion of the animal or vegetable fat used for frying. The cleaning must, therefore, be thorough to remove the soot and the excessive grease/oil combined together. The presence of soot left on the surface (or just below) will require extra coats of paint to achieve a solid opaque finish.

The presence of grease or oil can (1) cause any water-borne paint such as oil-bound distemper or PVA emulsion to cess and run off the surface and (2) can stop any oil-based paints from drying or cause them to dry more slowly and possibly leave a soft cheesy finish that will not stand up to normal wear and could well cause trouble later on when redecorating.

Any liquids used to remove the soot will obviously soak into the surface and take some impurities with them along with the cleaning agents. Detergent in water although cheap could activate any salts in the plaster and walls due to construction and could then cause efflorescence later on as the walls dried out.

White spirits should remove the greater part of grease and soot and while soaking in the surface somewhat would not create trouble later on as would water. The surface would dry out much more quickly and allow a second and third washing should they be required.

There would also be a greater chance of removing more grease than with detergent for the white spirit would act rather like a dry cleaning fluid. The spirit should be changed as it becomes dirty or oily and fresh spirit used.

It would be sensible to try out or test various decorative finishes to see which is the most successful on the cleaned surface. It could be that even with cleaning that an ordinary PVA emulsion would cess or ciss on the surface and be unsuitable.

Emulsion paints with an acrylic base are often found to be suitable in circumstances like this. Should these fail then a conventional oil-based system could be used e.g. plaster primer, undercoat(s) and suitable finish. Should any bleeding through of the soot into the primer occur it would be noticeable at the time of the test and the application of a coat of aluminium paint on the affected part would stop any soot stains bleeding through.

Aluminium paint is not normally specified for plaster, but it does have excellent sealing properties and it has been used with success in cases similar to this one. It would be followed of course with the undercoat(s) and finish of the desired colour.

Q258: *I have a problem regarding the preparation, treatment, and costing of some work involving a great amount of hardwood.*

The building was a new one when it was varnished eight years ago. Now, the varnishing needs to be re-done. Would the correct procedure be to sandpaper the original surfaces down, and then varnish on top of this; or would it be better to apply a stripper, rub down, and then re-varnish?

The hardwood is on skirting boards, architraves, and also on ceiling areas. At the moment the surface areas are not too bad.

Could you also explain how I should estimate for the above type of work?

A: A number of questions are posed which must be considered in detail, together with possible alternatives.

The hardwood concerned is stated to be in skirtings, architraves and ceiling areas. The latter may consist of panelling or beams and in view of the fact that wall panelling is not mentioned, it is assumed that the ceiling areas concern beams only.

The work is said to be varnished and it is necessary to be certain of this, since finishing materials will not always combine. French polish and polyurethane do not go together.

The surfaces 'are not too bad' and therefore the preparatory work could be the same for any treatment and a thorough washing and rinsing off should be carried out.

The original treatment may have been multicoat modern varnish work. When this has been determined, the surfaces can be lightly abraded with a fine wire wool and given two coats of varnish.

There are several other possible alternatives which may have been used originally and if doubt exists, an expert should be consulted.

To prepare an estimate all 'runs' and 'girths' should be measured and resolved into square metres. Material quantities can be determined by referring to the manufacturers' recommendations for surface covered.

Labour factors should be determined under headings of preparation and finishing, breaking each activity down into constituents.

A labour rate should be applied which will cover basic wages, insurances, etc. Add 30 per cent to this rate to cover overheads.

To the total estimated costs of all these items, a profit percentage of a minimum of 10 per cent should be added.

Q259: *Insufficient degreasing of the metal during manufacture is suspected as the cause of paint flaking away fron electric element radiators.*

It is proposed to remove the flaking paint with fine wet and dry paper and build up the affected patches with calcium plumbate.

Could you recommend a suitable paint that is heat resistant to a maximum of 3 kW, to restore the finish?

A: It would appear that 3 kW electric panel heaters can attain a heat of about 86 deg C plus the ambient temperature. In practical terms this means sufficient heat to make one withdraw the hand sharply, but not enough heat to burn unless the hand is held on the panel. To produce a panel hotter than this would, of course, be dangerous.

Many panel heaters do not in fact attain a surface temperature of this order and can be satisfactorily painted with most basic alkyd enamels, that is the general run of the mill enamels. The stipulated undercoat and a tetra chrome primer would be quite suitable as base coats. There should be no loss of adhesion or break down of the paint film, but there could be a slight discoloration of white and very pale colours. Deeper shades should not be affected at all.

It would be better to stick to the stipulated undercoats and finish and apply extra coats in order to build up to a level surface and carefully feathering off with smooth wet-or-dry than to introduce a further primer in the shape of calcium plumbate as querist suggests. When a level surface has been attained the panel can be painted in a normal manner.

It is most important that the panel should be cold each time it is painted and until it is finally painted.

If the querist's panel does get hotter than the temperatures discussed then a special heat resisting paint must be bought. These usually have to be ordered from most manufacturers and are sometimes difficult to obtain in small quantities as are the primers and undercoats necessary for these products.

Joy and Oro are two heat-resisting metallic paints which can be readily obtained in smaller amounts and which will stand temperatures higher than those we have been discussing.

Q260: *What paints are suitable for hot water radiators and pipes?*

A: Normal gloss paints will stand up to 90 deg C which is well above the temperature of most hot water systems. White and pale colours may yellow over 70 deg C. For steam and super heated systems consult the manufacturers.

As undercoats tend to become brittle on heating, it is often advisable to apply two coats of gloss which provide a more flexible film than one undercoat and one coat of gloss.

Q261: *A house built about 15 years ago has an exterior rendering of white spar which has been discoloured by smoke, etc., from a steelworks and railway line. Parts have become blackened by a greasy, sooty substance.*

Now, both the steelworks and railway line have closed and the outside of the house is to be smartened up. Washing with detergent does not brighten the surface sufficiently and painting is being considered.

Advice is required on the various commercial finishes obtainable.

A: White spar is an external rendering produced by the forcible application of white spar or similar sized chippings to a rendered surface while it is still wet. Difficulties for the decorator can arise due to:

1) The depth of the chippings on or actually in the surface.
2) The composition and porosity of the rendering.
3) Difficulty in cleaning prior to decoration.

The rendering is usually sharp sand/lime/cement in the ratio 4/1/1, but this can vary quite widely and if too alkaline can cause problems, as can differences in porosity. The depth to which the chippings have penetrated can vary from being half-submerged in the rendering and firmly fixed to being only just held by the rendering and thus relatively easily dislodged by cleaning, decorating and weathering.

Removal of dirt can be quite difficult as the surface offers an excellent hold for any grease and soot. Complete removal is virtually impossible, but conventional wire brushing to remove dirt and loose spar followed by a thorough brushing down afterwards is the usual practice. Greasy deposits can be alleviated somewhat with detergents and water, but time must be allowed for the surface to dry out thoroughly and alkalis such as soda and similar substances must be avoided as the residues of these cannot be removed from the rendering and interstices in and around the chippings. These residues could possibly cause later troubles with the chosen paint.

The sharp edges of the chippings present great difficulties for conventional paints although extra coats could eliminate this problem, but this, of course, is costly in labour and materials. The material must be applied evenly around any projecting chippings, for applying too thick a coat could tend to 'bridge' over much of the surface texture and so create an uneven and visually unacceptable finish. This 'bridging' could quite possibly lead to premature breakdown of the surface coatings later on.

It can be seen from these few facts that decorating white spar can be awkward if not difficult to obtain decorative and satisfactory lasting results.

Most manufacturers, however, are aware of these problems and produce first-class products specially designed for these relatively awkward surfaces. These materials can and do differ in composition rather a lot for each manufacturer has his own ideas on the subject. These finishes can be either basically oil-based and thinned with white spirits or emulsion-based and thinned with water. Clear instructions regarding thinning and thinning agents are always given.

Some of the finishes are intended to be smooth, but others have aggregates incorporated to give varying degrees of texture, strengths, durability and adhesion. The aggregates can be sand, powdered stone, mica, shredded nylon fibres and similar substances either used singly or in combination. Many contain fungicides which can be a consideration and advantage.

Some materials can be obtained in both smooth and textured finish, Sandtex is a good example of this.

The application of the water thinned paints is often easier than oil-based, some of which can be rather 'sticky', but the manufacturer would probably point out that this is offset by the greater durability of the oil/resin content. There is nowadays a good range of colours available in both types and there are very few re-decoration problems.

There are also some masonry paints based on cement and which set in a similar manner to cement. They are perhaps slightly more difficult to apply, are rather limited in colour and pose certain problems in re-decoration due to the nature of the film they produce.

Many manufacturers recommend and supply some sort of primer/sealer or stabilising liquid which will produce a satisfactory surface for further coats. Again, these are usually oil-based or emulsion-based. Each type will stand on its own merits, but it is considered more suitable to use one system throughout for technical reasons, that is, use an oily-based sealer under an oil-based system, or an emulsion-based stabiliser under an emulsion-type finish.

The ultimate cost for a given area can vary considerably due to a number of factors. One must consider the original cost of the material per litre or kg and the recommended spreading rate for any particular surface or surface texture, in this case quite a coarse surface.

One must also consider the number of coats needed to obtain a good solid opaque finish, and as this particular surface appears to be dirtier than most an extra coat may be necessary if white or any other light colour is used.

Leaflets are readily available for each product which gives spreading capacities for each type of surface, recommended thinners and thinning rates. Methods of application, be it brush, roller or spray are also considered. The latter can often prove difficult and wearing to the equipment due to the harsh aggregates which are sometimes incorporated in the material.

While white spar is already a texture finish a case could be made out for using a material which produces some slight texture in order to help mask and soften the sharp edges of the chippings. This would be an improvement visually and it would help in the weathering process for the razor sharp edges of the chippings are always the first part of the film to break down.

It would be invidious to make direct comparisons between various manufacturers' products, but I would suggest that while there is little to choose between the various makes the final choice of material should depend on availability of colour, spreading rate of material and the eventual cost in terms of durability and subsequent re-decoration.

Q262: Are wood stains the same as preservatives?

A: They are not. Wood stains are dye solutions applied to bare timber to darken it or change its colour. Some contain strong solvents which may have a slight preservative quality but it is not their main function.

Wood preservatives are applied to timbers which generally are not required to be painted, such as floor or roof timbers. Their function is to prevent the timber being attacked by wet or dry rot, or by wood boring insects.

Q263: What types of paint are waterproof?

A: Many paints will be impervious to water in the form of rain and snow but may not be suitable for continuous submersion such as coatings for water tanks and swimming pools.

For special conditions, paint manufacturers ought to be consulted but the type of materials which can be used include chlorinated rubber paints, epoxy resin paints, and polyurethane coatings.

Q264: *What can be done to overcome saponification?*

A: Saponification is a soapy formation of paint due to attack by alkalis upon the paint media. It usually occurs on plaster or cement surfaces due to their high alkali content.

It will require the complete stripping and cleaning of the surface before the re-application of decorative paint. The surface must dry out and become neutral, and should then be coated with an alkali resistant primer followed by the normal coats of paint.

Q265: *Can wallpaper paste cause damage to paintwork?*

A: It can. Some pastes will cause more damage than others depending on the kind used. If paste is allowed to dry on painted surfaces, flaking and staining may result. Even a small smear of paste left on a surface can cause staining.

Q266: *In painting, what is the remedy for grinning?*

A: Grinning is due to the poor opacity of a paint film which allows the paint coat beneath to show through the finishing coat. It is the result of poor workmanship, incorrect thinning of paint, or use of incorrect colours.

The remedy is simply to add further coats of paint until a satisfactory surface is obtained.

Q267: *I am renovating an old half timbered farm cottage. Over the years the interior beams have accumulated many coats of paint. I would appreciate your advice on the best way to restore them.*

A: Assuming it is gloss paint on the beams, the paint should be removed by using a water washable paint stripper (follow the manufacturer's directions). Several applications may be required. When you have got back to the original timber apply a primer and then the desired finish.

Q268: Where should the first length of paper be hung when a) papering a ceiling and, b) papering walls?

A: a) The first consideration should be where the main source of light enters the room. This is usually the wall with the largest window or a window facing south. The first length should then be hung nearest to and parallel with that wall.

In some cases it may be desirable to work from a centre line particularly if the paper has a dominant pattern, as this ensures a balanced effect at the edges. An immovable obstruction in the centre of the ceiling can provide a convenient starting point.

b) The first length on every wall should be hung to a plumbed line—never to an angle, window or door architrave. Papering normally starts by the window and proceeds away from the light in both directions meeting if possible in an obscure corner.

When using a paper with a large pattern the chimney breast or other focal wall should be centred and the paper hung from the centre line.

Q269: Are painted hardboards a cheap substitute for plywood?

A: No. Hardboard is not a substitute for any other material, but if it is used with care it can be the most suitable material for many jobs.

The smooth surface takes paint well without the need for filling and it provides the basis for many specialist applied decorative finishes. Much depends on the way in which the material is used, and if it is conditioned and fixed carefully there should be no trouble.

Q270: How do I go about painting wood which has been treated with creosote?

A: When surfaces have been previously treated with bituminous preparations of creosote they should not be painted at all unless the creosote is old and weathered, or the bitumen fairly hard and non-elastic, because they require sealing with a shellac preparation to prevent bleeding, and the hard-drying shellac coating is liable to crack if the ground is soft and plastic.

Given suitable conditions, however, two coats of tar-proof knotting should be carefully applied to ensure that the surface is effectively sealed.

Alternatively, the knotting may be pigmented with aluminium powder in the proportion of about 1 kg to 5 litres and applied with care to avoid misses or pin-holes through which the tarry substance might bleed.

One coat is usually sufficient in this case because the aluminium acts as a guide coat and its 'leafing' properties also make it a good sealer.

Q271: *Could you advise me on a clear grade floor sealer? I have used to different makes of polyurethane which seem to darken the wood from its natural shade. Neither have been acceptable by the customer.*

A: All clear grade polymer varnishes contain an oil which soaks into the timber, thus tending to slightly darken the timber due to the yellowness of the oil. All clear wax polishes for timber floors contain similar oils which will also lead to darkening of the timber.

Q272: *Some eight years ago I fixed 12.5 mm ply 2.4 m by 1.2 m sheets to stud work and to the plywood Magnalux oak faced ply with a contact adhesive and wax polished.*

The bungalow has changed owners and the new owner requires wall paper over the Magnalux. Please advise on best method of applying paper over the Magnalux without removing architraves and skirting if this is possible. There are five vees to each 1.2 m wide sheet of Magnalux.

A: Remove polish and thoroughly prepare surface. Aluminium primer may be required to seal the Magnalux board. If applied, allow to dry thoroughly before horizontally cross lining with medium grade lining paper.

The adhesive should be ready mixed Polycell, Clam Gold Label or Solvite ready mixed, as these use a PVA base with fungicide. Do not use a powder based adhesive.

The top paper can also be bonded with one of the above mentioned adhesives, but please check the manufacturer's instructions on the actual rolls.

Q273: *After redecorating the new paint is peeling off the wall in fairly large pieces. What is the likely cause of this and can anything be done short of redecorating once more?*

A: The most probable cause is that the old surface was not correctly prepared. The problems may have been caused because dirt and/or grease was not thoroughly cleaned off, or if loose paint films were not removed. If the old surface was a gloss surface it could be that this was not rubbed down as it should have been.

Some modern decorating materials are not always compatible with previous decorations such as distemper. If the previous surface was distempered it would be advisable to check with the manufacturer or the product you have used or intend to use for redecorating.

The only really effective remedy is to start again! Remove all decorations down to a firmly adhering, sound, clean surface. Rub down any gloss paint surfaces and redecorate with suitable materials.

Q274: *The painters in my firm use Vevic Cleaner for washing down paintwork and they say that it is not as good as it used to be.*

A: According to the manufacturers, Lanstar Coatings, the only change made to the product in recent years was to change the colour from white to yellow, purely for identification purposes (to avoid confusion with flour), which would have no deleterious effect on the function. The company stands by its product and asks anyone who has had poor results to return the packet for analysis.

Q275: *I have a timber framed, timber clad sunlounge at the rear of my house and the firm that constructed it recommended yacht varnish as the best treatment to give the Meranti cladding. Having used it, I find the timber has been degraded in patches by ultra-violet rays, and where this occurs the timber turns white and the varnish peels away, letting in the moisture. I have spent much time rubbing down and revarnishing.*

Is there a preservative/water repellent treatment which is easier to maintain and does not hide the natural beauty of the wood?

A: A number of firms now make wood finishes which are designed to enhance the beauty of the timber, resist ultra violet rays and are microporous to allow the timber to breathe. The new finishes do not need repainting so often.

Cuprinol makes a semi-transparent woodstain which is pigmented to keep out the ultra-violet rays; it will weather by erosion rather than cracking and flaking. The maker says that you will only have to clean it down and repaint (no rubbing down) about every two to five years depending on exposure. There is a selection of pigments, one of which is called Meranti, but the semi-transparent range is designed to show off the natural beauty of the wood.

Another product designed to protect timber is Demidekk, which is a combination of stain and paint, and is made by Jotun Decorative Coatings.

Q276: Is it possible to apply gloss paints effectively over other coatings?

A: Providing the surface is in sound condition—not flaking, cracking or blistering—is clean and abraded to provide a key, then standard decorative gloss paints can be applied over many other types of surface coating such as emulsion paint, water thinned paints, eggshell and flat finshes, cellulose finishes and varnishes.

They can be applied over primers, but full gloss, adhesion and hiding power is likely to suffer if this is done. For best result, gloss finishes should be applied over the appropriate undercoat formulated specially for the job.

Q277: What causes gloss paints to dry with an uneven sheen?

A: The absorption of the paint medium into the underlying surface. The most common causes are:
— absorbent undercoats due to being left too long before applying finish;
— applying gloss direct onto unpainted or only sealed absorbent surfaces;
— unsealed areas of filler;
— poorly prepared surfaces leaving rough areas which will refract light from the gloss finish.

15 Scaffolding

Q278: *What can be done in terms of care and maintenance to extend the useful life of scaffold boards?*

A: Every month or so scaffold boards should be scrubbed clean and the hoop iron binding examined and renewed if necessary. Projecting or loose nails are dangerous and should be dealt with.

Boards should not be painted or treated in any way that might conceal defects. Boards should not be dropped as this can start them splitting, as can using them as unloading ramps.

If scaffold boards are shortened, properly shape the ends and fit galvanised bands with large-headed galvanised clout nails 30mm long—six per binding.

Q279: *I have a number of wood ladders in need of repair. Can you give me some guidance on how to effect these repairs?*

A: Timber used in repairs should be straight grained and cut with the grain. New rungs should be of oak and cleft so that the grain is true to the length of the rung. Some shaping is necessary after the wood is cleft but this method gives a stronger rung than normal sawing would give.

Stiles must be sprung out so that the new rungs can be glued in, using a weatherproof adhesive. The stiles should then be cramped up and the rungs wedged. Iron tie rods (5 mm diameter) should be refixed, with washers at each end; the ends of the rod should be riveted over.

Rungs on extending ladders are often rectangular in section and should be tenoned and glued so that they are true and square to the stiles. They can be wedged in the middle or at both sides of the tenon—be sure to wedge with the run of the grain.

Repairs should be treated with a clear preservative. When this is dry the stiles and the ends of the rungs should be given four coats of clear varnish; the middle parts of the rungs should be left bare.

Q280: *What rules should be followed during the dismantling of scaffolding to ensure safety and what maintenance is necessary?*

A: It is a sensible idea to carry out all maintenance of scaffolding during dismantling. If all the damaged pieces are either repaired or discarded straight away, there should be no risk of them being used again.

During dismantling the following procedures should be followed:

An organised, systematic approach is required that does not allow collapse by irresponsible dismantling. Where temporary bracing or support is needed it must be incorporated, as must all warning notices and barriers at the end of each working shift or day.

Every scaffold must be inspected after erection, at every seven days thereafter, after structural alteration or after bad weather.

Where wind might create a hazardous situation, a suitable means of holding down all loose boards must be provided and implemented.

It is good practice to turn back the boards adjacent to the structure to avoid dirty splash marks. It is a good safety procedure to turn over all scaffold boards immediately after snow or frost, to reduce the risk of slipping on dangerous boards. The alternative is to use sand on snow but sand may blow away afterwards.

Keep an even distribution of loading and avoid point loading at any particular place.

Keep a clean scaffold while in use and make special checks for slippery boards after bad weather.

Clean, check and maintain all scaffold parts as they are dismantled. And damaged or otherwise unusuable items should be replaced.

Q281: *What are the regulations for the use of ladder cripples with a staging board for short duration maintenance work?*

A: The Safety at Work Act deals with all and any platforms over 2 m in height.

This states that they must have guard rails to prevent any injury to persons using the platform. In general, any working space 2 m or higher above ground level is treated the same as a scaffold.

Q282: *Recently I had a deal of trouble with scaffolding which was erected outside my building. Despite my best endeavours youngsters managed to scale the scaffolding, get onto the roof of a fairly high building and eventually to gain access.*

Is there any recognised means of erecting some sort of barrier round the base of scaffolding which could make it difficult, if not impossible, to get onto the scaffolding?

A: The problem outlined, regarding youngsters climbing scaffolds and causing damage, has been an age old problem in the building industry and there is effectively no guaranteed way to prevent it. The following steps are suggested.

The main actions would be to ensure that any ladders incorporated into the scaffold start at first lift level, rather than from ground level and that an easily detachable ladder be supplied for gaining access to the first lift; this should be removed at night.

Secondly, that the height of the first lift be made as high as possible i.e. 2.4 m or more, to deter casual attempts to climb the scaffold.

Finally, should problems still be experienced. 2.4 m high corrugated iron sheets could be built onto the scaffold uprights to form a continuous barrier all the way around, topped by barbed wire. However, this must be high enough to prevent accidental damage to passers by.

All the above actions would need to be specified to a scaffolding company before work commences and would obviously incur some extra cost.

Q283: *What are the main points to be observed when checking metal scaffolding?*

A: Inspect all tubes and fittings before use. Clean them by scraping, brushing or abrasive methods which do not affect the galvanising. Damaged protective coatings should be made good. if deterioration is suspected get an expert opinion before tubes or fittings are used.

Tubes once kinked, bent or dented are weakened and should not be used. Never attempt to straighten a bent tube except with a special machine and the necessary experience.

Never heat an aluminium alloy tube and never mix steel and aluminium tubes.

Take care of the fittings—these must not be used in a corroded state. Discard bent parts and joint pins with damaged threads. Clean the fittings after use and coat liberaly with oil. Store scaffold fittings under cover.

Q284: *How frequently should scaffolding be checked, and what are the key things to look out for during these checks?*

A: Tubular scaffold are required to be checked at least once a week and after bad weather. You should take note of the following:

— Has proper access been provided to the scaffold platform?

— Are all uprights provided with base plates or prevented in some other way from slipping or sinking?

— Have any uprights, ledgers, braces or struts been removed?

— Is the scaffold secured to the building in enough places to prevent collapse?

— Have any ties been removed since the scaffold was erected?

— Are there sufficient boards at all working platforms in use?

— Are all boards free from obvious defects and are they arranged to avoid traps?

— Are there warning notices to prohibit the use of any scaffold that is incomplete (e.g. not fully boarded)?

— At every side where a person can fall more than 1.98 m are the platforms, gangways and runs provided with guardrails and toeboards?

— Who is responsible for the inspections, are they carried out and recorded?

— The loading for which a scaffold has been provided should be known and should be evenly distributed.

Q285: *What safety precautions should be taken when using platform hoists on construction sites?*

A: A platform hoist must be protected by a substantial enclosure and the enclosure must be fitted with gates where access is needed. A platform hoist can be dangerous if the gates are not kept shut.

Hoists are required to be inspected weekly, and thoroughly examined every six months by a competent person. Check:
— Who is responsible for these inspections? Are they recorded?
— Is there an enclosure, where necessary, to prevent people being struck by any moving part of the hoist or materials on it?
— Are gates provided at all landings?
— Are the gates kept shut except when the platform is at the landing?
— Is the control rope so arranged that the hoist can be operated from one position only?
— Is the safe working load clearly marked on the hoist?
— Is there a proper signalling system?

Q286: *What precautions can be taken to prevent damage to hoist ropes and to extend their usefulness?*

A: It is bad to leave ropes of any kind unnecessarily exposed to the weather, although only natural fibres will rot. Ropes should be dried naturally by festooning over pegs.

The life of natural fibre ropes is improved by waterproofing with a repellant preservative or zinc napthenate (do not use creosote).

Securely whip all rope ends. Take care in uncoiling and coiling not to overtwist the rope or you will never be rid of the harm done. Do not 'unwind' a rope by allowing a suspended load to revolve.

Keep ropes clear of paint strippers. It is illegal to use ropes which have been attacked by corrosive substances.

Friction over siezed pulleys can cause natural fibre and synthetic ropes to burn. Blowlamps must be kept away from ropes. Synthetic fibres such as nylon, polythene, terylene and polypropylene are all affected by heat.

Nylon ropes in particular should not run together as the friction may cause them to melt. All ropes should be stored in coils, dry and away from the heat.

Rust can cause wire ropes an cables to deteriorate so that they are not reliable. The best safeguard is to clean them regularly with a wire brush and apply a light lubricant dressing.

Ropes and cables to be stored should be similarly treated. In uncoiling, loops should be drawn out vertically but never pulled as this causes kinks and permanent damage.

Q287: *What are the rules concerning the reporting of accidents?*

A:A notifiable accident is one which arises out of or in connection with work and; (a) results in the death of or major injury to any person or, (b) in the case of an employee results in that employee being off work for more than three consecutive days.

Where a notifiable accident results in the death of or a major injury to any person or there is a notifiable dangerous occurrence, this must be notified to the enforcing authority forthwith by the quickest practicable means, and a report sent within seven days on the prescribed form (Form F2508).

Where death follows within one year of the accident or dangerous occurrence the enforcing authority must be notified in writing. Where an employee suffers injury and is off work for more than three days and the Department of Health and Social Security is notified for the purposes of industrial injury benefit, then the D.H.S.S. must notify details of the accident to the Health and Safety Executive.

There are exceptions to the notification procedure contained within Regulation 6. Records must be kept of accidents and dangerous occurrences at the place where the work to which is relates is carried on.

"Major injury" means: (a) fracture of the skull, spine or pelvis; (b) fracture of any bone, (i) in the arm, other than a bone in the wrist or hand; (ii) in the leg, other than a bone in the ankle or foot: (c) amputation of a hand or foot; (d) the loss of sight of an eye; or (e) any other injury which results in the person injured being admitted into hospital as an in-patient for more than 24-hours, unless that person is detained only for observation.

An accident is notifiable if it arises out of or in connection with work and either; (a) results in the death of or a major injury to any person; or (b) in the case of an employee at work, results in that employee being incapacitated for work for more than three consecutive days excluding the day of the accident and any Sunday, or if Sunday is not a rest day, one rest day.

A dangerous occurrence is notifiable if it arises out of or in connection with work and is of a class specified in Part I of Schedule 1.

The "responsible person" means; (a) in the case of a notifiable accident to an employee, his employer; (b) in any other case, the person for the time being having control of the premises in connection with the carrying on by him of any trade, business or other undertaking (whether for profit or not) at which the notifiable accident or notifiable dangerous occurrence occurred.

Regulation 4. Notification and reporting of accidents and dangerous occurrences.

Subject to Regulation 6 (exceptions) where there is (1) a notifiable accident resulting in death of or major injury to any person, or (2) a notifiable dangerous occurrence, the "responsible person" shall; (a) forthwith notify enforcing authority by the quickest practicable means, and (b) within seven days send a report to enforcing authority on prescribed form.

Regulation 5. Duty to notify the death of an employee.

Subject to Regulation 6 where an employee suffers an injury as a result of a notifiable accident or notifiable dangerous occurrence which is the cause of his death within 1 year of the accident or dangerous occurrence the employer shall inform the enforcing authority in writing.

Regulation 6. Cases to which Regulations 4 and 5 do not apply.

Regulations 4 and 5 shall not apply to; (a) any notifiable accident to, (i) a self-employed person not engaged in work under control of another person; (ii) a patient undergong treatment in hospital or surgery of doctor or dentist; (iii) member of armed forces or visiting forces whilst on duty. (b) any notifiable accident arising out of or in connection with the movement of a vehicle on a road.

Regulations 4 and 5 shall apply if the person killed or injured was himself engaged in, or was killed or injured as the result of activities of another person who at the time of the accident was engaged in work on or alaongside a road concerned with the construction, demolition, alteration, repair or maintenance of; (a) road, markings or equipment; (b) verges, fences, hedges or other boundaries; (c) pipes and cables, under, over or adjacent; (d) buildings or structures adjacent to or over the road.

Regulation 4 shall not apply to any accident or dangerous occurrence required to be notified under Schedule 2.

Regulation 7. D.H.S.S. to notify accident particulars to H.S.E.

Where an employee is injured and an employer sends particulars to D.H.S.S., a copy of particulars to be sent to H.S.E. by D.H.S.S.

Regulation 8. Records.

An employer or self-employed person shall keep a written record of; (a) all notifiable accidents and dangerous occurrences; (b) all enquiries for D.H.S.S. concerning claims by his employees in respect of any disease under Section 76, Social Security Act 1975 for the purpose of industrial injury benefit.

Information shall be as prescribed in 3rd Schedule.

The record shall be kept for 3 years at the place where the work is carried on. If this not reasonably practicable at the usual place of business.

The employer/self-employed person shall send to the enforcing authority any extract from the record as may be required.

Regulation 9. Defence in proceedings.

It shall be a defence for a person to prove; (a) he was not aware of the accident or occurrence; (b) that he had taken all reasonable steps to have all notifiable accidents/dangerous occurrences brought to his notice.

Schedule I: Notifiable Dangerous Occurences

Part I: Dangerous occurrences which are notifiable wherever they occur.

Part II: Dangerous occurrences which are notifiable in relation to mines.

Part III: Dangerous occurrences in relation to quarries.

Parat IV: Dangerous occurrences in relation to railways.

Schedule 3

Particulars to be kept in records of accidents or dangerous occurrences.

1. Date of accident or dangerous occurrence.

2. In the case of an accident, the following particulars of the person injured: (a) name; (b) sex; (c) age; (d) occupation; (e) nature of injury.

3. Place where the accident or dangerous occurrence took place.

4. A brief description of the circumstances.

Particulars to be kept of ill-health enquiries.

The following particulars shall be recorded of the person concerning whom the enquiry was made:

(a) sex; (b) age; (c) occupation; (d) nature of disease for which the claim was made; (e) date of first absence from work.

Schedule 5: Repeals.

16 Tools

Q288: *Are there any recommended maintenance procedures for the care of powered hand tools?*

A: Powered hand tools should be cleaned regularly. The dust produced by electric cutting tools and abrasive tools can damage the motor. To avoid these problems, tools in regular use should be cleaned daily.

To remove dust from inside the tool blow it out with an electric blower or a compressed air line, alternatively a pair of bellows will do.

Follow the maker's recommendations regarding lubrication, as this is an essential part of maintenance.

Cutting edges and teeth must be kept sharp. As well as giving poor results and slowing up a job, blunt tools are a potential cause of danger and injury to the operator.

Each tool should be inspected and tested at intervals not exceeding seven days and each time it is returned to store.

Cables and hoses should be examined and replaced where necessary; threaded couplings should be cleaned and oiled; screws should be tightened where necessary; and bearings must be properly lubricated.

Q289: *What is the best way to sharpen cold chisels?*

A: Once the hardened and tempered tip is removed and the taper made blunt, a cold chisel cannot be sharpened effectively. The chisel must be drawn-out by a blacksmith and the tip re-tempered. Then the head can be ground back to its original shape.

Q290: *How are grooves cut in the timber in the direction of the grain?*

A: You should use a special plane with an adjustable fence, adjustable depth guage and a variety of single cutters of from 4 to 12 mm wide.

When setting up the plane it is important to allow the blade to project slightly from the side of the main stock and to set it fine to make the plane easier to push. The blade should be kept sharp and the fence kept in close contact with the working edge of the timber.

It makes the cutting of rebates and plough grooves much easier if the cut is started at the forward end of the timber, gradually working backwards. If long rebates or plough grooves are being cut this method will also save a lot of walking up and down along the bench walk.

Q291: *Can a plane be used to clean up rebates?*

A: It can, but the type of plane used depends on the width of the rebate. If the rebates are wide, as in door frames, a badger or bench rebate plane would be most appropriate. This is similar to the metal smoother and jack plane, but the blade extends to the full width of the plane and even projects somewhat from either side.

Smaller rebates can be cleaned up with the rabbet plane or fillister. This kind of plane has a single iron 38 mm wide and is not meant for working wide surfaces. With a fence and depth gauge fitted, the plane can cut rebates. When setting the iron in the plane it should project slightly beyond the edge of the plane. This will prevent the step effect caused by a badly set plane.

Q292: *Are there any guides for good practice concerning the care of cables to powered hand tools?*

A: Cables should be secured to the tool by a cordgrip or adjustable gland so that the weight is not supported by the terminal connections.

Never lift or drag a tool by the cable as this causes loose connections and damage to the cable. Do not let cables drag on the ground—they will last longer if unwound from reels.

Do not extend cables by twisting wires together and taping them over, always use proper plug and socket connections.

Extension cables must have at least the same capacity as the cable fitted to the tool. Where long cable runs are necessary use the next size up, to allow for voltage drop.

Q293: Are there any precautions that should be taken when storing paint brushes and rollers?

A: Never store rollers or brushes until they are clean and dry. Never stack, lay or wrap in a manner which can distort and damage the filling or pile. Always suspend rollers and always store both in clean dry and well ventilated conditions.

Q294: In the interests of safety what guidelines should be followed when operating portable power tools?

A: Portable power tools, whether fitted with a revolving blade or abrasive disc are always a potential hazard and danger. Be sure that the machine you operated has been manufactured to high safety standards.

A fixed guard must be fitted to enclose the blade above the sole plate and a retractable, spring loaded guard fitted to cover the blade below the sole plate. Check the latter frequently to ensure that it works freely with the manual operating lever when fitted. Never wedge the guard open.

Keep the blade sharp. Apart from giving a clean, effortless cut, it will not jam and attempt to 'kick back' dangerously from the material.

Disconnect the power supply when changing blades or adjusting the machine. Use goggles when cutting material likely to splinter with an abrasive disc.

If you convert a portable tool for use as a bench saw, the installation must then comply with additional safety regulations and mandatory requirements specified in the Woodworking Machines Regulations. The important points to note are that a correct guard, designed for use with a bench saw must be fitted, together with a riving knife.

Q295: How do cartridge operated tools work and what are the major hazards involved in using this type of equipment?

A: There are two basic types of cartridge tool; high velocity and low velocity. With high velocity tools the exploding cartridge fires the fixing device down the barrel of the tool in free flight and so into the work surface. This sort of tool has a muzzle velocity approximately equivalent to that of a small firearm.

Low velocity is where the exploding cartridge acts on a retained piston which drives the fixing device into the work. Here the power is about one quarter of that of the high velocity tool.

When using these tools there are three main hazards to be aware of. First, firing through a soft material, when the fixing device goes right through and becomes a dangerous missile.

Secondly, there is the possibility of a ricochet when the fixing device is deflected and can turn back on itself and strike the operator or another person.

Thirdly, the surface being fired into may splinter, with splinters flying off and striking the operator or other workers.

Q296 : *Are lasers quite safe to use on construction sites? What precautions should be taken if there are any safety problems?*

A : The lasers used on construction sites are a far cry from James Bond or Star Wars, but nonetheless can be dangerous if certain basic safety measures are ignored.

Laser equipment should only be set up and operated by trained operatives. Manufacturers and suppliers should be able to give safety training to end users.

Areas in which lasers are being used should be posted with laser warning signs and all equipment must be labelled to indicate the maximum output power.

When aligning the laser great care should be taken. Ideally, mechanical or electronic means should be used as direct viewing along the beam could be dangerous should any reflection take place. If a laser beam enters the eye the lens will focus the beam to a small spot on the retina which will lead to burning. Make sure that nobody looks directly into the beam—ideally the beam should always be above eye level.

The beam must be efficiently terminated at the end of its path and never permitted to go beyond the bounds of the site. Reflective material in the path of the beam should either be removed or covered over.

At all times the manufacturer's instructions should be followed.

Q297 : *Can you summarise regulations applicable specifically to circular saws, i.e., not general woodworking machinery regulations?*

A: • The part of the saw blade which is below the table should be guarded as efficiently as possible.

• A strong, rigid and easily adjustable riving knife must be securely fixed directly behind the line of the blade. This is to separate the timber as it passes through the saw and to make sure that it does not jam.

• On a saw of 600 mm diameter or less, the riving knife shall extend above the saw table to within 25 mm of the highest point of the blade. On a saw larger than 600 mm the riving knife must extend above the table by a minimum of 225 mm.

• The part of the saw blade which is above the table must be fitted with a strong and easily adjustable guard which can be positioned not more than 12 mm from the top edge of the material being sawn.

• An adjustable extension piece should be fitted to the front of the guard. The flange of the extension piece must extend below the roots of the teeth.

• No saw blade must be used which has a diameter of less than sixth-tenths of the largest saw blade permitted on the saw.

• A notice must be fixed to all circular saws specifying the diameter of the smallest saw allowed on the machine.

• Circular saws must not be used for cutting rebates, tenons, moulds or grooves.

• A suitable push-stick shall be provided and be available for use at all times.

Q298: *Could you provide some guidelines for the safe operation of hand-held power drills?*

A: Always disconnect the tool from the power supply before changing drill bits.

A common hazard is to attempt drilling holes larger than the rated capacity of the tool. Make sure the work piece is properly held and remember to ease the pressure as the drill bit breaks through. Failure to observe these points can result in serious injury.

In the first instance, the drill should be accidentally started and the chuck key ejected as a dangerous missile. Drilling a hole beyond the rated capacity of the tool can damage the drill bit and/or overload the machine, but more seriously, it can 'snag' and stall the motor against the operator's hold resulting in a sprain or worse.

Drill 'parts' fitted in the 'engineers' geared chuck must be securely fixed by applying the chuck key firmly to all three holes. Always keep morse taper sleeves and shanks clean and drill bits sharp.

17 Roofs

Q299: *Some modern houses in my area are roofed with concrete tiles. These are showing signs of grey-green growths.*

I feel that if left unchecked these growths might eventually prevent efficient shedding of rainwater and cause disintegration of the tiles.

Could you tell me what these growths are and whether there are any available treatments?

A: The growths are probably lichens or moss and should not cause any damage to the tiles, which have to pass stringent tests for watertightness.

If the appearance of these growths is unacceptable the roof can be treated. A toxic wash is suggested, comprising a 3 to 5 per cent solution of copper nitrate with a wetting agent such as 0.01 per cent pyredenium chloride, which should be applied during the drier summer months.

All loose moss and lichens should be brushed off before the wash is applied. Afterwards, gutters, downpipes and brickwork which have been contaminated with the wash should be hosed down.

Q300: *In converting a bungalow loft into bedrooms, is it possible to cross joist the existing ceiling joists in order to avoid moving water pipes, electrical wiring, etc?*

A: There is no reason why querist should not lay the joists of his loft floor at right angles to the ceiling joists, provided that the ceiling joists themselves do not have to take any of the weight.

The floor joists should be preferably kept about 10 mm clear of the ceiling joists to ensure this while accommodating any irregularity in their depth. This may mean however that, assuming 150 to 200 mm joists are necessary it may be difficult to conform to the Building Regulations with regard to ceiling height and area to the loft.

The regulations require:

(1) The general ceiling height shall be at least 2.3 m

(2) This height shall be maintained, in the case of lofts with raking sides, over an area of at least half the floor area taken at a height 1.5 m above the floor, which in most cases will be the area of the floor itself (assuming 1.5 m vertical walls).

I suggest that about 100 mm in height could be saved by using binders between the existing ceiling joists, (Fig. 63) each formed from two members coach screwed and glued together using resorcinal resin gap-filling glue. The bottom being say 90 mm deep so that it could have its upper edge level with the ceiling joists carrying services and give 10 mm clearance above the existing plaster ceiling while the upper member could be say 110 or more according to span and notched over existing service pipes or cables.

The breadth of the binders could be 100 mm or more to allow for loss of strength by drilling for the coach screws, but the actual sizes would depend upon conditions of span and load.

Information is available from Schedule 6 in the Building Regulations.

As the span of floor joists (supported by cleats nailed to the binders) is only 1.5 m, 100 by 50 joists should be acceptable. The tops of the joists should be just above the binders to give room for the heads of the coach screws.

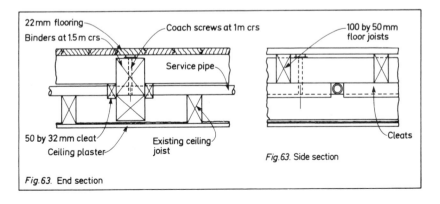

22mm flooring
Binders at 1.5 m crs
Coach screws at 1m crs
Service pipe
100 by 50 mm floor joists
50 by 32 mm cleat
Ceiling plaster
Existing ceiling joist
Cleats

Fig.63. Side section

Fig.63. End section

The only purpose of the coach screws is to pull up the glued joint between the members of the binder until the resin glue sets, so they only need to be slender. The shank hole for the screw needs to be about 1 mm greater than the shank and the thread hole about ⅔ the shank diameter.

Washers under the screw heads are necessary. The joint between the members of the binders should be planed to a reasonable fit and should be clean.

When glued together, the two parts of the binder should act as one. Under load the maximum tensional and compressional stresses will be in the extreme lower and upper fibres. The middle depth which is notched for the services will only be subject to sheer and will be more than sufficient to resist this.

The best way to notch for pipes is to bore a hole slightly larger than the pipe, if an auger is available, and to saw into this to form the notch. Any pipe passing through timber must be loose enough to expand and contract with changes.

Q301: *Advice on the construction of the valley beams/ tie beams, etc., shown in Fig. 64, is required.*

Also details of the joists used where the 250 mm by 75 mm valley beams meet the 25 mm by 75 mm tie beams.

As shown in Fig. 64, one will meet the other at an angle and it is necessary to keep in mind, that all the roof timbers are exposed to view.

A: There is not sufficient information to enable a full answer to be supplied with confidence.

It is not clear why the valleys could not be carried by wall plates or by the tie beams. The height of the tie beams also is not given or their relationship to the valleys.

What is the purpose of the tie beam — is it to carry some other load?

As the roof spans are 5.5 m and 5 m respectively as delinated by the valley positions the end roof must be a flatter pitch than the middle one.

The pitches are shown in Section MM and Section NN (Fig. 64a). By studying these in relation to the plan it will be seen that the eaves levels are at different heights, so that wall plates will also be at different levels unless that at b can be taken in.

The bevels needed have been shown in the earlier answer, but as the hips are not at 45 deg. on plan the backing bevels will be

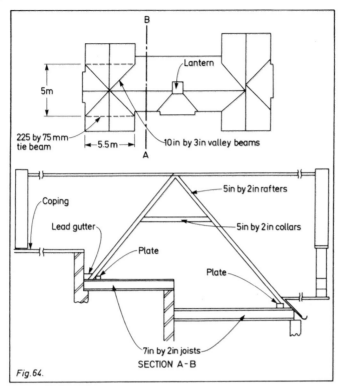

Fig. 64.

different on both sides of the valley. It is doubtful if this will be needed, however, for valleys as it would mean cutting a shallow sinking into the top edge of the hip—not an economical job. The cripple jacks are usually kept a little above the hip edge or the bottom corner of the valley gutter board slightly bevelled each side.

As regards cutting the roofing bevels, the best way to mark on the bevels and at the same time cut to the correct length is to draw the timber thicknesses over the centre lines on the plan and then, noting the basic principle that any measurement taken on any timber off the plumb cut is a plan measurement, place the centre line length on the timber, (rafter, etc.), mark on the plumb cut and square over the edge. Then measure square to the plumb cut the dimensions taken direct from the plan intersection details.

In the detail of intersection of valley with tie beam, I have assumed that the valley will cut over the top of the tie beam

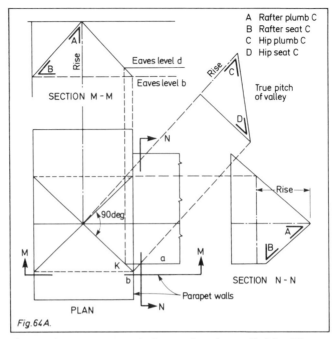

A   Rafter plumb C
B   Rafter seat C
C   Hip plumb C
D   Hip seat C

Fig.64A.

although to what extent no information is available. The centre of the edge of the valley must of course come in the roof line.

Where the valley cuts against the side of the tie beam will be the plumb cut. In the plan at "K" (Fig. 64b) it has been assumed that the centre of the valley coincides with the centre of the tie beam. The top of the notch where it rests on the top edge of the tie beam will be the seat cut.

The method of taking the measurements from the plan and transferring to valley square off the plumb cut should be clear from

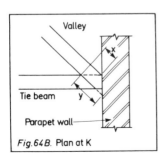

Fig.64B. Plan at K

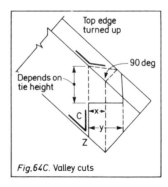

Fig.64C. Valley cuts

consulting the two relevant diagrams 64B and 64C. The bevel shown on the top edge of the valley must be of course marked on the bottom edge as the plan bevel of the vertical cut.

Querist emphasises that the roofing timbers are lift exposed and seen from underneath. This means primarily of course that all timbers should be paned and joints cut to a joinery standard. I note, however, that the construction includes parapet walls and presumably metal-lined wooden gutters. This timber work is likely to be untidy seen from below and should be cased in by some kind of sheeting, matchboard, ply, etc.

Q302: *Fig. 65 is a typical roof layout of a council project on which I am employed.*

The joists, with economy in mind, are of unregistered timber. The architect, while agreeing that an undulating ceiling must be expected at centres of rooms, has insisted that he should get a straight line where the ceiling meets the wall, as all joists should be sitting on a level course of bricks or wall plate.

However, the carpenters say that in nailing firrings to joists, undersize joists are being lifted and a ceiling free from undulations is not possible, even at perimeters of rooms, without extra labour being involved.

The problem only affects the firring nearest the point where the joists have bearing on wall. The architect will accept these undulations in centres of rooms. Ways of dealing with this problem are various and relatively simple. Expert advice is sought as to the most straightforward and economical approach.

A: Though simple at first sight this question is quite involved. The architect is asking for a straight line across the ceiling, even

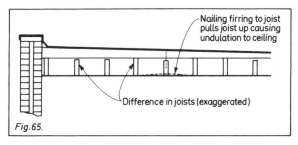

Nailing firring to joist pulls joist up causing undulation to ceiling

Difference in joists (exaggerated)

Fig.65.

if the straight line is only in one place. I can say, quite certainly, that with this form of construction he is most unlikely to get a straight line anywhere, and if he does manage to get one today he will not have it next week!

To get a straight ceiling at least two coats of plaster must be used and the first coat must be screeded. A "screed" in the sense I am using it is "a straight piece of wood". At least three of these screeds are required, two are fixed to the ceiling and lined in, i.e. made level and straight with each other, the first coat is applied and struck off with the third screed. Instead of the third screed a long "Darby" would probably be used. The finishing coat can now be applied. This is the only way of getting a straight and level surface, and if the architect wants this he must say so in his specification so that the contractor can insert the appropriate amount of money in his tender.

A skilled plasterer can get quite a true surface by using a Darby alone without the use of the two fixed screeds, but he will be the first to admit that the use of screeds produces a better result—but at a much higher cost.

Having gone to all this trouble to get a straight and level surface the moisture content of the roofing timbers will change, the shape of the timber will change accordingly, and the straight line of the ceiling no longer exists!

The carpenter is quite right that the fixing of the firrings will lift any undersized timbers and throw the undersides out of line. The effect can possibly be minimised by not driving the nails fully home, but this is undesirable. Anyway, if the two ends of the ceiling are brought to line the other two sides will probably be out since the joists are unlikely to be perfectly straight.

"Regularised" timber does not cost so very much more than ordinary, but is not worth the money if plasterboard or lath is to be used with a single coat of plaster on it. No matter how even and regular the line of the joists may be the plasterboard will show undulations, especially if a fluorescent light fixed flush with the ceiling is used.

Q303: *A quote is to be given for the replacement of the copper flashings on a built-up felt roof. Because of movement in the copper the pointing keeps falling out.*

It is proposed to adhere felt to the parapet wall and on to the roof, then render down to the roof over the new flashings, but will the rendering crack as before? The

remaining rendering will be waterproofed with a propriet-
ary surface treatment.
  See Figs. 66 and 66a.

A: I am not very happy with the proposal to render over the felt
as shown in Fig. 66A. I should think cracking and failure is
inevitable if this were done.

I would have liked to have seen a dpc in the parapet wall,
however, we have to deal with the situation as it is, and in a
reasonably economic fashion I imagine.

An upstand should be formed with a suitable built-up roofing, eg
Ruberoid, as shown in Fig. 66B. A chase 32 mm deep and 25 mm
high should be cut into the parapet wall and carefully brushed out.

The upstand should be bedded with an appropriate compound
or mastic.

The underlayer is dressed tightly into the junction of the roof and
parapet wall, and the built-up layers applied as shown. This may
be done by making the material pliable with a blowlamp, carefully
used.

For ease of handling lengths should not exceed 1 m and should
always be cut from the length of the roll and not across the width.

The final layer of the upstand should extend at least 75 mm on to
the main roof area, and the top should be turned over 25 mm into

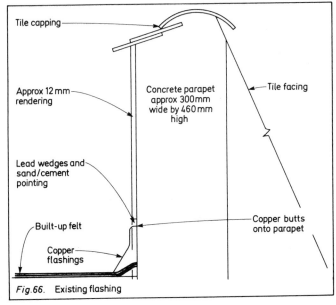

Tile capping

Approx 12 mm rendering

Concrete parapet approx 300 mm wide by 460 mm high

Tile facing

Lead wedges and sand/cement pointing

Built-up felt

Copper butts onto parapet

Copper flashings

Fig. 66. Existing flashing

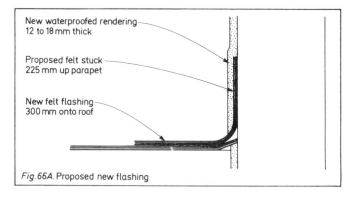

Fig.66A. Proposed new flashing

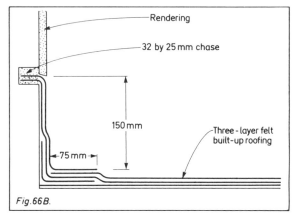

Fig.66B.

the chase as shown. Both underlayer and top layer should be bedded to the bottom of the chase and then pointed.

The overall upstand and flashing should be not less than 150 mm high.

Rendering can finally be brought down to the level of the top of the upstand.

Q304: *A bungalow built 15 years ago was constructed with 75 mm by 50 mm ceiling joists running lengthwise—see Fig. 67 – and two rows of 75 mm and 50 mm binders.*

Now, the binders have dropped in the middle and there is a noticeable dip in the ceiling.

To make it safer, the alternative to taking down the ceiling appears to be placing a heavy joist across the centre and bearing in the chimney breast, probably through the flue—unless a method of pulling up the joists from within the roof space can be suggested.

A: From the details to hand this problem reminds me of the old-style country labourer who had a job to keep his work-a-day trousers up. He'd used up all the adjustment on his braces, the elasticity had long since gone and he'd no money for either belt or braces until he received his yearly "hiring" which wasn't due for another four months.

What did he do? Someone each day had to tie together his braces with binder-twine as high up his back as possible!

We are faced with a similar situation here. It must be accepted that although the 75×50 mm ceiling joists span the longest way they are essentially ties for the rafter feet and since the roof spans 5.79 m the width of the bungalow (given), they have no alternative. This does give an advantage to the binders spanning the short way 3.502 m which is correct.

It is an accepted practice where a hip-end occurs, to tie in the feet of these jack-rafters by reversing the direction of say from about

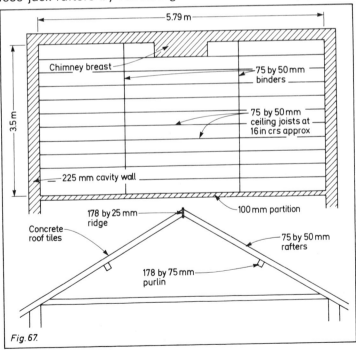

Fig. 67.

15 mm of the main hip-rafter length, all those joists occurring beneath this point. Where possible they are notched over any plates they encounter and fixed at right-angles into the main joists. This is rather loosely termed as "tying-in the flank wall".

The position of the binders is alright, but on account of their size 75 by 50 mm they are not serving any useful purpose. In addition I have no knowledge of size, position or method of fixing regarding any hangers which are usually notched over binders and nailed to them. Presumably the 178 by 75 mm purlins are supported at one end by the chimney breast gable wall and at the 100 mm partition some 3.502 m away.

If the partition is loadbearing (let's hope so), we encounter the first place for any adequate strutting. I wonder if struts are placed at intervals and propped from the binders. A system combining strut and hanger would cause the present failure!

So what shall we do? Firstly, the installation of a lighting point in this area of false roof if one doesn't exist. It's better than pulling inspection lights around. Now I propose that the two binders will have to come out and be replaced by 150 by 75 mm rsj's with suitable timbers bolted on each side of the web.

Select one of the binders. Locate its position in the room below by drilling two small holes down through the ceiling by the sides of the binder at each extremity. Strip away the polystyrene carefully from this area across the ceiling exposing the plaster and join these holes by pencil lines.

Move a pair of stout trestles say 1.830 m high immediately below and some 762 mm from each wall. Use the forks at the head of each trestle to cradle a 100 by 75 mm timber and spanning across these, place a 178 by 75 mm flat. On top a pair of small screw-jacks, themselves underneath another 178 by 75 mm which should be about 25 mm from the ceiling. Place something suitable like a hardboard strip as "cushioning" on top of the timber.

Having centralised, wind the "jacks" up and just "take the strain" at the ceiling. Repeat this process at binder No. 2, and when we have the ceiling "held", release carefully all hangers attached to these binders and/or joists in the immediate vicinity. Make sure that no electric cable or joint boxes are attached to binders and indeed release any other stapling thought necessary.

The binders may be nailed down to the joists. They may be attached by nailing up through the joists. In addition they could be skew nailed from the top.

So we will saw through each joist twice (actually there will be 10 of them) in such a position to leave an adequate gap to accommodate our girder-plus-joists combination. Thus the complete binder plus short ends and nails will all come away with little disturbance. Care will be needed where any odd plasterboard nails are holding.

When one binder is out carefully fix suitable metal joist-hangers to the joists concerned. Turn one appropriate zinc-plated countersunk screw to hold plasterboard to joist at a position near the metal joist hanger to compensate for any nails removed. Slowly and carefully turn each of the four screw-jacks to evenly take out the sag in the ceiling.

On account of the top flange on the joist hangers, each rsj unit will have to go in through a hole cut in the chimney-breast wall at the appropriate position and be gradually "coaxed" along to gather up each pair of joist-hangers as it encounters them. For this reason make sure that the top edge of each timber bolted to the girder is planed absolutely straight. Your level ceiling line is dependent upon it.

You have to decide as work progresses whether to take out both binders before inserting a girder, just as I have to have the courage of my convictions to tell you to do all this unorthodox indiscriminate cutting.

Perhaps querist could pick up a couple of small girders from a demolition contractor and even joists as well. Usual precautions regarding rust should be taken and the girder kept up 18 mm above the underside of joists.

Having no details regarding any strutting of the actual roof in question, the rsj's could serve to carry two cross-members or "booms" to form a built-up system of trussed purlin, using the existing purlin as the top boom, and so strutting the roof.

I may be wrong, of course, but I'm still of the opinion that the present struts are also the hangers. Conversely, the hangers have turned themselves into the struts. If you screw instead of nail, gently ease instead of force, you're ceiling will be perfectly safe. Take the same care in releasing the screw-jacks, lowering slowly and evenly.

Q305: *A circular turret roof 6 m in diameter is to be cut and fixed and I require the construction and cuts for such a roof.*

A: The wall plate or curb needs to be built of two thicknesses, say 50 mm each of circular ribs so that the joints in the top layer are central on the bottom (see Fig. 68).

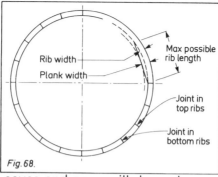

Fig. 68.

The detail at eaves and apex will depend upon design details, but assuming the simplest, Fig. 69 shows the shape of the first pair of rafters. As all the rafters will radiate on plan the birdsmouths at the eaves will be cut square. Some massing of timbers at the apex will be unavoidable.

This may, however, be greatly reduced by cutting in horizontal ribs between the two main pairs of rafters near the apex. Thus the first pair of ribs is butted together and the second pair cut against them. Four horizontal quadrants are cut between these with vertical edges.

The rafters may be birdsmouthed against these, Fig. 70. The rest of the construction depends upon the type of roof covering.

If this is to be sheet metal, then one or more layers of plywood (external grade) may be bent around the rafters and nailed to them to form the base for the covering. If shingles are to be used thin battens may be fixed as for normal roofing. Where they cannot be kept horizontal on their edges near the top of the roof they may be made wider and merely bent one way. The extra width will then accommodate the error.

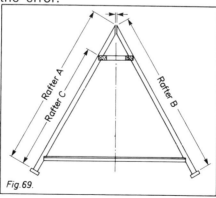

Fig. 69.

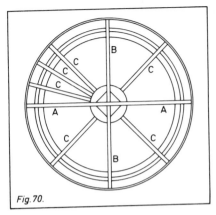

Fig. 70.

If the apex is to be brought to a point the top curve will have to be formed in solid timber. Stout triangular boards will have to be nailed to the four rafters and rib and the shape planed with a jack plane afterwards (see Fig. 71).

The tops of the rafters will have to be splayed as in Fig. 72 to give a flat nailing for these boards. The method of obtaining the shape of sheet metal or plywood coverings is shown in Fig. 73.

If as is sometimes done the ends of the rafters are left square and the fascia nailed to them, the shape of the fascia is also shown in Fig. 73.

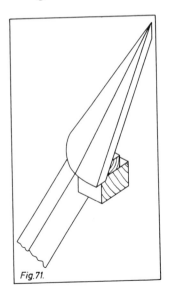

Fig. 71.

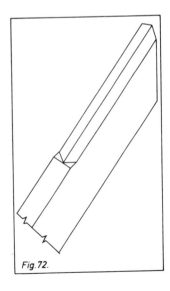

Fig. 72.

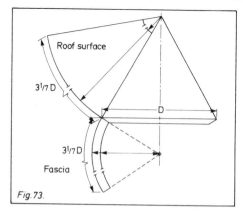

Fig.73.

Theoretically, assuming all the rafters to be evenly loaded the curb will be in tension only from the total of the pressures radiating from the rafters. However some irregularity will occur due to wind loads, etc., and it would be advisable to tie across the main rafters, one tie above the other.

If a resin glue is used in assembling the curb this will stiffen its resistance. It can be built on the ground and lifted into position in two halves.

Irrespective as to the general roof covering used, the apex is most likely to be metal covered so the cap formed should project above roofing materials to permit flashing.

Q306: *Winds and storms have spoilt the ceilings of a dozen houses roofed with Roman tiles without underfelt. Please suggest an alternative way of underfelting satisfactorily other than stripping and re-roofing complete.*

A: The old time method of weatherproofing Roman and/or pantiled roofs was to 'torch' them.

This was to place a haired mortar fillet along the top of each tile lath so that it sealed the gaps between the tiles, this was reasonably satisfactory. But it did in time tend to work loose and crack, and if repairs were carried out, it meant disturbing the mortar fillet, and very rarely indeed was it ever replaced properly.

To weatherproof the existing roofs, one could 'torch' the roof, but there are two other methods which can be done, neither of them is easy and it does mean a difficult job in fitting materials to the underside of the roof tiling.

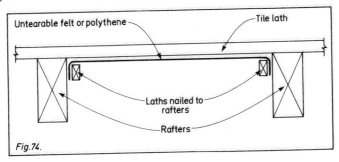

Fig.74.

Method 1. (Fig. 74)

Untearable roofing felt or black 1000 gauge polythene sheet, is cut into strips 75 mm wider than the distance between rafters, then with the aid of thin wood laths the felt is turned down so that the laths can be nailed through the felt into the side of the rafters. If this felt is kept close up to the underside of the tile laths and it is weathered properly at any joints it will keep out any water, but it must be carefully dealt with at the eaves and the felt must be draped over the wall plate so that any water penetration does not get passed down into the inner side of the wall or cavity. (Note if the tile nails protrude through the tile laths, then the felt must be kept away sufficiently so that the nails do not penetrate the felt or polythene).

Method 2. (Fig. 75)

Is similar to Method 1, except that 25 mm thick expanded polystyrene is used. This could be cut into strips just slightly under the width between rafters, and then held in place with laths nailed to the side of the rafters. Where any joints occurred they could be sealed by applying a strip of Secomastic to the joining edges. This material is fairly impervious to water and it would considerably assist the insulation of the roof at one and the same time and would be easier to do than the felt or polythene sheeting.

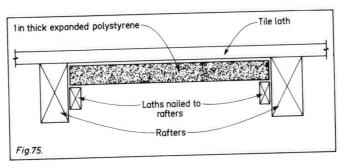

Fig.75.

Q307: *I am the owner of a house built in 1938 with a clay tile roof which was torched. The torching has deteriorated and has begun to fall off. Having investigated the cost of completely stripping the roof, felting and lathing and re-using existing tiles where possible, I am considering the possibility of re-torching the roof myself. Could you advise please?*

A: Torching is not a recommended practice. Torching is generally considered undesirable, because of its tendency to retain water, but in some circumstances torching of slated or clay tiled roofs may be required. It should be carried out with haired/lime mortar in accordance with good local practice, and should not be specified unless craftsmen experienced in this work are likely to be available.

Concrete tiles or asbestos-cement slates should not be torched with mortar.

Retention of water is undesirable as it may lead to rotting.

Q308: *Could you please provide answers to the following questions which relate to the drawing (Fig. 76)?*
1) Do I connect the collar and rafters by tooth plate connectors?
2) Do I need a ridge piece?
3) Do I need to birdsmouth the rafters over the wall plate?
4) Does the timber need to be stress graded?

A: *Question 1:* Assuming that the walls will not be expected to take any lateral pressure, the use of a tooth plate connector is probably the most satisfactory method by which the joints between the rafters and collars can be made. The joints can be designed as follows:

Lengths taken from the drawing appear to be roughly as follows: common rafter, 4 m; roof rise 2.8 m, distance of collar above wall plates 760 mm. Tiles are taken as 450 N/m²; plasterboard 92.6 N/m²; timber 5760 N/m³—imposed loads as per Building Regulations for 37 deg pitch.

Imposed load on 1 rafter
$= (720 - 100) \times 0.4 \times 9.25 \times 0.305 = 700N$

Tiles load on 1 rafter
$= 450 \times 13 \times 0.35 \times 0.4 = 713 \text{ N}$

Weight of rafter
$=0.125 \times 13 \times 0.305 \times 0.05 \times 5760 = 142.5$ N
Half weight of collar
$=6.5 \times 0.305 \times 0.15 \times 0.05 \times 5760 = 86$ N
Plasterboard to rafter and half collar
$=97.6 \times 10 \times 0.305 \times 0.4 = 119$ N
Total load on 1 rafter
$=700 \times 713 \times 142.5 \times 86 \times 119 = 1760$ N

If the rafter was at wall plate level the tension on the collar, which is load on connector, would be $1760 \times$ cotan 37 deg, but as the rafters now act as cantilevers the actual load $= 1760 \times$ cotan 37 deg $\times (7.5/5) = 1760 \times 1.303 \times 1.5 = 3440$ N.

In the connectored joint, the connection of the rafter is the weakest. A 50 mm connector will take 4.752 kN parallel to the grain (P) and 3.33 kN perpendicular to the grain (Q). If N=load at $37\frac{1}{2}$ deg to the grain on rafter, then N=

$$\frac{PQ}{P\sin^2 0 + Q\cos^2 0}$$

$$\frac{4.72 \times 3.33}{4.72 \times 0.3706 + 3.33 \times 0.7934}$$

$=3.58$ kN $=3580$ N.

So a 50 mm connector will be safe with strength to spare and we can ignore the slight load from the collar.

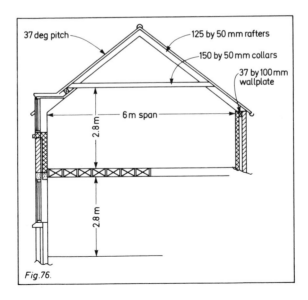

37 deg pitch

125 by 50 mm rafters

150 by 50 mm collars

37 by 100 mm wallplate

6 m span

2.8 m

2.8 m

Fig. 76.

Question 2: The main purpose of the ridge is to help in the assembly of the roof in situ and position the rafters at the tops, the nailing through the ridge giving some additional rigidity. As the collar tie roof will be made up before and lifted into place, a ridge is not necessary. The rafters can then be halved together at the apex.

Question 3: Fig. 76 does not give any detail of finish at the eaves. If the rafters cut down onto the plate (not over it) a birdsmouth is most convenient as the seat cut will finish a long way inside the plate taking away support for the plaster ceiling. If the rafters overlap the plate to give overhanging eaves, the birdsmouth is necessary to give a bearing on the plate.

Question 4: The timber sizes are robust and the spacing of rafters quite close, a lower grade timber should be acceptable.

Q309: *What is a typical sequence of working for laying mastic asphalt roofing?*

A: First, make sure the base on which the asphalt is to be laid has been checked and ensure that all the necessary preparatory work has been completed.

Break up the mastic asphalt blocks and melt them in the pot or mixer-boiler. The surface on which the asphalt is to be applied should be brushed clean and should be dry. Lay the underfelt and set out gauges about 2 m apart, of the same thickness as the asphalt to be spread.

The melted asphalt is brought by bucket (dusted), tipped at the working position keeping the working edge hot, and spread evenly by hand float; an even surface is achieved when the initial spreading is completed by repeated sweeps of the float.

New supplies of melted asphalt are spread slightly over the edge of the previous onee to keep it soft, and the join is welded together by float. This overlap joint welded by float and temporary application of hot material enables the join to be formed. Blows are pierced and made good while the asphalt is still warm.

On additional coats the joins are staggered—150 mm for horizontal work and 75 mm for vertical work should be adequate. All joins must be clean and free from sand or dust.

Graded sand is then rubbed into the top surface by float, unless some other treatment has been specified. This sand rubbing removes the thin skin of rich bitumen and restrains the development of crazing.

On some roofs it may be necessary to lay white spar, or similar chippings, in bitumen dressing compound, to prevent excessive heat transmission through the asphalt membrane. Alternatively, it may be dressed with reflective paint.

Q310: *Can you give calculations regarding the structural analysis of a collar trussed roof?*

The walls will not be "expected" to take any lateral pressure, but obviously the wall will be subjected to lateral pressure, which could cause fractures of the brickwork.

A: Timber.

Species Group 53
Grade 50
Emean 8,300 N/mm^2
Rafter 30 by 125 mm
$Zx=113\times10^3$ mm^3
$Ix=6.77\times10^6$ mm^6
Tile load per metre run of span$=450\times0.40=180$ N/m.
Component of tile load per metre at right angles to span$=180\times\cos\times37$ deg.$=144$ N/m.
Component of span reaction at right angles to span$=1.76\times\cos$ 37 deg.$=1.405$ kN.

Consider Bending
Bending moment at B$=1.405\times1.397=1.962$ kN/m.
Bending stress$=1.962\times10^6/113\times10^3=17.36$ N/mm^2.
Permissible bending stress$=6.2\times1.1=6.82$ N/mm^2.

Thus the section is very much overstressed and will not meet the requirements of CP 112.

Consider deflections
Case 1: Deflections due to reaction of 1.405 kN.
Moment at B$=1.405\times1.397=1.963$ kNm.

$$\text{Slope at B} = \frac{2\times1.963\times10^6\times2261}{6\times8300\times6.77\times10^6}$$

$$=0.0263.$$

Deflection of foot of span due to slope at B
$$0.0263\times1397=36.74 \text{ mm}$$
Deflection of foot of span due to cantilever from collar
$$= \frac{1.405\times10^3\times1.397^3\times10^9}{3\times8300\times6.77\times10^6}$$
$$=22.72 \text{ mm}$$

Total 59.48 mm

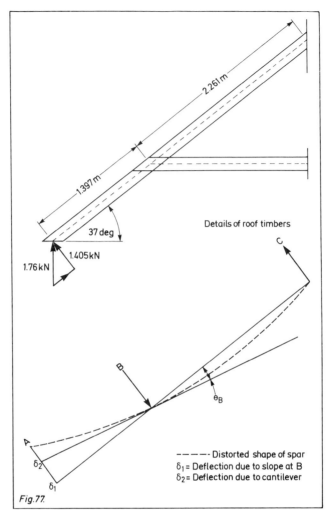

Fig.77

Case 2: Deflections due to weight of tiles on span

Slope at B
$$= \frac{144 \times 10^{-3} \times 2.261^3 \times 10^9}{24 \times 8300 \times 6.77 \times 10^6}$$
$$= 0.0012$$

Deflection of foot of span due to slope at B
$$= 0.0012 \times 1397 = 1.67 \text{ mm}$$

Deflection at foot of span due to tile loading

Slope at B $\qquad = \dfrac{144 \times 1.397 \times 1.397^3 \times 10^9}{8 \times 8300 \times 6.77 \times 10^6}$

$= -1.2$ mm

Total 0.47.

Total deflection at foot of span, at right angles to span
$= 59.46 + 0.47 = 60$ mm

Vertical component of deflection $= 60 \times \cos 37$ deg. $= 48$ mm.

Horizontal component of deflection $= 60 \times \sin 37$ deg. $= 36$ mm.

The horizontal deflection will cause the wall to spread at the wall plate, and most likely would cause a horizontal crack to appear in the brickwork and plaster.

Q311: *Regarding thermal insulation and condensation in roof spaces I would appreciate your advice on a proposed loft conversion to form a new bedroom as shown on the drawing (Figure 78), specifically on the following points:*

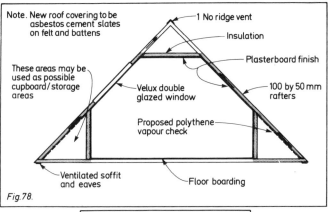

Fig.78.

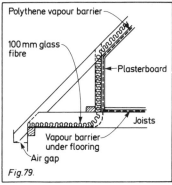

Fig.79.

1) Need for any vapour barriers—position and type;
2) Thickness and position of ventilation (existing rafters are
100 mm deep);
3) Need for any ventilation behind plasterboard surfaces.

A: The reason for a vapour barrier is to provide a moisture-resistant envelope into which habitable rooms are placed. The vapour barrier is placed onto the framework of the structure after insulation is installed and should be fixed to ceiling joists, rafters and stud walls and lapped onto floor joists.

Normally 500 gauge polythene is specified, being stapled to timbers with the lap of 225 mm horizontally and joist width vertically.

Insulation of 100 mm is normally used as the Building Regulations require a minimum of 80 mm. Insulation is placed behind the vapour barrier from the room side. (See Figure 79).

Ventilation of the roof space will require a vent at either end of the ridge to allow for through air passage.

Q312: *With regard to dormer windows, it is necessary to put soakers at the junction of the dormer cheeks and the main roof?*
We are assuming that if the felt is continued from the main roof and up the dormer cheek this would make it weather-proof, lead flashing at this junction also being unnecessary.

A: Soakers and lead flashings are only necessary for the abutment of slates and tiles against a wall or dormer cheek, chimney. In the case of a roof covered with felt as a finish, the felt of the main roof may be turned up against the dormer cheek under the covering of the cheek. The fold is a weak line; it may, with differential movement in time, possibly develop a split. A second covering layer is therefore needed to reinforce this particular area.

Q313: *Can you please provide structural calculations for a collar roof, pitch 30 deg., span 4 m, collars, 0.5 m up rise?*

A: The collar type of trussed rafter construction is not structurally economical when the collar is high as in the design requested.

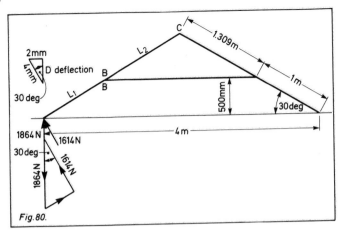

Fig. 80.

The reaction at the support creates a high cantilever effect at the foot of the rafter which must govern its design. If there is no resistance to lateral thrust rafter sizes may, according to the position of the tie, have to be excessive.

The amount of lateral thrust exerted on the supports depends upon deflection.

Assume timber is from group S2 grade SS, then values are $f_{gpar}=6.9$ N/mm^2 $E_{mean}=8900$

Fig. 80 is a centre line diagram of the truss.

It is first of all necessary to obtain roof loads as follows:

Average weight medium tiles and battens   537 N/m^2
Self weight of rafters say   147 N/m^2
Imposed load (building regs) on plan=720 M/m^2=
720 cos 30 deg in slope   624 N/m^2
Total unit load on slope   1344 N/m^2
Assuming spacing of rafters=0.6 m load m run   807 N/m
Length of rafter=2000×sec 30 deg   2309 mm
Length 1=2×500=   1000 mm
Load on 1 rafter=2.309×807   1864 N
Reaction at support square to rafter=1864 cos 30 deg   1614 N

Take bending moment at B,

$M=1614\times10^3$

$f_z=M=\dfrac{fbd^2}{6}$ assume b=41 mm

$d=\sqrt{\dfrac{6M}{fb}}=\sqrt{\dfrac{6\times1614\times10^3}{6.9\times41}}=185$ mm

So ignoring axial stresses which are small 41×194 mm would do for bending. For deflection, influences are deflection due to bending in L_2, deflection due to cantilever effect on L_1 and deflection due to loading from roofing in L_1 and L_2. The latter are small and tend to balance out in extreme cases, as this.

Formula for deflection due to bending in L_2 is $D = L_1 \dfrac{2ML_2}{6EL}$

Assume deflection $= 0.003 \, L_1$ then the equation in terms of I will permit selection of timber sizes. Thus $I = L_1 \dfrac{2ML_2}{6ED}$

$$= \frac{10^3 \times 2 \times 1614 \times 10^3 \times 1309}{6 \times 8900 \times 0.003 \times 10^3} = 26.38 \times 10^6 \text{ mm}^4$$

From table 56 CP 112 part 2 timber section 47×194 mm gives $I = 28.6 \times 106$ mm^4.

This can now be checked for full deflection.

1 Slope above B. $D = L_1 \dfrac{2ML}{6EL} = \dfrac{10^3 \times 1.6 \times 10^6 \times 1309}{6 \times 8900 \times 28.6 \times 10^6} = 1.38$ mm

2 Cantilever below collar. $D = \dfrac{RL_1}{3EI} = \dfrac{1614 \times 10^9}{3 \times 8900 \times 2.6 \times 10^9}$

Total deflection $=$ say 4 mm (allowing for weight of tiles on rafter spans). Horizontal deflection $= 2$ mm.

Q314: *Could you please supply me with any information on techniques in lead brazing, lead burning and lead dressing?*

A: Information on lead burning (welding) and lead dressing and bossing is contained in *Lead Sheet in Building*, published by the Lead Development Association (available from 34 Berkeley Square, London W1). It covers all aspects of the use of lead sheet for roofing, cladding, flashing and weathering. Two other useful publications are Lead Sheet Flashings and Leadwork No 3, the current edition of the technical/promotional series.

I am not familiar with the term 'lead brazing' and think you are referring to lead welding. Traditionally the term used for welding lead sheet and pipe was lead burning but since the term is sometimes applied to burning off lead paint we now prefer the more correct term lead welding.

Q315: *Could you please advise me on how to construct an eyebrow window in an existing roof covered with 265 mm by 150 mm plain tiles.*

A: There are basically four variations of the eyebrow window which are illustrated here. Fig. 81 shows the camel's hump or police helmet, considered something of an eyesore, and which also gives the tiler a headache. It should be a gabled or hipped dormer with tile hung cheeks. Fig. 82, is a hump-back bridge which is still too high for its proportions. Fig. 83, the human eyebrow with its ratio of 1:4 is proportionally better though the extremities of the curve finish too abruptly at the sill.

Fig. 84, is considered the ideal eyebrow window with the window head cut to curve. If the curved window head is continued beyond the window jambs as a reserve curve to meet the

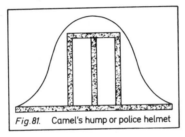

Fig.81. Camel's hump or police helmet

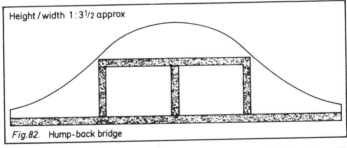

Height / width 1 : 3½ approx

Fig.82. Hump-back bridge

Height/width 1 : 4 approx

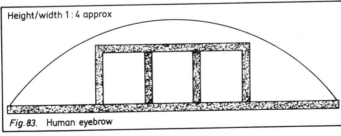

Fig.83. Human eyebrow

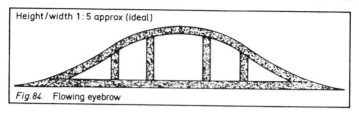

Fig.84. Flowing eyebrow

extremities of the sill (the length just over five times the window height) the whole is claimed to be the perfect eyebrow.

Fig. 85. The size of the window frame is 1371 mm by 610 mm high in the centre, 406 mm the actual jambs. Overall width to extremities of sill 3.35 m. Divide the frame into three and have the centre sash opening. The feature looks best on a large expanse of roof. Bonnet hip tiles, half timbering and, to a lesser extent, tile hanging complement it nicely.

Two methods of devising drawings follow:

Method 1 (Fig. 85): determine rise from D on centre line CE. Join AC, Bisect this line, and where this meets the centre line at E place the compass point and draw the arc ACB (CD is 200 mm). Similarly, the sweep reverse curves can be drawn giving about 75 mm to 100 mm rise.

Method 2 (Fig. 85): Using the intersecting chords principle, if CE is the diameter of a circle of which ACB is an arc, then AB and CE will be intersecting chords. So AD×DB=CD×DE and CD is 200 mm (fixed).

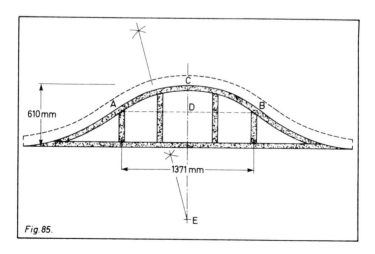

Fig. 85.

Therefore 675×675=200 DE (millimetres).
Therefore

$$DE = \frac{675 \times 675}{200} = \frac{455625}{200} \text{ 2278.125 mm.}$$

Now DE is 2278.125 mm, DC is 200 mm, so circle diameter= 2278.125 mm.

Therefore radius=1139 mm. This distance is marked from C and used to draw the arc or segment outline ACB. Again similarly with the "sweep" curves. Broken line over frame outline is approx. height ready for tiles.

Q316: *A timber constructed flat roof is to be designed either as a 'cold' or 'warm' structure. It is suggested that the 'warm' roof method is more expensive to construct. I am designing a means of complete through cross ventilation airflow to the standard timber board and three layer felt flat roof to replace the normal vertical flashing, an would welcome comments.*

A: The flashing upstand shown in Fig. 86 is designed to replace existing methods of sealing close boarded flat roofs of new or existing buildings to parapet or house walls, and to provide internal ventilation to roof areas.

The ventilated adjustable flashing upstand is to be manufactured in two adjusting parts: a lower section and upper section preformed in a zinc metal sheet material in interlocking lengths of one metre external; and internal angles to be manufactured in two adjustable units: a lower section and upper section preformed in a zinc metal sheet material and interlocking to above lengths.

One piece preformed end stops with top lipped angle and predrilled lower angle to be fitted to close cavity of ventilated flashings.

Ventilation airflow is acquired through predrilled holes incorporated in upper section of flashing and right angled internal ribs fitted inside upper and lower sections of ventilated flashing with a 10 mm gap between roof board and vertical structure.

The continuous ventilated adjustable flashing upstand is to be used in conjunction with the 50 mm thick sheet polystyrene and preformed air flow ducts and fitted to underside of roof deck and a continuous soffit or fascia board ventilator.

The external areas of the continuous ventilated adjustable flashing upstand will be coated with a durable weathercoat of a dark colour.

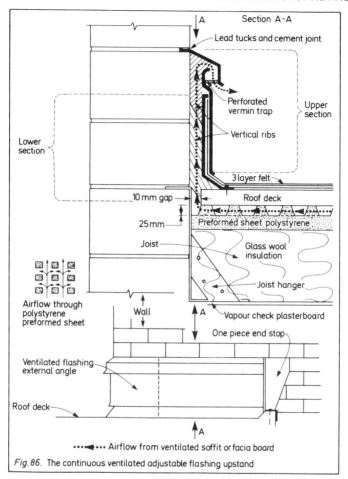

Section A-A

Lead tucks and cement joint

Perforated vermin trap

Upper section

Vertical ribs

Lower section

3 layer felt

10 mm gap

Roof deck

25mm

Preformed sheet polystyrene

Joist

Glass wool insulation

Joist hanger

Airflow through polystyrene preformed sheet

Wall

Vapour check plasterboard

One piece end stop

Ventilated flashing external angle

Roof deck

····◄···· Airflow from ventilated soffit or facia board

Fig. 86. The continuous ventilated adjustable flashing upstand

The continuous ventilated adjustable flashing upstand is to be fixed on site with the lower section tacked to roof deck and upper section tucked and cemented into chase in brickwork.

End stops to be fitted as above.

Q317: *Do roofs ever have to comply with specific regulations concerning fire resistance? If so, what are the relevant standards which should be followed?*

A: On some occasions a roof may be required to be able to contain a fire. For example, where it forms part of an external escape route or is required to give protection against fire spreading to higher storeys of the same development from a podium or other lower structure.

The roof must then be constructed to achieve the necessary period of fire resistance under Section 3 of BS 476: Part 8 (as for floors). It will also be necessary for any supporting structure to be fire resisting.

In some cases, although the fire resistance of the complete roof is not necessary, it may still be necessary to protect the supporting structure—for example, where the collapse of the roof structure might otherwise endanger the stability of other fire resistant elements.

Q318: *Please explain the detailing of built-up roofs.*

A: To achieve the best performance from a built-up roofing system it is essential that during its installation particular attention should be paid to roof details such as outlets, abutments, verges and eaves.

The eaves drip should be welted and formed out of mineral surfaced roofing. To complete the finish, the drip should extend below the bottom edge of the drip batten and turned back on to the flat roof at lest 100 mm. The top layer of the built-up system can then be sealed to the apron, again with an overlap of at least 100 mm. (Fig. 87. Welted apron to eaves).

Usually, verges must be raised about 25 mm above the roof level to stop rain driving over the edge. Again, it is recommended

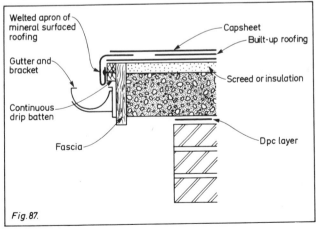

Fig. 87.

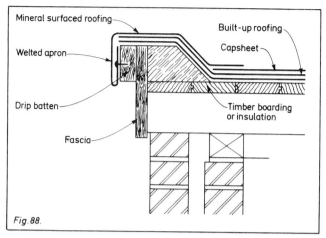

Fig. 88.

practice to advance the drip beyond the verge board and the apron welted as for the eaves. (Fig. 88. Welted apron to verge).

Alternatively, a metal trim may be used but care must be taken to ensure that cracking does not occur at the joints between the trim.

Upstands: As a general rule, if the roofing is cut from a 1 metre wide roll it should only be cut lengthwise, parallel to the grain, thereby assisting in the folding of the material.

At abutments such as brick walls or chimney stacks, roofing failures can be prevented by dressing the underlayer tightly into the corner with the upstand against the wall. Upstands should also be at least 150 mm above the highest point of the roof and their edges pointed in the brickwork joint. Where upstands exceed this height the flashing should be mechanically fixed to prevent slipping.

Where British Standard roofings are used, triangular fillets may be placed between the roof and abutment to minimise stresses which may cause roof failure. These fillets should be made of cork or polystyrene but not of timber which may warp and pull the roofing away from the wall. With high performance roofings, fillets are not necessary. (Fig. 89. Upstand detail).

Where insulation is used it is important that the vapour retarder is sealed over the edge of the insulation board in accordance with BS 5250.

At internal and external angles it is essential to ensure a waterproof joint and to reinforce if possible. On pitched roofs the roofing felt should be turned up a minimum of 75 mm and covered with a stepped flashing.

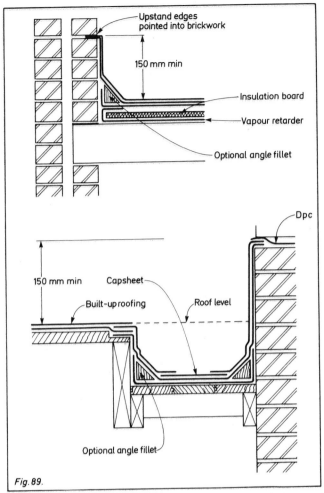

Fig. 89.

Internal gutters: All outlets should be at low points on the roof and allowance must be made in levels for the build up of laps in the roofing layers.

Q319: *As so many serious accidents on site concern men working on roofs, can you set out some basic safety precautions?*

A: Check the following:
- Is work being done on a sloping roof of more than 30 deg., or

less than 30 deg. but which is slippery. If so, are there crawling ladders or crawling boards? Are these being used? If crawling boards or ladders are not provided, does the roof structure itself provide a safe handhold and foothold?
• For sloping roofs or work near the edge of flat roofs, is there sufficient edge protection to prevent falls of materials and persons?
• Are any men working on or near fragile materials such as asbestos sheets or glass? If so, are crawling boards provided and used? Are warning notices posted?
• Have all rooflights been properly covered or provided with barriers?
• During sheeting operations, are precautions taken to prevent men falling from the edge of the sheet?
• Where other men are working under roofwork, are precautions taken to prevent debris falling on them?

Q320: *Advice is required on the roof construction for a semi-bungalow with the lounge, one bedroom and box-room in the roof.*
The main items are the construction of the flat dormer roof without supporting purlins showing in the lounge ceiling and the sizes of the roof timbers. Fig. 90 is a plan of the proposed bungalow.

A: I have modified querist's roof section to try to render it more stable and architecturally sound.
By doing this the 228 mm by 75 mm purlins can be accommo- dated above the ceiling tie, as shown in isometric detail and section Fig. 91 and Fig. 92. End bearing can be obtained by rearranging or running up the load bearing walls up to roof space.
With this form of roof construction, stability of the roof is most important, that is another reason for running rafters down and connecting them to 228 mm by 50 mm floor joists. All these and other connections must be well made, I suggest a "butt" joint with 9 mm exterior plywood gussets nailed and glued both sides of members.
The roof will be formed of three basic trussed rafters, as can be seen from the section and isometric detail (Figs. 91 and 92). On this detail (Fig. 92) pay attention to joints A and B. Querist will have to work out, from the elevation, how many of each type he will require, at 610 mm centres.

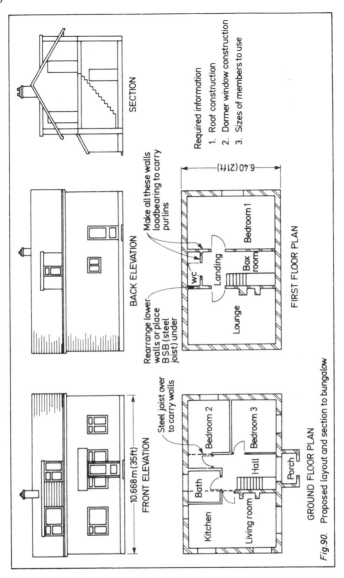

Fig.90. Proposed layout and section to bungalow

To construct the roof, first bed 100 mm by 50 mm wall plates in sand/cement mortar. If required, plates can be nailed to wooden pads built into top course of brickwork, or hoop iron straps can be built into brickwork, about four courses from the top.

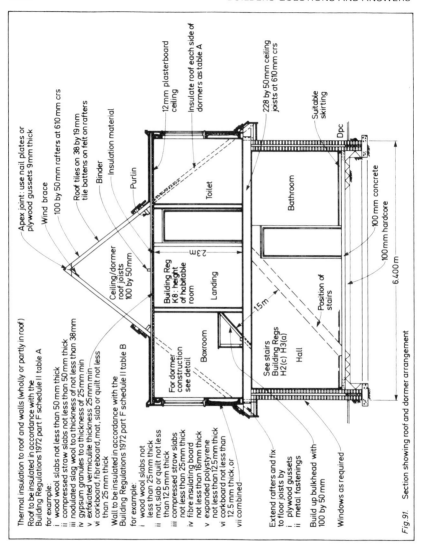

Fig. 91. Section showing roof and dormer arrangement

Hoop iron is then bent up and over wall plates and nailed, see D Fig. 92.

Next, mark out truss positions on wall plates, mark these locations on a gauge lath, use a floor-board or similar sized material for this purpose. This will be used at ridge to give required spacings for trusses, and left in place as "wind brake", until purlins

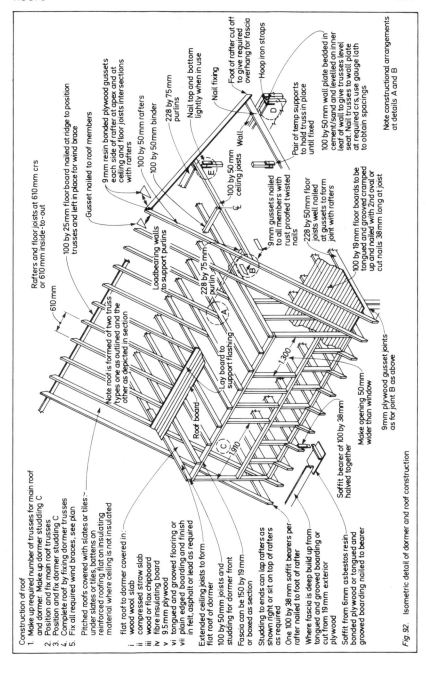

Construction of roof
1. Make up required number of trusses for main roof and dormer. Make up dormer studding C
2. Position and fix main roof trusses
3. Position and fix dormer studding C
4. Complete roof by fixing dormer trusses
5. Fix all required wind braces, see plan

Pitched roofs covered with slates or tiles:-
under slates or tiles, battens on reinforced roofing flat on insulating material where ceiling is not insulated

flat roof to dormer covered in:-
i   wood wool slab
ii   compressed straw slab
iii wood or flax chipboard
iv   fibre insulating board
v   9.5 mm plywood
vi   tongued and grooved flooring or
vii plain edged boarding and finish in felt, asphalt or lead as required
viii plywood

Extended ceiling joists to form flat roof of dormer

100 by 50mm joists and studding for dormer front

Fascia can be 150 by 19mm or boxed as section

Studding to ends can lap rafters as shown right or sit on top of rafters as required

One 100 by 38mm soffit bearers per rafter nailed to foot of rafter

Where fascia is deep build up from tongued and grooved boarding or cut from 19mm exterior plywood

Soffit from 6mm asbestos resin bonded plywood or tongued and grooved boarding nailed to bearer

Fig. 92.   Isometric detail of dormer and roof construction

Rafters and floor joists at 610mm crs or 610mm inside-to-out

610mm

100 by 25mm floor board nailed at ridge to position trusses and left in place for wind brace

Note roof is formed of two truss types one as outlined and the other as depicted in section

Loadbearing walls to support purlins

228 by 75mm purlin

Lay board to support flashing

Roof board

1 300

190

Make opening 50mm wider than window

9mm plywood gusset joints as for joint B as above

Soffit bearer of 100 by 38mm halved together

9mm resin bonded plywood gussets each side of rafter at apex and at ceiling and floor joists intersections with rafters

Gusset nailed to roof members

100 by 50mm rafters

100 by 50mm binder

228 by 75mm purlins

Nail top and bottom lightly when in use

100 by 50 mm ceiling joists

Wall

9mm gussets nailed to all members with rust proofed twisted nails

228 by 50mm floor joists well nailed at gussets to form joint with rafters

100 by 19mm floor boards to be tongued and grooved cramped up and nailed with 2nd oval or cut nails 38mm long at joist

Nail fixing

Foot of rafter cut off to give required overhang for fascia

Hoop iron straps

Pair of temp supports to hold truss in place until fixed

100 by 50mm wall plate bedded in cement/sand and levelled on inner leaf of wall to give trusses level seat. Nail trusses to wall plate at required crs, use gauge lath to obtain spacings

Note constructional arrangements at details A and B

are fixed, see isometric detail Fig. 92. Position first truss 50 mm inside and away from end gable wall.

Trusses may be too heavy to lift completed, without a crane, so leave off floor joists and by using a pair of props and purlins, see E Fig. 92, trusses can be supported ready for framing to floor joists. Continue to fix other trusses in similar manner.

Next, position and fix fronts to dormers, these will need temporary bracings until roof joists are securely nailed to them.

When constructing dormer fronts, make openings, to receive standard windows, 38 mm maximum larger in both directions see C Fig. 92, this will help when fixing windows later.

As stated earlier, the roof in total design, is not architecturally sound. Querist may consider reducing the width of rooms in the roof and bringing the dormer farther back onto the roof, thus giving a larger area of roof under the dormer windows.

Also, the bathroom layout will have to be modified to allow the soil and vent pipe to run vertically down inside a duct, in the bathroom and up through the roof.

Q321: *In designing a house with traditionally constructed roof should the long span rafters over the porch and garage area (Fig. 93) be split into two separate rafters or should one long rafter be used?*

Details at the eaves (points 1, 2 and 3) for this particular type of roof are also required.

A: The sketch provided with the query (Fig. 93) does not give any sizes, but assuming that garage door and porch are of average

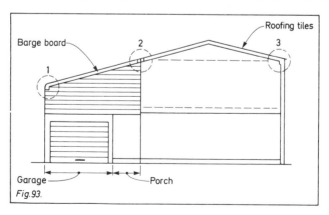

Fig.93.

dimensions it would appear that rafters over the lower slope, will only need to be about 4 m long.

I, therefore, presume that the query refers to the whole length from ridge to eaves. This would be well over the 6 m usually accepted as maximum length obtainable in commercial sizes unless especially ordered.

If a scarfed joint is formed in the rafters 450 mm beyond the wall plate supporting the upper members so that the lower member is carried by the upper one, this will not only reduce the span of the lower rafters, but will also reduce the maximum bending moment in the top ones by contraflexure.

50×100 mm rafters spaced at 400 mm crs, carrying between 50 and 75 kg/m² may have a maximum unsupported span of 2.49 m. If the span is greater than this, heavier rafters will have to be used or an intermediate support (purlin) introduced. This would need to be carried at its ends by cross on end walls if available or strutted off lower load-bearing partition walls.

The size of the purlin depends upon the load it has to carry and the span or spacing of supports but 63 by 150 purlins spaced at 2.4 m (the width of the load they have to carry) need support at 2.12 m centres with normal tiled roof construction.

Regarding the constructional details asked for, the finish at (1) and (3) in Fig. 93 may be identical with the probable exception that ceiling joists may be needed in one case and not the other. These are therefore indicated by dotted lines in the section "external wall" Fig. 94.

The pitch of the roof given by the querist is only 15 deg. This is very flat and some care should be taken in selecting and using a suitable tile.

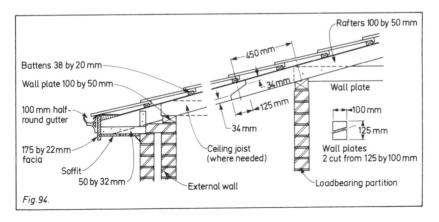

Rafters 100 by 50 mm
450 mm
Battens 38 by 20 mm
Wall plate 100 by 50 mm
34 mm
Wall plate
100 mm half-round gutter
125 mm
100 mm
34 mm
125 mm
175 by 22mm facia
Ceiling joist (where needed)
Wall plates 2 cut from 125 by 100 mm
Soffit
50 by 32 mm
External wall
Loadbearing partition

Fig. 94.

If the upper rafters are cantilevered over the partition wall as suggested and shown they will be subject to flexural stresses directly over the support, they should not be weakened by birdsmouthing, but the wall plates should be bevelled to fit them as shown.

These are best cut in pairs from 125 by 100 timbers as in Fig. 94. If the ceiling joists are splay-notched to fit this will provide an additional anchorage to tie the feet of the upper rafters which will in turn restrain the lower ones.

18 Extensions

Q322: *Details of the following are required for an extension to an existing house shown in Figs. 95, 96, 97 and 98.*

1. Size of U beam.

2. Piers to support U beam and any special requirements for foundations.

3. Specification for the flat roof suitable for regular foot traffic.

A: I will answer the questions in order.

U Beam:

The universal beam across the sitting room has to carry:

(i) Half of the bedroom and gallery floor and superimposed load.

(ii) The stud partition to bedroom and handrailing to gallery.

(iii) Part of the weight of the new roof and its superimposed load and ceiling (purlin needs supporting).

(iv) Self-weight of beam and casing.

I make out loads to be:

Floor: kg.

$\frac{1}{2} \times 7.25 \times 3.02 \times 222$ kg/m^2 =   2430

Stud partition and half-return:

Studs $3.7 \times 2.25 \times 17$ kg/m^2

Plasterboard (2) at 33 kg/m^2 total 50   =   420

Handrail 3.5×1 m $\times 5$ kg/m^2 =   20

Roof:

Consider half the width down the slope as the correct width and three quarters of the span for the length (remainder carried by purlin ends on walls).

This gives $3.25 \times 5.25 \times 200$ kg/m^2 = 3420

Self-weight with casing:

7 m $\times$ 40 kg/m   = 280

                                    6570

                            = 65 kN

U Beam to span 7.25 m

Tables for 43 grade steel give $305 \times 102 \times 33$ kg takes 75 kN. This is the least weight of steel suitable in 43 grade. There are no more economical figures for 50 grade steel as deflections are likely to be excessive.

The piers

The calculated force imposed by a beam end is about 33 kN. Pads should be placed under the ends of the beam to distribute the weight on the brick piers. Basic stress for normal brickwork may be 1.45 N/mm^2. Reduction for a slenderness of 2.5/0.2 ie. 12.5 is 0.75

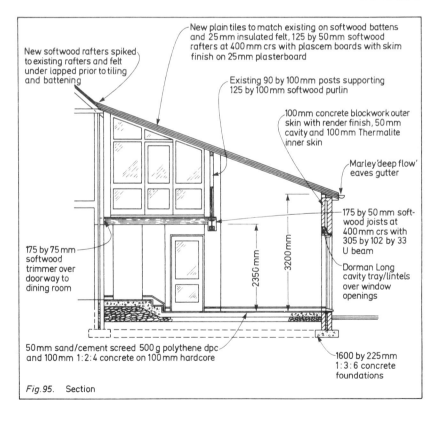

New plain tiles to match existing on softwood battens and 25mm insulated felt, 125 by 50mm softwood rafters at 400mm crs with plascem boards with skim finish on 25mm plasterboard

New softwood rafters spiked to existing rafters and felt under lapped prior to tiling and battening

Existing 90 by 100mm posts supporting 125 by 100mm softwood purlin

100mm concrete blockwork outer skin with render finish, 50mm cavity and 100mm Thermalite inner skin

Marley 'deep flow' eaves gutter

175 by 50mm softwood joists at 400mm crs with 305 by 102 by 33 U beam

Dorman Long cavity tray/lintels over window openings

175 by 75mm softwood trimmer over doorway to dining room

2350mm

3200mm

50mm sand/cement screed 500g polythene dpc and 100mm 1:2:4 concrete on 100mm hardcore

1600 by 225mm 1:3:6 concrete foundations

Fig.95. Section

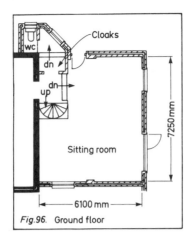

Fig.96. Ground floor

giving a working stress of 1.1, say 1 N/mm². Therefore area required=33000 m².

Suppose the thickness=225 mm then the length works out at 147 mm, which is absurdly short. For practical purposes take the pier to be 1 B thick (HB thickened by an extra ½ B) and two bricks long (450 mm).

The load becomes spread along the wall and no special details or alterations of foundations are needed on normal soils.

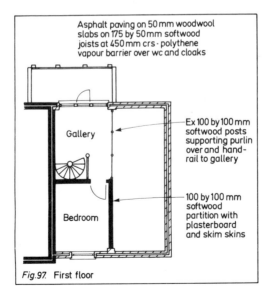

Asphalt paving on 50 mm woodwool slabs on 175 by 50 mm softwood joists at 450 mm crs · polythene vapour barrier over wc and cloaks

Ex 100 by 100 mm softwood posts supporting purlin over and hand-rail to gallery

100 by 100 mm softwood partition with plasterboard and skim skins

Gallery

Bedroom

Fig.97. First floor

Fig.98. East elevation

The flat roof

The details of the construction are not very clearly shown but the SW joists 175×50 mm at 450 mm centres as noted should suffice. Presumably one end is supported on the brick-built wc and cloaks extension, and the other end on the U Beam which has to project through as a cantilever. This will impose a small negative bending moment on the beam, but reduce the main positive bending moment on which the selection of the beam was based thus adding a little to the safety margin.

The SW joists would be satisfactory and woodwool slabs 50 mm thick as suggested may be used. The question of foot traffic and a suitable surface remains to be considered.

If of asphalt as suggested, although this is a small piece of work in size to employ an asphalt contractor to execute, then a suitable 'isolating' membrane which also waterproofs would be bituminous felt (not polythene to receive hot asphalt). The mastic asphalt for light foot traffic for terraces should be laid in two thicknesses, one 10 mm, followed by 16 mm with a little grit in the second thickness.

The question of edging is important. It would appear from the plan that one if not two eaves' gutters are to be provided at the ends, with slight falls to same. This fall can be achieved by thin firrings on the joists.

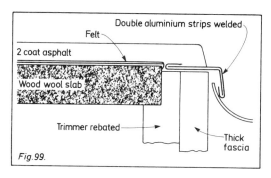

Fig.99.

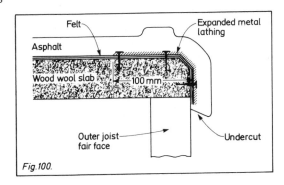

Fig.100.

A detail of the turn down into the eaves gutter is shown in Fig. 99, and a water check along the front edge in Fig. 100. A normal asphalt skirting is required along the brickwork.

If querist considers an alternative such as quarry tiles for the balcony floor these would be laid on a cement and sand screed reinforced with chicken wire, with polythene under the screed. In such case there is always the difficulty of obtaining a satisfactory edge to drip into the gutter which would be efficient and permanent. Another possible surface is asbestos decking tiles, but there is still the difficulty with the edge.

Note. The handrail posts must be fixed in such a way that they are independent of the asphalted surface, taking support on the side and end joists.

There is one point I notice on inspecting the annotated drawing, which appears to be unsatisfactory, that is the covering for the roof of the extension at a pitch of 20 deg. Plain tiles as specified require a pitch of at least 35 deg., slates 30 deg., interlocking tiles 30 deg., diagonal asbestos tiles 30 deg. with 76 mm lap or an increased lap if shallower. It looks rather as if querist may have to resort to three coat roofing felt on boarding.

Q323: *With regard to the building of an extension, I would be interested in your opinions on the best method of supporting the ends of upper storey floor joists lean-to rafters, or roof trusses at right angles to the outside face of the existing stone built building.*

A: There are various solutions to this problem dependant on the condition of the stonework.

If the stonework is of good quality and in good condition then the simplest way to provide support would be to fix an ordinary timber wall plate with resin anchor bolts at appropriate centres. However, if the wall is in a very poor state of repair then one solution would be to support the joists, etc., from a RSJ channel section spanning between the new extension walls, with appropriate piers to give adequate end bearing.

Using this method no loads would be transferred to the existing building which could be an extra advantage with old buildings with foundations which could be inadequate for the extra load from the extension floors and roof.

Q324: *I propose to build a bedroom extension above an existing garage which involves providing a new pier at the front and increasing the size of the other piers. The plans have been given the okay subject to the submission of 'detailed calculations required to prove the stability of the garage wall'.*

Can you help to prove the structural stability of the garage wall, particularly the front pier.

A: The piers are designed as piers with the sizes given accepted, as they are largely point-loaded, and the stresses that are present are calculated. The permissible stresses based on ordinary Fletton brickwork in 1:1:6 mortar, piers handed in, are given and are shown to be considerably greater.

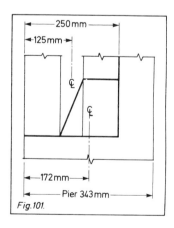

Fig.101.

Front corner pier

Point loading

	kN
Floor 0.75 m × 1.09 m × 2 kN/M^2	= 1.64

Half front wall on Catnic
1.2 m × 2.75 m × 3.25 kN/m^2 = 10.73

Part side wall apportioned to pier via Catnic
Length (behind front) 0.7 m
Height   2.75 m
Weight   0.7 × 2.75 × 3.25   = 6.26
Roof 0.75 m × 1.1 m × 1.3 kN/m^2 including snow   = 1.07
                                                                                    ─────
                                                                                    19.7
                                                                                    ─────

                                                        Say 20 kN

Self weight of pier applicable at ground level
0.45 m × 0.228 m × 2.2 × 17.6 kN/m^3 = 4 kN

Normal stress$\dfrac{20.000}{450 \times 228} = 0.195$ N/mm^2

Eccentric Stress

From front Catnic carrying part front wall and floor

                                                        Load W = 12.37 kN

Eccentricity = $\frac{1}{3}$ thickness   = 76 mm
Moment = We   = 12.370 × 76 = 940.000 Nmm

Section modulus of pier (z) $= \dfrac{bd^2}{6} = \dfrac{450 \times 228^2}{6}$
                                                = 3.898.800 mm^3

Eccentric stress = moment/modulus   = 0.24 N/mm^2
Total stress (combined) = 0.195 + 0.24   = 0.435 N/mm^2 at top
At bottom add self wt./area

                $= \dfrac{4.000}{450 \times 228}$ = 0.039 N/mm^2
                                                                    ─────────────
The total is   **0.476 N/mm^2**
                                                                    ─────────────

Basic Stress CP 111, on Brickwork. Say, Flettons to 27.5 N/mm^2 in cement-lime mortar 1 : 1 : 6.
        Stress given as 1.585 N/mm^2, general.
For small piers multiply basic stress by reduction factor

$0.75 + \dfrac{\text{area (m}^2)}{1.2} = 0.75 + \dfrac{0.10}{1.2} = 0.83$

Basic stress with applied reduction factor for small size

$$= 1.585 \times 0.83$$
$$= \mathbf{1.32 \ N/mm^2}$$

Reduction for Slenderness

Effective height = actual height = 2.2 m
Effective thickness = actual = 0.228 m
Ht/thickness $\quad = 2.2/0.228 = 9.64$. Say 10
Reduction factor for slenderness, CP 111 with eccentricity $\frac{1}{3}$ from
Table 4 $\qquad = 0.76$
Permissible stress $= 0.76 \times 1.32 = 1.0 \ N/mm^2$
This is to be compared with calculated actual applied stress of
$$\mathbf{0.476 \ N/mm^2}$$

Side pier

0.45 m × 0.343 m

Point loading

	kN
Floor 2 m × 1.1 m × 2 kN/m²	= 4.4
Side wall on Catnic 2 m × 2.75 m × 3.25 kN/m²	= 18.0
Roof 2 m × 1.2 m × 1.3 kN/m²	= 3.1
	25.5

Normal stress $\dfrac{25.500}{450 \times 343} = \mathbf{0.165 \ N/mm^2}$

Self weight $0.45 \times 0.343 \times 2.2 \times 17.7 \ N/m^3 = \mathbf{6 \ kN}$

giving a stress of $\dfrac{6.000}{450 \times 343} = \mathbf{0.039 \ N/mm^2}$

Eccentricity e = 47 mm (see sketch) W = 25.500
Moment = W e = 25.500 × 47 = 1.198 × 10⁶ Nmm

$$z = \frac{bd^2}{6} = \frac{450 \times 343^2}{6} = 8.824 \times 10^6 \ nm^3$$

Eccentric stress = 1.198/8.824 = **0.136 N/mm²**
Total actual stress at top = 0.165 + 0.136
$$= 0.3 \ N/mm^2$$
or at bottom **0.339 N/mm²**
Basic stress (as before) $\qquad = 1.585 \ N/mm^2$
Reduction factor for small piers

$$= 0.75 + \frac{area}{1.2} = 0.75 + \frac{0.154}{1.2} = 0.88$$

Applied to basic, gives 1.585 × 0.88 = **1.4 N/mm²**

Slenderness effect

$$\text{Slenderness} = \frac{\text{Ht.}}{\text{thick}} = \frac{2.2}{0.343} = 6.4$$

With eccentricity $\frac{1}{6}$ and slenderness 6.4 the reduction factor from
Table 4 is 0.98 giving 1.4×0.98 $= 1.37 \text{ N/mm}^2$
  Permissible stress $= 1.37 \text{ N/mm}^2$
Compare with the calculated actual value of 0.339 N/mm^2
The Catnic at the front should be bolted down into the brick pier at the
left end.

Q325: *One builder quotes £1,600 for a bathroom back
addition with all-white suite, and another £10 per sq.ft.
complete or £8 per sq.ft. for the fabric.*

*Construction is to be cavity wall with concrete floor and
lean-to felted roof. Work to include minor alterations to
kitchen, such as closing up existing door opening and
making good; cutting a new door opening in rear wall and
providing and fitting a new door. A ventilated lobby would
be formed between the kitchen and bathroom. The lobby
would also include a new back door.*

A price for the work is required for:
*(a) Middle of terrace property with no secondary access,
and*
(b) As (a) but with secondary access.

A: The floor size of the proposed addition is not given. For the
purpose of this answer I am assuming the following sizes:
bathroom (and lavatory) 2.4 m by 2.4 m plus a ventilated lobby
2.4 mm by 0.9 m between, combined floor area 7.82 m², three
external walls and one side being the existing building.

If my supposition of size is about correct, then one builder's
estimate of £10 per sq.ft. floor area equals £880, a little over half
the £1,600 estimate by the other builder. It appears that each
builder is estimating on a different guesswork system.

Using my supposition of size combined with the detail stated I
give the accompanying approximate quantities and cost analysis.

It appears that the builder who used the approximate prelimin-
ary floor area price came very near to my estimate. I find the £1,600
quite inexplicable.

An estimate for a job of this nature should be based first on
some detailed measurements and quantities. Last of all check the

current wage rates and costs of materials from BTJ's Estimating Guide. It is necessary to add 5 per cent, 10 per cent or 45 per cent to cover these shortcomings, whichever profit margin is best suited for.

Q326: *The Town and Country Planning General Development Order 1977 provides for the erection of a porch without planning permission subject to certain conditions. While the condition in paragraph 2(a) states 'the floor area does not exceed 2 m²', the rules for measuring seem vague—some local authorities insisting on external measurements, some allowing internal.*

The difference in floor space can be a deciding factor in whether or not to have a porch built, as can the delay caused by planning applications. Is there a definitive answer?

A: If one looks at the General Development Order as a whole, Class 1(1) relates to increasing the cubic content of dwelling-houses by 70 m³ 'as ascertained by external measurement'. This is clear, as also is Class VIII for industrial purposes, when the content of buildings may be increased 'as ascertained by external measurement'.

That situation existed long before the introduction of the proviso which allows a porch 'so long as the floor area does not exceed 2 m²'. When this provision was introduced the lack of 'as ascertained by external measurement' was widely noted and the fact that the area of porch is being interpreted in that is a source of surprise.

Thus the answer to your question is really in what the clause does not say. If the floor area measured in a conventional building manner does not exceed 2 m² and the other conditions with regard to position and height are also fulfilled, we are of the opinion that it is 'permitted development' and does not require a local planning authority's permission.

Q327: *Calculations have to be submitted to the local authority for the two RSJs shown in Figs. 102 and 103. These will provide support in the kitchen extension where two sections of the existing walls are to be removed.*

Above the higher joist there is 9 ft. by 10 ft. of 9 in. solid brickwork to the underside of the roof and the area above the lower joist is 3 ft. wide by 10 ft. high with a window 3 ft. high by 1 ft. 6 in. wide. There are no windows above the upper joist.

The rear end elevation is a hipped roof with a pitch of 40 deg. to 42 deg.

The upper floor is normal construction and the bedroom joists run parallel with the rear elevation; the ends resting on the top of the upper joist. The 7 ft. span lower joist would carry the point load from the upper joist. There is 1 ft. 6 in. height of brickwork above the lower joist on the left hand side.

For the flat roof extension 5 in. by 2 in. timber joists will run across from a new external garage wall and will be staggered in between the floor joists on the upper RSJ. The roofing is board and felt and there is no access on to the flat roof except for maintenance. (Please keep answers in imperial).

A: The difficulty with calculations of beam sizes, etc., is usually one of deciding how much load is likely to be borne by the beams.

There is always some uncertainty and it is advisable to allow enough load and in the present case I will allow for all the vertical load directly above the beams that is apparent.

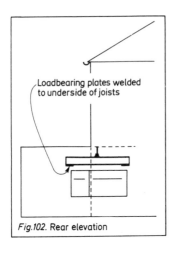

Fig.102. Rear elevation

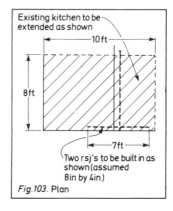

Fig.103. Plan

It can be contended that in the case of brickwork, which is by far the major load here, that two 60 deg. upward slopes can be drawn from the beam ends to meet and form an equilateral triangle and that only the work in this triangle has to be supported, the rest being self supporting. In this present case this would hardly apply anyway, as it is irregular with the lower joists and there would be a very limited bearing length at one end of the upper joist.

So reckoning the full vertical load to be found above the beams I make the figure to be:

Upper beam(s)

The figures for length (width) and height in ft. and load in lb/ft² are:

		lb.
Brickwork, plastered 8×10×100	=	8000
Triangle of roof (hipped) ½×8×10.6×20	=	848
Superimposed on roof ½×8×8×11	=	352
Wind on portion of roof reckoned as vertical component ½×8×10.6×4.5	=	190
Upper floor, half, + superimposed 8×6×(10+30)	=	1930
Bedroom ceiling 8×6×10	=	480
Eaves, say	=	100
Load imposed by flat roof ½×6×8×(10+15 imposed)	=	600
Total	=	12490
	=	**5.6 ton**

Taking grade 43 steel (ordinary mild steel) safe load tables for uniformly distributed loads for a span of 8 ft. (2.44 m) give:

8 in.×4 in. (203×102 mm) 120 kN	= 12 ton for one
	= 24 ton for two
7 in.×4 in. (178×102 mm) 90 kN	= 9 ton for one
	= 18 ton for two
6 in.×3½ in. (152×89 mm) 62 kN	= 6.2 ton for one
	= 12.4 ton for two
5 in.×3 in. (127×76 mm) 40.N	= 4 ton for one
	= 8 ton for two

Since it is more practical to carry a 9 in. wall on two rather than one RSJs it would seem that either of the latter two sizes above quoted are ample.

Lower steel joists

Span 7 ft. Point load at centre from upper steel joists	= **2.8 ton**
Direct UD load over right half only	lb.
Brickwork 3.5×10×100	= 3500

Triangle of roof $\frac{1}{2}\times4\times5.3\times20$ = 212
Superimposed $\frac{1}{2}\times4\times4\times11$ = 88
Wind $\frac{1}{2}\times4\times5.3\times4.5$ = 46
Eaves, say   = 54

     3900 lb.
     = **1.75 ton**

Left half of beam   lb.
Brickwork $3.5\times2\times100$ = 700 lb.
     = **0.31 ton**

As we have a mixture of point and UD loads it would be simpler in order to use safe load tables, to consider the point load of 2.8 ton as double this as UD load (bending moment for point load at centre is double that for UD load)—hence reckon 56 ton. In addition there is 1.75 ton UD on right half, but less on left half.

As a simplification and erring on the heavy side reckon 1.75 ton on both sides. Total $5.6+1.75+1.75=9.1$ ton.

This, as I said, allows more than necessary. I find that a first principles calculation gives the equivalent of 7.7 ton UD.

Safe load tables for span of 7 ft. (2.14 m) give the following: 6 in. by $3\frac{1}{2}$ in. (152×89 mm$\times$17.09 kg/m) in 43 grade steel bears 71 kN say 7 ton each, i.e 14 ton for two.

These allow ample margin. The load bearing plates at the ends welded to the underside of the pair as shown is a good idea.

Bearing of these joists on brickwork

Since a window opening occurs close underneath these joists it is desirable to check for length of bearing.

The reaction at right end of beams is maximum and is about 2.8 ton by using the above calculated loads and then taking moments.

Fletton brickwork in 1:1:6 cement/lime/sand mortar will take a basic stress of 14 ton/ft^2 which is reduced to about 11 ton/ft^2 owing to slenderness. To accommodate 2.8 ton an area of 2.8/11 ie. 0.26 ft^2 is required. An area of 0.56 ft^2 is provided by a bearing of 9 in. by 9 in. and so this should be sufficient. The length of bearing then should be at least 9 in. beyond the window reveal at each end.

19 Plant/Machinery

Q328: *I have recently purchased a small dumper and would be grateful for guidance on daily maintenance and good operating practice.*

A: Special attention must be paid to regular maintenance of dumpers as they are often used and misused by many different people. Each dumper whould have only one or possibly two drivers.

Surplus concrete must always be removed from the skip before it has a chance to set. The machine should be thoroughly cleaned down at the end of each day especially around brake drums or discs.

In the interests of safety, people should never be allowed to ride in dumpers. In addition, tipping should be supervised and tipping boards should be fixed where possible. Accidents may also be caused by the driver remaining on his dumper while it is loaded by excavator.

Q329: *Preventive maintenance is recommended for plant. What does this involve?*

A: This is a series of checks and inspections performed at regular intervals and designed to extend the working life of the machine, and prevent premature and unexpected failure of components.

The inspection will be of the whole machine for general wear and condition of parts (such as bucket teeth), to allow ordering of replacement parts and the arrangement of machine time so that repairs or replacements can be effected with the least interruption of the work schedule.

The operator's contribution to preventive maintenance is of prime importance, and it is essential that adequate time and facilities are given to him, and that supplies of materials are always to hand.

Q330: *Could you illustrate the standard signals which should be used when directing crane drivers?*

A: See Fig. 104.

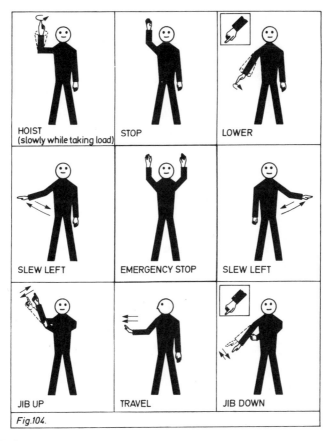

Fig.104.

Q331: *How does a diaphragm pump work?*

A: The pump works by means of a flexible diaphragm of rubber or rubberised canvas being raised and lowered in a closed cylinder by a pump rod attached to a rocker bar, which is in turn connected to an engine driven crank.

As the diaphragm is raised, water is sucked into the cylinder through a valve from the suction pipe. The down stroke of the diaphragm closes this valve and forces the water through a second valve into the delivery pipe.

This type of pump may also be called a lift and force pump and is capable of handling most liquids found on a building site, and in some circumstances will handle liquid containing up to 15 per cent solid matter.

Q332: Does the use of mufflers or silencers affect the efficiency of pneumatic concrete breakers? What kinds of silencing devices are in use?

A: Tests by the Building Research Establishment show that noise from pneumatic concrete breakers can be effectively reducd without any loss in performance. Silencing will not make the job take longer but the silencer must be carefully matched with the breaker and be specially designed for it.

Manufacturers will recommend the type of muffler or silencer most suited to their tools. Commercially available damped steels also contribute to a reduction in overall breaker noise.

Mufflers, acoustic shields or exhaust silencers can be incorporated in the design of the breaker. The muffler or silencer need not be bulky or heavy, or interfere with the operator's view of the work.

Q333: What safety precautions should be followed when using concrete breakers and similar equipment?

A: Concrete breakers, chipping hammers and similar tools should be fitted with a tool-retaining spring to prevent the tool from falling out and possibly onto someone.

When using a breaker stand firmly and brace one leg against it—never steady the tool point with your feet. If working near an excavation, or an elevated floor or flat roof, check that there is a secure guard rail. If the breaker slips it can take the operator into the excavation with it. When working overhead make sure the platform is stable.

Operators should wear non-conducting safety footwear with steel toecaps and steel insoles. Dust masks, ear protectors and a safety helmet should also be worn. Goggles must be worn in accordance with the requirements of the Protection of Eyes Regulations.

Q334: *For a large part of the working day I operate near noisy machinery. While I am used to this noise, and can conduct conversations over it, could you tell me if my hearing is likely to be damaged in the long term?*

A: Without knowing the precise noise levels that you are subjected to it is not possible to give a complete answer. However, there are some general points which should be borne in mind.

Almost everyone is aware that violent noise, such as that from explosions or even concrete breakers can rupture the ear drum, but it is often forgotten (or overlooked) that continual exposure to noise which might be regarded as acceptable in a working environment can also cause deafness.

This sort of damage is frequently slow to develop and it may take as long as ten years of exposure to noise, all day every day, before the effects become serious. Although deafness often develops with age, it is much worse in people who work in noisy conditions—as many who have operated plant all their lives will readily testify.

There are, of course, some obvious precautions which should be taken (and some which are laid down by law). Hearing protectors should be worn by people exposed for 8 hours to a noise level exceeding 90 dB(A).

Ear plugs, if properly fitted, can be a great benefit. They are certainly preferable to cotton wool or similar materials. However, the best things to use are ear muffs, as they afford greater protection because of their size and can be seen to be worn. Models are available to wear with a safety helmet or as an attachment to a helmet.

Q335: *How can one position plant on a site so as to minimise the amount of noise generated?*

A: The characteristics of the site and construction will restrict what can be done, but it is obviously desirable to locate noisy static plant as far as is practicable from people living and working nearby. The noisiest side of plant should also be orientated away from noise sensitive areas.

It is often possible to take advantage of the screening effect of buildings under construction. Noisy compressors, generators and pumps can be put in a basement, the shell of which has been completed.

When using such internal combustion engined plant in enclosed areas, see that exhaust gases are discharged directly to the outside air—or that there is good cross ventilation to prevent the build-up of poisonous carbon monoxide fumes.

Access to the site can often be arranged at points where the noise of vehicles will cause least disturbance.

In demolition work, form a break in solid connections (eg concrete paving) between the working area and adjoining buildings to reduce the transmission of vibration and structure-borne noise.

Q336: Noise on site is a problem that arises time and time again. Can you give some ideas for practices to be followed which can help reduce the amount of noise from piling, engines and machinery?

A: Very noisy processes can often be avoided if alternative and quieter constructional methods are considered at design stage.

Where piling is required, careful attention should be given to the selection of the most suitable system of piling, keeping in mind the prevailing sub-soil conditions, design loads, programme and the noise levels produced.

High tensile bolts can be used to assemble steel frames instead of riveting.

If noisy processes cannot be avoided the best way to reduce noise is to use 'sound reduced' plant, together with acoustic screens in some cases.

Noise from engines and machinery can be reduced by the more efficient silencing of exhaust systems and by better fitting working parts such as gears. Anti-vibration mountings at the engine supports and covers lined with sound absorbent material to form an acoustic shield also help.

It may be possible to overcome engine noise by using electric motors instead of the more usual diesel or petrol engines.

Q337: Can you give some hints on the general day-to-day care of compressors as it is most important that these machines work efficiently as and when required?

A: A compressor must be supported on firm level ground with parking brake applied and, if necessary, with the wheels chocked.

Ensure that all outlet nozzles are clear and the safety valves and gauges are functioning properly.

At the end of every day's work drain any condensate that may have accumulated in the main casing sump and cooler. Drain the control system water trap at least twice daily.

Remove all water during frosty weather or ensure that sufficient anti-freeze is added and circulated in the water cooling system.

Q338: *What provisions should be made on site for access of ready-mixed concrete trucks?*

A: Make sure in good time that the trucks can get to the place where you want the concrete discharged. A fully loaded ready-mixed truck weighs about 24 tonnes, and so your roads and access points must be firm enough to carry this load even in wet conditions.

They have to be stronger than is necessary for normal temporary site traffic access roads and, ideally, should be equivalent to at least 200 mm of fully compacted hardcore.

It is more economic to build an access road to the full required thickness at the start of the job, rather than to add to it as it fails after trucks have been bogged down.

The average truck mixer is 8 m long, 2.5 m wide and 3.5 m high, and needs a turning circle of at lest 15 m. You should, therefore, provide enough space to allow the truck to be turned round.

Remember that you will be wasting your time and the supplier's time if delays occur because you are not completely ready.

Q339: *What types of breaker are available and to what uses can the different types be put?*

A: The concrete breaker is the most common percussive tool used in building and construction. The 'steel' is solid and driven without rotation to provide a straightforward chiselling action.

Breakers are classed as light, medium and heavy duty and their weights, depending on the robustness of construction for a particular duty, range from 13.6 to 40.8 kg. Heavy breakers are used to demolish concrete foundations and walls, to break concrete pavements and for trenching in hard ground.

Medium breakers are used for breaking light concrete pavements and floors, tarmac and similar surfaces.

Light breakers are used for demolition work on floors, paving and masonry walls, and as general utility 'trimming' tools. Air consumption varies considerably with size and duty.

Various kinds of steel are available. Pointed and chisel-edge steels are used on concrete and other hard materials; wide chisel steels are for cutting softer materials, such as asphalt, and various spade-shaped steels are for digging, trenching and clay-cutting.

A similar range of steels is also available with renewable tips. Sound dampened or muffled steels assist in noise reduction. Further attachments adapt the breaker for tamping, ramming and driving, and extracting sheet piles.

The spader is a lightweight breaker and generally has a D shaped handle. An extension handle can be fitted so that the tool can be handled more easily when digging narrow trenches. The spader may be used for light demolition work by fitting a moil or chisel point instead of the spade.

The pick is another lightweight version of the breaker, designed to be held at shoulder height for working on vertical or overhead surfaces. It can also be suppied with a connection for water supply, producing a fine spray round the pick point to damp down dust.

Breakers should never be used without silencers. Several models are now fitted with built-in silencers; mufflers are available for others. Tests have shown that they give considerble noise reduction without loss of power, provided they are used only with breakers for which they are designed.

Q340 : *I have about half a dozen items of plant and feel that I should apply a logical approach to the maintenance of this equipment. Can you give any guidelines as to an efficient way to organise this maintenance?*

A: Often serious problems and delays to work are the result of insufficient maintenance or, quite often, a complete disregard to routine servicing and attention. The regular maintenance of plant on a small site is probably even more important than on a large one because broken-down plant cannot so easily be replaced.

As a result, delays are likely to be longer and more costly. Maintenance should be supervised by a responsible person who should see that each machine is regularly inspected and over-hauled at the correct times.

A company with five or more machines—for example, two concrete mixers, two dumpers, a small excavator and a hoist—

should consider employing a fitter. He should be able to attend to all but major overhauls and look after lorries or other vehicles.

Each driver must know how to operate his machine and be able to look after it. He should be given a schedule of the maintenance items to which he must attend, together with the manufacturer's instructions. Mark the items to which he must attend. Make sure that he is given the time (and, idealy, somewhere dry) to do these jobs. A 'tick off' maintenance sheet is a useful guide.

Keep a record of the hours worked and the lubrication and mechanical maintenance completed, with dates, for each machine. This will be a very useful check on running and maintenance cost, and will indicate when the next overhaul, oil change, etc. is due.

When a machine is not in use, have it checked and/or serviced to ensure that it will not break down on the next job. Machinery out of use for any length of time should, if possible, be stored under cover and have all exposed parts treated with a suitable rust preventive.

There are generally three stages of maintenance: the daily check, usually by the operator, of the oil, fuel, water, tyres, brakes, steering and controls. All defects should be reported. The machinery should also be cleaned daily.

The weekly inspection should be by a competent fitter. This incorporates the items covered in the daily checks, but in greater detail.

Thirdly, there is the periodic servicing and overhaul in a workshop. Each stage of maintenance must be carried out in accordance with the manufcturer's instructions.

Q341: *As a self employed builder I seem to be in a catch 22 situation in respect of trying to open my first account with a building equipment hire company. I have not had anything on account in the past two years because I used the deposit hire system.*

When I mention opening an account, they always want two previous two year old accounts as references or a very large bond of good faith.

Have you any suggestions because the deposit system is getting out of hand with larger and larger sums being required.

One suggestion of mine would be to take out a temporary insurance with the hire contract. What do you think of this?

A: You seem to have been unfortunate in your dealings with plant hire firms. Most require two trade references and a banker's reference to let you open an account.

If you have not traded before most would let you work on a cash basis for a few months until they got to know you. Then, with a bank reference would be prepared to let you start an account, small to start with, and then building up over a period of time.

Some ask for a letterhead of the company, two trade references for the last six months and a banker's reference. Once checked you could open an account.

Q342: *If plant is hired, who is responsible for its condition—the user or the person from whom it has been hired?*

A: The operator is responsible for the safe use and sound mechanical condition of plant even though it may be hired. Normally, repairs to hired plant are only undertaken by the owners. It may be possible for the hirer to make minor adjustments but only after obtaining the owner's approval.

Any defects discovered during the daily check should be reported. Dangerous machinery must be taken out of service until it can be repaired.

Q343: *Are there circumstances where excavators can be used as cranes? I am thinking of small lifting jobs where the workload does not really justify the cost of hiring a crane.*

A: In theory, the answer is no. Certain regulations governing the use of cranes do seem to make the use of excavators as cranes impossible. However, it is recognised that there are times when the temporary adaptation of an excavator is sensible and the Health and Safety Executive issues an exemption certificate so long as certain criteria are met.

An excavator which has been adapted may only be used as a crane for work immediately connected with an excavation it has dug. The bucket must not be removed (except in the case of a dragline) and the hook or other lifting gear must be attached to the bucket safely.

It is not permissible to wrap a set of chains around the bucket arms. A responsible person must specify the maximum load to be lifted, which must be the same whatever the radius of the jib, and which must not exceed the weight of the load which the machine in its least stable configuration is designed to lift.

This maximum load must be clearly marked on the machine and also entered on a certificate, signed by the competent person, a copy of which must be kept on site.

20   Structural Calculations

Q344: *House plans submitted to a local authority included stairs with tapered steps or winders to a specification worked out on the Building Regulations.*
The specification was:
Regulation H4 (1) and (2), going 233 mm, 13 risers of 210 mm, pitch 42 deg., quarter turn with winders of 30 deg., notional width 854 mm, 100 mm by 100 mm newel. See Fig. 105.

This was rejected because of non-compliance with H4 (3) (b)—(the going of any tapered step shall be not less than 75 mm).

It was pointed out that under H2 (h) taper step must comply with H4 (2) or (3), but the building inspector would not withdraw his objection.

A: Although there is a considerable amount of confusion over these regulations, regulation H4(3) is simple and plain enough. It is indisputably the only one which specifically requires a minimum width of tapered step at the end (it is easier to speak in practical terms and avoid legal exactitudes).

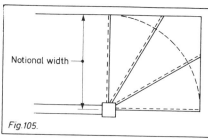

Notional width

Fig.105.

The 75 mm minimum requirement, however, does prevent the use of the normal newel post construction and if one is required an effort must be made to satisfy regulation H4(2).

In attempting to dispel the confusion over this regulation I will first of all put aside those rules which are generally understood, but which added to the others increase their appearance of complexity.

It is generally accepted that:

The going and pitch of tapered steps shall be measured on pitch lines each end 270 mm in from the notional width.

Measured on these pitch lines 2×rise+going shall be min. 550 mm, max. 720 mm.

All tapered steps shall be uniform in every way.

The rise and nosings shall be the same as the parallel steps in the stairs. The projection of the nosing over the back of an open tread below shall be a minimum of 16 mm.

The regulations as to head-room and clearance shall apply equally to tapered steps.

The interpretations some people give, but I do not agree, are:

(1) That the rule of 20 mm minimum going for parallel steps should also be applied to tapered steps on the pitch line.

(2) A pitch of 42°. maximum should also be applied on the pitch line.

These interpretations come from the rather vague wording of Regulation H4(2)(c) which says "The tapered steps shall otherwise comply with any relevant requirements of regulation H2 or H3 (as the case may be).

Regulation H2 applies to private stairways with which we are concerned in this case, while H3 is concerned with common

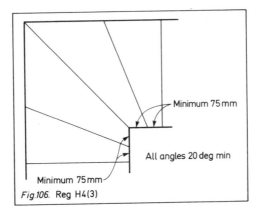

Minimum 75 mm

All angles 20 deg min

Minimum 75 mm

Fig.106. Reg H4(3)

stairways for which regulations are more stringent, (mostly in numerical values).

The two regulations not covered in previous references here are (f), the rise of a step is not more than 220 mm and the going of a step is not less than 200 mm and (g) the pitch of the stairway is not more than 42 deg.

The second part of (f) and (g) cannot be applied to tapered steps. For instance, taking (f), the rise of a tapered step is uniform along its length and therefore the term can be applied equally to parallel and tapered steps. You cannot however refer to the going of a tapered step as it varies all along its length.

Similarly (g) refers to the pitch of the stairway, not the pitch of one step. You cannot have a pitch to a set of winders; a line taken along either of the pitch lines would be a helical curve.

Now looking at the matter from a practical point of view. The pitch line 270 mm from CL of handrail is not the walking line; this will be found to be from 400 to 450 mm from CL of handrail and on this line a reasonable pitch will be obtained.

Finally, taking regulation H4(3) and the extreme case of maximum permitted rise 220 mm and minimum permitted taper of 20 deg., then taking the pitch line at 270 mm, the going on this line will be $75+2$ $(\tan 10° \times 270) = 170$ mm which is a lot less than 220 mm also with a going of 170 and rise 220 the pitch will be very much steeper than 42 deg; surely it was not meant that precautions should be unworkably severe under one regulation and comparatively thrown to the wind under another?

Coming back to the example provided by querist.

Going on inner pitch line = $\sin 15° \times 2 \times 270 = 145$ mm. Rise = 210 $2R+G=575$ mm, which is satisfctory, ie. above 550 mm.

Going on the outer pitch line = $\sin 15° \times 2 \times (854-270) = 304$ mm. $2R=+G=724$ which is 4 mm too high.

It seems ridiculous to reject the work for this value but if this is insisted on the width of the stairs must be reduced by $4/\sin 15° =$ 15 mm bringing the width back to say 840.

This is the situation as I see it but what you can do about it if the building inspector is adamant I do not know, a lawyer can no doubt advise you.

Q345: *Is there any timber saving if manufactured roof trusses are used at 450 mm centres?*

Is there a simple way to find the timber sizes necessary for hipped areas for traditional roofing? Please show the methods involved, particularly for a building 7.3 m 25mm o/a brickwork, for a pitch of 35 deg.

Where the hipped areas join the ridge line, on to roof trusses, do the trusses need strengthening?
LEGEND (figs. 107 and 108)
a—Whole trusses
b—Truncated trusses
c—Untrussed jack rafters
d—Braces nailed under rafters
e—Hips

A: British Standard Code of Practice CP 112 Part 3 states that its values are based on recent research, prototype testing and experience gained in use. In other words it is not based on mathematical structural analysis and indeed if this is applied from data at the present available lower strength values will result.

Therefore, it seems to the writer that the only way to answer the first question and arrive at values to suit trusses spaced at 450 mm is to take a look at methods of analysis and see in what proportion reductions can be made.

First of all, most of the loading is collected on the joists and rafters from uniformly distributed loads and consequently the loads carried by trusses at 450 mm crs will be 0.75 per cent of loads carried at 600 mm crs. Besides the uniformly distributed loads, however, the rafters and ceiling tie should be designed each to carry concentrated loads of 0.9 kH but the writer feels that this also is likely to be reduced if rafters are closely spaced.

Secondly, consider what would be the stress diagram for trusses spaced at 600 and 450 mm respectively. As the two sets of loads are proportional the diagrams would also be similar and all the vectors representing individual stresses in the proportion 1:0.75. Where bending is involved in ceiling ties and rafters spans will be the same but loads will be reduced and consequently the bending moments in the same proportion of 0.75:1.

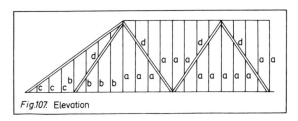

Fig.107. Elevation

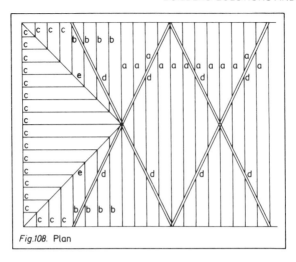

Fig.108. Plan

Thirdly, taking all the stresses developed in a roof truss or trussed rafter these are compression and bending in rafters, tension and bending in ceiling ties, pure tension in ties and pure compression in struts. Resistance to bending varies as the square of the depth of a beam and in direct proportion to its thickness or breadth. The resistance of a tie varies as its cross-sectional area the resistance of a strut varies as its cross-section area and its slenderness ratio.

Therefore, ignoring, for now, the slenderness ratio, if the section of all the members in a truss is taken from the code to suit the required pitch and span, but the thickness of the truss is reduced to 75 per cent, all the conditions will be met with the exception that the slenderness ratios of the rafters and struts will be reduced. However, the slenderness ratio is really the ratio of the unsupported length to the least dimension.

As the rafters will be tied every 450 mm by roofing battens the reduction in the ratio will not matter and as the roof pitches are low and the struts short, again the increase in the slenderness ratio should not matter.

It remains now to select suitable sized timbers from the tables and then reduce their thickness. As a practical requirement for nailing the reduced thickness should not be less than a nominal 37 mm so obviously be must start with 50 mm timbers. The effective span of the truss as specified in CP 112 Parat 3 is the length along ceiling tie between intersections of centre line of the rafters.

In the querist's case this will presumably be about 7.3 m.

Querist does not say which type of truss he is using, but assuming that it is the fink or W type then a suitable section for both rafters and ceiling ties is 41 by 72 mm finished size after planing giving truss thickness of 41 mm for spacing of rafters at 600 mm. Therefore, thickness can be reduced 0.75 by 41=30.8 mm so that if the timbers are ex 38 by 75 mm finishing at 35×72 mm these will be on the safe side.

Although the internal struts and ties will be less heavily loaded than the rafters and ceiling joists they are better made to the same dimension to give a greater stability at the joints when erecting and give wider surfaces for gluing or nailing the plywood or metal gussets.

Querist does not make it clear whether he is referring to the hipped outline as 'traditional' and still wishes to construct his roof using modern trussed rafter construction, or whether he is going back to traditional construction using rafters and hips supported by purlins strutted at intervals of about 2 m off internal load-bearing walls.

Assuming the latter, then common construction is to use 100 mm by 20 mm rafters supported by purlins at intervals of not more than 2.4 m. The size of the purlins depends upon the unsupported

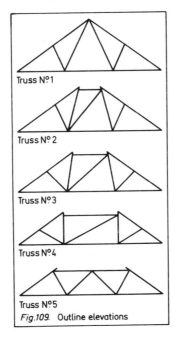

Truss Nº1

Truss Nº2

Truss Nº3

Truss Nº4

Truss Nº5

Fig.109. Outline elevations

span, but assuming that this is not more than 2 m, 125 mm by 75 mm or 150 mm by 50 mm is satisfactory.

Hips are traditionally 200 mm by 35 mm. The purlins are carried across the hipped end and help to support the longer jack rafters.

If, however, it is wished to use hipped ends to roofs of modern prefabricated trussed rafter construction, there is the problem not only of supporting the longest jack rafters at mid span, but also of carrying the ceilings under the hips without the use of any load-bearing walls.

The outline layout of the method used is shown in Figs. 107 and 108.

The trussed rafters are continued into the hipped end to half-way towards the end wall plate, the tops being levelled off or truncated so that they come belong the face of the hipped end and give partial support to the end jack rafters. The bottom halves of the jack rafters and the last three jack rafters at the sides are beyond the trussing system and are supported by the last truss and hip respectively and the wall plate and nailed to them in the usual way.

Figs. 109 and 110 show details of the truncation of the trusses in the hipped end and the method of supporting giving intermediate support to the last three or four ceiling joists.

The horizontal top members are kept low to support the hip rafters and the hips which rest on them. The last truss No. 5 should be of heavier construction using, say, nominal 100 mm by 50 mm timbers as it has to carry extra weight from the jack rafters in the hip and the last three or four ceiling joists through the short binders seen in Fig. 110.

Querist has not stated whether plywood gussets or plates are used in the construction, so this has not been discussed, but the writer suggests that these be kept of the same strength as before.

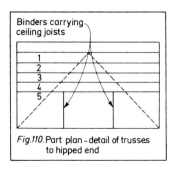

Fig.110. Part plan - detail of trusses to hipped end

It is presumed also that he is aware of the precautions to be observed as identified in the Codes of Practice CP 112 Parts 1 or 2 and Part 3, as well as BS 4978 dealing with grading of timber.

Q346: *A timber upper floor in a building is to be used as a store area.*

The existing floor is plasterboard and skim ceiling (weight 22 kg/m², 305 mm by 76 mm joists at 305 mm centres in Douglas fir Group I timber and finished with 38 mm thick boarding (weight 22.4 kg/m²).

The span of the floor is 3.2 m and the weight of the joist 599 kg/m³. Take f=7 N/mm² and please calculate the permissible uniformly distributed load.

A: This is unusually heavy construction with thick flooring and closely spaced joints. Some unusual values may be expected and it will be necessary to investigate floorboards and joists for their load capacity in bending, deflection and shear. As the overall size of the floor is not given it is presumed that the load per m² is required.

It is better to work in metres for all dimensions and Newtons for stresses and loads. The span in m is therefore L/1000 and the load in kg N/10. Symbols and the units in which they are represented are as follows:

L = Span of member acting as a beam in mm.
S = Spacing of joists in mm.
b = Breadth of member or assumed breadth in mm. (1 m = 1000 mm for flooring).
d = Depth of member in mm.
$E = 1.17 \times 10^4$ N/mm² (CP 112 for Douglas fir).
f = Safe fibre stress as given in N=7.
$I = bd^3/12$
D = Deflection assumed at 0.003L (as required by CP 112).
V = Maximum shear
v = Unit shear stress = 0.90 N/mm² (given in CP112 for 50 grade Douglas fir).
W = Total load on one joist or load on floor boards spanning between joists over width of 1 m
w_1 = Load over unit area of 1 m².

First of all taking floor boards acting as beams partly continuous over supports.

$$= 1.246 \times 10^5 \text{ N}$$

$$= 1.245 \times 10^4 \text{ kg}$$

which is the lowest value for flooring.

Taking the joists, assuming they are simply supported then:
For bending

$$\frac{WL}{8} = \frac{fbd^2}{6} \quad W = \frac{w_1 Ls}{10^6}$$

$$\frac{w_1 L^2 s}{8 \times 10^6} = \frac{fbd^2}{6}$$

$$w_1 = \frac{8 \times 10^6 \, fbd^2}{6 \, L^2 s}$$

$$w_1 = \frac{8 \times 10^6 \times 7 \times 76 \times 305^2}{6 \times 3200^2 \times 305}$$

$$= 2113 \times 10^4 \text{ N}$$

$$= 2.113 \times 10^3 \text{ kg}$$

Deflection
Deflection formula

$$= D = \frac{5}{384} \frac{WL^3}{EI}$$

$$D = 0.003 \, L \quad W = \frac{w_1 Ls}{10^6}$$

$$0.003L = \frac{5 \times w_1 L^4 s}{384 \times 10^6 \times EI}$$

$$w_1 = \frac{0.003L \times 384 \times 10^6 \times EI}{5 \, L^4 s}$$

$$= \frac{0.003 \times 384 \times 10^6 \times 1.17 \times 10^4 \times 76 \times 305^3}{5 \times 3200^3 \times 305 \times 12}$$

$$= 4.881 \times 10^4 \text{ N}$$

$$= 4.881 \times 10^3 \text{ kg}$$

Bending moment.

$$\frac{WL}{10} = \frac{fbd^{2\cdot}}{6}, \quad W_1 = \frac{w_1 L}{10^3},$$

$$\frac{w_1 L^2}{10^4} = \frac{fbd^{2\cdot}}{6}$$

$$w_1 = \frac{10^4 fbd^2}{6 L^2}$$

$$= \frac{10^4 \times 7 \times 10^3 \times 38^2}{6 \times 305^2}$$

$$= 1.811 \times 10^5 N$$

$$= 1.811 \times 10^4 \text{ kg.}$$

Deflection

$$D = \frac{3}{384} \frac{WL^3}{EI}$$

$$0.003L = \frac{3}{384} \frac{w_1 L^4}{10^3 EI}$$

$$w_1 = \frac{0.003 \, L \times 384 \times 10^3 \, EI}{3 L^4}$$

$$= \frac{0.003 \times 384 \times 10^3 \times 1.17 \times 10^4 \times 10^3 \times 38^3}{3 \times 305^3 \times 12}$$

$$= 7.241 \times 10^5 \text{ N}$$

$$= 7.241 \times 10^4 \text{ kg}$$

Shear. $V = 0.6 \, w.$ $V = \dfrac{2bdv}{3}$

$$\frac{0.6 w_1 L}{10^3} = \frac{2bdv}{3}$$

$$w_1 = \frac{10^3 \times 2bdv}{0.6 \times 3L}$$

$$= \frac{10^3 \times 2 \times 10^3 \times 38 \times 0.9}{0.6 \times 3 \times 305}$$

Shear

$$\text{Formula} = V = \frac{2bdv}{3} \quad V = \frac{w}{2}$$

$$W = \frac{w_1 Ls}{10^6}$$

$$\frac{w_1 Ls}{2 \times 10^6} = \frac{2bdv}{3}$$

$$w_1 = \frac{2 \times 10^6 \times 2bdv}{3\,Ls}$$

$$w_1 = \frac{2 \times 10^6 \times 2 \times 76 \times 305 \times 0.9}{3 \times 3200 \times 305}$$

$$= 2.85 \times 10^4 \text{ N}$$

$$= 2.85 \times 10^3 \text{ kg}$$

The lowest value and the one which controls the loading on the floor is therefore the strength of the joists in bending which is 2.113×10^3 gross including self-weight of floor.
Volume of joist per m^2 of flooring
Therefore net load per m^2 on floor = 2113-89.4 = 2023.6 kg

$$= \frac{10^3 \times 305 \times 76}{305 \times 10^6} \times 599 \text{ kg}$$

$$= 45 \text{ kg}$$

Flooring per m^2 $= 22.4$ kg
Ceiling $= 22$ kg

Total self-weight $= 89.4$ kg
Therefore net load per m^2 on
floor $= 2113 - 89.4$

$$= 2023.6 \text{ kg}$$

Q347: *Because, under Building Regulations H4 Tapered Steps, one cannot use less than three steps, please illustrate suggested arrangements at newel, how a 75 mm tread is achieved?*

A: The traditional way of fitting winders around a newel post cannot be used as this will not give sufficient width of step at the narrow end. There is, however, no reason why all four risers should not be housed in the newel; for sound construction it is better if only two are housed.

These are placed in the middle of the newel face to give a solidly enclosed housing. The details are shown in Fig. 111, which also illustrates the method of spacing out the winders on the centre line. They can no longer be at angles of 30 deg. and 60 deg. to the fliers.

The requirement to fix a handrail on the outside of the winders, and that it should be continuous, brings in a new condition. Again, the diagram indicates a satisfactory and economical solution.

Before taking sizes it is important to survey the area and look for restrictions to access which may limit the size and therefore the degree of the assembly of stair units; e.g. it may be necessary to leave all newel posts and balustrades loose.

The space under the stairs may be left open, in which case a plaster soffit is the usual finish. Alternatively the space may be enclosed to form a cupboard by taking the newel post to the floor and enclosing the area with rectangular and triangular panelling, known as spandrel frames or drags. These are rebated under the strings and housed into the continuous newel posts.

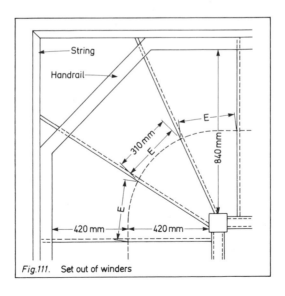

Fig.111. Set out of winders

Q348: *I enclose a sketch (Fig. 112) of a building used as a temporary living unit. It is my intention to change it into a store by removing the existing wall from 'A' to 'B' to 'C' leaving only a pier/column at 'B' (see drawing). To allow maximum headroom I intend to take away existing cavity wall and place an RSJ from A to B to C immediately under the wallplate.*

Could you please let me know what size RSJ should be used. I would prefer a clear wall without pier or return at A, if possible.

A: As this is a very long joist I would design it as if it were jointed in the middle over the pier, whether or not it is in two pieces. This makes calculations easier and more certain. Lateral support at the middle is necessary in any case and must be provided.

For the RSJ (or channel) the calculations (in metric) are as follows:

Size of sloping quarter of whole roof taken as 4.3 m×5.37 m on flat=26.5 m². Or 23 m² on flat, for snow.

Dead Load	kg/m²
Timber	14
Ceiling	12
Slates	14

40×26.5	=1060 kg
Add snow	=10.4 kN
23 m²×0.75 kN/m²=	$\dfrac{17.25\ \text{kN}}{27.65}$
Self weight	$\dfrac{.70}{28.35\ \text{kN}}$

Bending moment=W L/8
where L=5.2 m
$\qquad$ =(28.35×5.2)/8
$\qquad$ =18.4 kNm
$\qquad$ =18.4×10⁶ Nmm

This is f×z. For mild steel take
f=165 N/mm²
z=(18.4×10⁶)/165=1100 000 mm³
$\qquad\qquad\qquad$ =110 cm³

The choices are, of RSJs

152×89 mm×17.09 kg

$z = 115.6$ cm^3

178×102×21.54 kg

$z = 170.9$ cm^3

or the channel

152×89×23.84 kg

$z = 153$ cm^3.

If there are any added loads do not use the first RSJ.

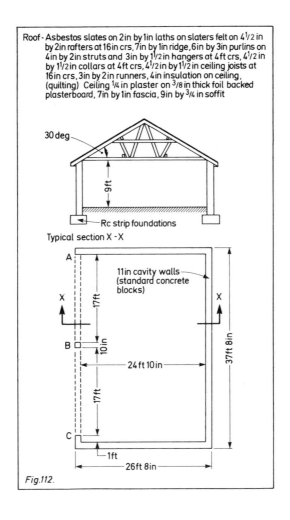

Roof - Asbestos slates on 2in by 1in laths on slaters felt on 4½ in
by 2in rafters at 16in crs, 7in by 1in ridge, 6in by 3in purlins on
4in by 2in struts and 3in by 1½ in hangers at 4ft crs, 4½ in
by 1½ in collars at 4ft crs, 4½ in by 1½ in ceiling joists at
16in crs, 3in by 2in runners, 4in insulation on ceiling,
(quilting) Ceiling ¼ in plaster on ³/8 in thick foil backed
plasterboard, 7in by 1in fascia, 9in by ³/4 in soffit

30 deg

9ft

Rc strip foundations

Typical section X - X

A

11in cavity walls
(standard concrete
blocks)

X

17ft

B

10in

X

37ft 8in

24ft 10in

17ft

C

1ft

26ft 8in

Fig.112.

Note: Sideway restraint must be provided, whether the steel is jointed over the central pier or not. Whatever is provided should stabilise the central support.

Possibilities are:

1. A bolt, say 20 mm threaded at one end to pass through the wall plate on the far side, or through the top course of blocks, with plates on both sides, nuts and washers. Against the new RSJ (or RSJs) or channel a forged plate with shoulder piece bored for the bolt, the whole welded together and to the joist or joists.

2. An angle also with plates welded at right angles at each end, bolted to the wall plate or blocks at one end and to the joints at the other end, or welded.

I am rather doubtful if you can get away with no return pier at A.

21 Surveying

Q349: *What is the first stage in setting out a building?*

A: 'First stage setting out' is a term commonly used for the setting out of a building. The first procedure when setting out a building is to establish two corners of the proposed construction from the baseline, site grid or traverse stations.

From these two corners, the sides will be set out using a theodolite to establish the right angles. Corner positions should be accurately marked in the top of the wooden pegs by surveyor's nails.

Ideally offset pegs should be positioned at that time. Next the diagonals must be checked. On completion of the diagonal check, the marker nails must be repositioned in the tops of the pegs if it proves necessary.

When that is completed, the next stage is to erect profile boards at the corners or a continuous profile board. Excavation for the foundations can then begin.

Q350: *Never having had any formal training in setting out on site I have always 'muddled through'. Now I intend to approach the work more scientifically and wonder whether you could, for a start, advise me on the basic principles by giving me a simple example?*

A: The first operation is to set out the position of the walls with pegs and lines, and this is followed by using profiles.

Commencing with the first operation, an accurate and, if possible, large-scaled plan of the site must be obtained and dimensions marked thereon of all distances shown between the letters marked on the illustration. These measurements must then be translated on the ground using a steel tape. Linen tapes should not be used for any setting out schemes.

Measure the line C–E and fix a marking stake at E. Check the line A–E to ensure that E is correctly placed. From J measure to H and erect a marking stake at H. Stretch a length of binding wire from E to H. Along the line E–H mark off L and G and drive pegs at these points. Measure A–B and stake out point B, similarly C–D and fix D to B and along this line points K and L can be established.

It is now necessary to fix profiles. These are placed at all angles of the building and at any cross walls. The profiles consist of plain-edged boards securely fixed to stout posts which are driven firmly into the ground. The profiles should be of sufficient length to enable the supporting posts to be driven outside the width to be excavated and should be set with the boards truly horizontal by levelling them with a spirit level.

The position of points L, K, M and G must be accurately fixed by driving a nail in the top of each peg (as shown in Fig. 113). The lines are then transferred to the profiles, each line marking the outer face of the wall. The position of all lines is marked on the profile by saw cuts and from the fixed lines three further saw cuts

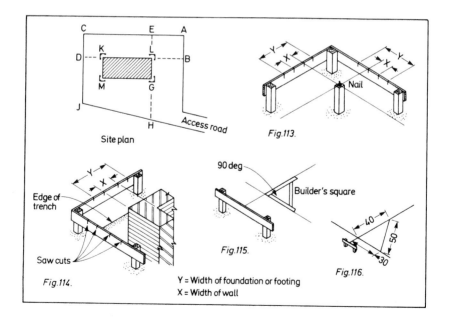

Site plan

Fig.113.

Edge of trench

Saw cuts

Fig.114.

90 deg

Builder's square

Fig.115.

Fig.116.

Y = Width of foundation or footing
X = Width of wall

are made, one cut representing the inside face of the wall (as shown in Fig. 114) and the other two cuts marking the outer edges of the foundations or footings.

The spacing of these cuts is shown at X and Y (Figs. 113 and 114). At the point K it is necessary to set out a right-angle to locate M. This can be set out by using a builders' square (as shown in Fig. 115) or by constructing a triangle with measuring tapes in the proportions of 3, 4 and 5 being base, perpendicular height and hypotenuse respectively. This method is illustrated in Fig. 116. Other useful numbers are:

8	15	17
7	24	25
15	20	25
20	21	29
40	42	58

Q351: *Access to the garage of a new house in the north of Scotland is by a ramp so steep that the owner's car cannot climb back to the road. The drive has a gradient of 1:3.8 and the site is very exposed. Snow falls are termed moderate for the area, but drifting and hard frost can be expected in the winter.*

Fig. 117 shows the house in question and the neighbouring property with the two attached garages at the rear approached by a common access between the two.

Taking the ramp between the houses may contravene the regulation that the ground level outside the house must not exceed the level of the underfloor surface inside the building. What is the solution and what gradient is recommended?

Would a concrete or tarmacadam surface be better in this situation from the point of view of traction and durability? Should stepped access be provided for foot traffic?

A: There are a number of problems here, as the drive should be extended so that the slope is such that it can be used under weather conditions in that part of the country. It is possible that during ice and snow it will be almost impossible to drive on the flat, so the slope is only part of the difficulty. Finished surface, drainage, and safety in remaining on the drive in icy/skid conditions have to be taken into account so it must be as wide as practicable and provided with a safety barrier on both sides.

The drawing, provided by querist (Fig. 117) is exceptionally good and discloses all the required facts.

If the exterior immediately adjacent to the house is as required by the council there is nothing to prevent the builder keeping his double ramp say a reasonable distance by a concrete wall which will allow an airflow between them to prevent damp.

The council's exact requirements should be discovered in this direction as any ramp could exceed its requirements. If the council asks for say 3 m this would take both houses both past the middle of the ramp.

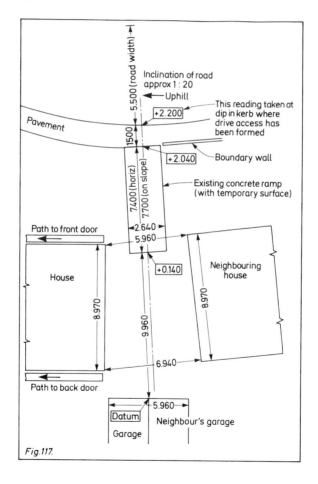

Fig.117.

What protection is given against surface water between the property and the rising ground in the front and between the path, which should be lower than the under-floor surface inside the buildings?

A must is a safety rail on both sides to prevent anyone falling down the slopes from the ramp.

Any good builder would provide, for safety in winter conditions, standard precast steps, from the path to the road, at pavement level, making sure the treads retain the foot at all times.

As soon as the ramp gets level with the property, the required air gap can be covered at concrete drive level with detachable cast iron grids, for both cleaning and safety.

As it is a party ramp, it is very necessary, for this to be completely covered in the deeds. A non-car owner of the neighbouring house might be able to shut off half of same and thereby preventing its use for its original purpose. I do not mean the existing owner, but over a lifetime I have seen boundaries cost their owners thousands in litigation.

Another point is the garage being built on to the adjacent one, so make sure that it has a completely fireproof party wall, many are a fire hazard.

A car must never be left on the ramp, and no one should at any time be between the moving car and the garage as the loss of braking and any control could be fatal.

Q352: *What checks should be made on an erected timber frame prior to proceeding with finishing work?*

A: The site manager should inspect the frame. This inspection should establish that the frame has been correctly manufactured, is complete and complies with the frame drawings and specification. The following is a check list, comprising the principal items the inspection should cover.

- Dimensional accuracy including location and size of joinery, openings and stair well positions.
- Plumbness of panels.
- Squareness of dwelling.
- Quality of frame manufacture.
- Quality of material.
- Correctness of connections and arrangement of panels.
- That any loose components supplied with the timber frame package have been provided.

The site manager should acquaint himself with the extent of permissible tolerances, the acceptable quality standards and the engineering principles adopted by the timber frame manufacturer, to enable him to complete a responsible inspection.

Q353: *In setting out, what are slope rails and travellers?*

A: Slope rails are employed to control side slopes on embankments and cuttings. They may also be referred to as batter boards. Travellers are also employed to define a slope.

In the case of an embankment, the slope rails are employed to indicate a plane parallel to, but offset from, the proposed embankment slope. They are offset so that they will not be covered during the filling of the cutting.

In the case of a cutting, the stakes supporting the slope rail are usually offset from the edge of the proposed cutting so that they will not be disturbed during excavation.

Travellers are portable and similar in configuration to a single support sight rail. The length from upper edge to base should be a convenient dimension to the nearest half metre.

Travellers are normally employed in conjunction with sight rails. The sight rails are established at a convenient height above the required plane, the travellers being so constructed that their length is equal to this height.

What happens in practice is that the traveller is sighted in between the sight rails and employed to monitor the cutting or filling. It rises or falls according to the filling operation or excavation.

Excavation or compaction ceases when the tops of the sight rails and the travellers are all brought into line.

22 Legal

Q354: *A builder owns a field on the outskirts of a village. As planning permission is very difficult to obtain could this be circumvented by selling the field to a smallholder? If the smallholder reared pigs, calves or poultry, would he be able to build a house to live in?*

Another field would make a good small caravan site. How is permission obtained for this? I understand the Caravan Club can give permission for sites used for two or three nights.

A: You are quite correct in saying that planning permission is now very difficult to obtain for development in the countryside, particularly where it extends a village into open countryside rather than solidifying the existing village structure.

Information about a particular village can usually be obtained from the local council offices where inquiries may be made about overall planning policy for an area and whether any local plan affects the land in question.

The way to tackle this problem is first to discuss the idea with the local planning officer, and even if he suggests that consent is unlikely, to make an outline application for the council to consider and issue a formal decision. If this is 'no', that is not the end, as an appeal may be made to the DoE.

With regard to the caravan site, the law does allow the Caravan Club to list a site where its members may make short stays and they may be used on a very limited basis.

Q355: *A new house is to be built with a paved patio at the rear with a flight of steps down to the lawn.*

Are these steps subject to the control of Part H of the Building Regulations?

Fig. 118 is a sketch of the proposed work.

The local authority building inspector considers that they come under the control of Part H as being an external stairway.

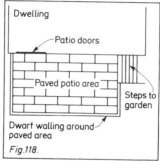

Dwelling

Patio doors

Paved patio area

Steps to garden

Dwarf walling around paved area

Fig.118.

A: Before seeing the query this particular application of Part H of the Building Regulations had just not occurred to me. What do the regulations say?

H. 1. 'Private stairway' means an internal or external stairway of steps with straight nosings on plan which forms part of a building and is either within a dwelling or intended for use solely in connection with one dwelling.

H. 2. A private stairway shall be so constructed that between 'consecutive floors', etc., etc.

Therefore one must decide whether a terrace is 'part of a building' and is a 'floor' and whether the lawn at a lower level is also a floor. If this is so then the steps must comply and also there must be a guarding of the terrace in the terms of H. 5.

I am compelled to the opinion that the regulations were not devised to require this and do not relate to this terrace or to the steps thereto.

Q356: *My company has been building on a particular site for some years and we have recently received a demand for rates for site and storage huts.*

We are told this is because we have not moved the huts for two years. The District Valuer states that rates can be demanded after one year. Could you advise whether this information is correct?

A: It is not possible to give a simple yes or no answer to this question because rating decisions vary throughout the country.

Certainly, in many cases, contractors' site huts are probably rateable. As a general rule, if huts are on site for what is termed a sufficient time rates become due. It is the phrase 'sufficient time' which causes problems – in one area it may be a year or more in another less.

Intention is also important. If, for example, the contractor intends to leave the huts on site for a long time, rates may be chargeable from the outset.

When setting up a site it is a good idea to consult with a rating surveyor or the local valuation officer to establish local procedures and to get an estimate of likely costs.

If you do receive a rates demand that you consider to be unreasonable any objections should be lodged within 28 days. Following that, if agreement cannot be reached, the case will go to the local court, where you may be represented by a rating surveyor. This action would not be costly, but the final step – should you consider it necessary – might be: this is the Lands Tribunal and should only be used as a last resort.

Q357: *Has the role been repealed that the sale of a house within five years of the payment of a grant for renovation requires the payment of the grant?*

A: The legal position regarding repayment of a house renovation grant has changed as a result of the Housing Act 1980. Although the five year rule remains there is now a much wider definition of the person who qualifies to enjoy the benfit of the grant. In particular the sale of the house by the owner occupier who received the grant to another person who occupies the house or who allows the house to be occupied by a close relative of his or of his spouse does not mean that the grant must be repaid. The occupation of the house by a close relative of the applicant of the grant does not now require repayment of the grant. In addition to this a local authority still has power to decide not to demand repayment or demand only part of the grant when they are entitled to require repayment.

Q358: *I live in the upper maisonette in a two-storey block. A builder altered a flue from the lower maisonette while converting my attic. The builder did the work badly,* *with the result that smoke entered the attic, and there was a fire hazard. Can I claim against the builder, and if so, how?*

A: You do have a claim against the builder, for the breach of the implied term in all building contracts that the builder will carry out the work in a good and workmanlike manner.

You should see a Solicitor, preferably one who is experienced in building disputes. If you do not know any Solicitors you should consult the Citizens Advice Bureau. You should also ask to be considered for legal aid.

It is essential in all such cases involving defective building that adequate evidence be collected to support the action, especially if the defects are to be remedied prior to the action. Such evidence is best provided by an independent professional (surveyor, architect or engineer), and must include suitable photographs.

Q359: *I am renovating a semi-detached house in a light industrial and residential area. I intend building an extension to the side of the house and so extending the frontage; the two points in question regarding planning are:*

(1) As the roof covering is in slate at present, as is a terrace close by, can the planning authority insist on slates being replaced, as the intention was to re-roof in concrete interlocking pantiles;

(2) Most of the windows nearby are sash types or bays but the intention was to put in modern windows and increase the size horizontally.

The planning department have held the plans up for some time, but recently suggested that one intention be changed – that is, either the roof or the windows. The house is not of any architectural or preservation interest. Are there any rules of laws I can quote to help my case?

A: This is the kind of question most difficult to answer authoritatively without having seen the property and its surroundings. The aesthetics of the proposal are therefore ignored.

The following points may be taken into consideration.

(1) With the exception of listed buildings, one may re-roof an existing dwelling with different materials and replace existing windows with new ones of different shape or size. In doing this work the roof must not be raised any higher than the existing roof, and windows may not project further in front of a wall than those

which existed. This is called 'permitted development' and planning permission is not necessary.

(2) If the council really wished the building to keep its present appearance it could serve a 'Building Preservation Notice' which would hold good for six months and if not confirmed by the Secretary of State, would fall into abeyance.

(3) As the planning decision is overdue you may write to the Secretary of State and lodge an appeal against the council's lack of action. At the same time, tell the council – it may speed things up!

(4) It is open for the applicant to withdraw his present application; undertake the roof and window work as 'permitted development' and submit plans only for the work involved in making the extension.

(5) Unfortunately all these options take time, but it may be rewarding to discuss these possibilities with the planning officer, particularly as the Secretary of State does not like too much interference with design and has been critical of delays in decision making.

Q360: *What is the position with regard to making a claim against an insurance company: is the six year period under the Limitation Act 1939 the fixed period or are there circumstances where a claim may be made much later?*

A: A claim made under an insurance policy is a claim under a contract. Since most insurance companies are ones to which the six year period under the Limitation Act apply it means that a claim must be made within the six year period.

A claim may be made outside the six year period where there has been fraud. This, however, is unlikely to apply to a contract with an insurance company. In addition, it should be noted that policies usually require prompt notification of claims.

Q361: *I built a pair of houses 25 years ago. Recently I built five garages with access by way of a private drive which I own. The flank wall of the old detached house (see Fig. 119) has been affected by subsidence for more than 25 years.*

The present owners have engaged a surveyor who tells me that he can get permission to excavate the drive for the purpose of underpinning the flank wall. Is this correct?

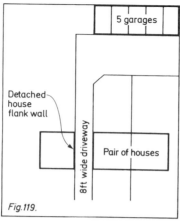

Fig.119.

Cannot the underpinning be carried out from within the house, thus avoiding excavating the driveway?

A: There is no general Act of Parliament which gives a person a right to enter his neighbour's property for a private purpose. A Private Act of Parliament may do so, but it is not likely that such an Act is available in this case.

Thus there is no statutory person from whom permission might be sought. The neighbour may, however, have a right of entry without permission by virtue of a 'profit', 'licence' or an 'easement', but the neighbour must prove his right prior to exercising it, and there is not likely to be one in this case.

The surveyor may prevail on the local authority to use its powers under the Public Health Act or the Housing Acts if the house has become, or is likely to become, a dangerous structure.

Underpinning can be carried out from within the house, indeed it is a method commonly used. However, external shoring may be required if the underpinning is to be carried out safely. The sensible solution would be to use flying shores since these would not interfere with access to the garages, but this would require the permission of the owner of the semi-detached house.

Q362: *Is it correct that the Building Regulations impose a duty on local authorities to enforce compliance but grant discretion to the local authority to inspect a proportion of the buildings only? Would non-inspection which resulted in a major structural defect in a building make the local authority liable?*

A: The duty of a local authority with regard to the enforcement of building regulations and their discretion in making inspections was considered by the House of Lords in the case of Anns v London Borough of Merton 1977.

In this case the Law Lords recognised that although there is a duty on local authorities to enforce the regulations it was not so extensive as to require them to inspect every building which was being erected.

The Lords recognised that local authorities have limited resources and that they may therefore have to make a decision as to what buildings to inspect and the number of inspections to be made. They did however indicate that a failure to make inspection may amount to a breach of the local authority's duty of care.

Failure to inspect therefore is not apparently a complete defence, and if a major structural defect is not detected because of a failure to inspect, this is probably negligence on the part of the local authority.

Q363: *Could you give me advice and guidance on setting up a private limited company.*

A: This answer is based solely on English law and does not attempt to deal with matters of finance or financial practice.

Any individual can set up a company, since in the main it is only necessary to register certain documents with the Registrar of Companies in order to create a company under the Companies Act 1948–81.

A not uncommon practice, however, is for a person wishing to form a company to purchase a 'ready-made' company. That is a company which has already been formed but has not yet been brought into operation. Where the activities the company intends to undertake are not extensive and are possibly related, such as several works building contractor, purchasing a ready-made company is a suitable course to adopt.

The cost of such a company is in the region of £100 and as this includes the formation fees and the appropriate documents.

The law now is that a private company may have one director only but more than one is common.

Companies which are 'ready-made' can be brought into trading operation in a matter of days. Where companies are being formed specially then from the start of the operation to trading will be a number of weeks.

The loss which any director or other shareholder may suffer in the event of the company failing is the amount unpaid on his shareholding. In practice shares are issued fully paid so this liability ought not to arise. It is, however, the practice of banks to ask directors of small companies to give personal guarantees for loans which consequently puts the directors at risk personally.

The duties of directors are extensive and in part are set out in the articles of association of the company. Very briefly, a director must act as a trustee of the company, act lawfully and use his powers for the good of the company.

Q364: Who are the persons in common law entitled to have access to a building site?

A: To deal with this question fully would require considerable space but in brief the position is the following. The person who is in occupation of a building site gives access to those persons he either invites or permits to come on the site.

In some circumstances, to put the matter beyond doubt, a building contract will state that certain persons are to be allowed on the site. Otherwise persons legally have access by either the occupiers express or implied invitation or permission.

Those persons an occupier wishes to exclude he may do by either giving named persons notice that they are not to enter the site or by giving a general warning that certain persons are not to enter. Any person who disregards this notice or warning and enters the site then becomes a trespasser.

Q365: When were planning fees introduced and to what do the regulations apply?

A: The decision to introduce fees in respect of planning applications was taken as part of the Local Government Planning and Land Act 1980. Section 87 of that Act enables the Secretary of State for the Environment to make regulations requiring the payment of fees.

The regulations came into effect on April 1 1981 and the ful title is the Town and Country Planning (Fees for applications and deemed applications) Regulations 1981.

The regulations apply to the following classes of applications, all of which attract a fee: applications made for planning permission; application for approval of reserved matters; applications for

consent for the display of advertisements; applications for planning permission deemed to have been made when an appeal is
lodged against an enforcement notice; and, application for
planning permission deemed to have been made in connection
with an application for an established use certificate. Planning fees
are mandatory.

There are, however, some exemptions – work to aid disabled
persons; permitted development; renewal of temporary permis-
sions; and revised applications.

Q366: *A labour-only sub-contractor received payment from a contractor from which had been deducted the amount of surcharge made by the scaffold hirers for the contractor having released the scaffolding late. Is this legitimate?*

A: The answer depends on both law and fact. If the contract
between the contractor and the sub-contractor was such that the
sub-contractor agreed to complete by a certain time, then the
sub-contractor would be entitled to extra time in respect of any
default on the part of the contractor which caused the sub-
contractor to be delayed.

The sub-contractor might also be entitled to extra time due to
events not within his control which caused him to be delayed (such
as bad weather, strikes, force majeure, etc.), but only if there was
an express term in the contract to that effect.

If the contract was such that the sub-contractor did not agree to
complete by a certain time, then his duty was to proceed regularly
and diligently.

The answer now depends on the facts. In the first case, was the
sub-contractor entitled to extra time? If not, did he complete within
the agreed time? If extra time was justified, how much, and did he
complete within the extended completion date?

In the second case, did the sub-contractor proceed regularly and
dilligently? If the sub-contractor failed to complete in time (first
case) or failed to proceed regularly and diligently (second case)
then he has committed a breach of contract, and the contractor is
entitled to contra-charge such damages as he has suffered as a
result of the breach. Such damages would include scaffold hire
surcharge.

Q367: *We would be grateful for your advice about the following: (1) The standing of verbal communications from*

VAT officials; (2) the VAT rating of continuation of construction following an incompetent builder; (3) The VAT rating of remedial work to sections unapproved by a building inspector.

Inquiry was made of VAT officer about the possible inclusion of some prime cost invoices paid by the client for the job and upon inquiry he learned of the situation where we had been engaged to follow a builder put off for incompetence.

To our surprise he expressed the opinion that all of our work could be positive rated because a structural shell (unprotected) was already erected when we quoted. Alternatively he indicated that he would expect to see all repairs of faulty work positively rated.

In quoting we sectioned the estimate to help the client's surveyor obtain reparations into 'remedial work' and 'general building'.

We have held the view that the construction as taken over stood up but did not serve anyone any use and the remedial operations were not repairs but were simply preparatory to and in order to complete a new construction eligible for zero rating.

A: Standing of verbal communications from VAT officials: A verbal communication does not alter the law, i.e. if the official was wrong his comment has no standing. You should get a ruling in writing which you can then challenge if you disagree.

The VAT rating of continuation of construction following an incompetent builder: This is what is euphemistically described as a 'grey area'. In other words, the VAT man usually wins! In theory, if the construction was taken over from an incompetent builder, the work should be regarded as new construction. Customs and Excise said that, in general terms, a change of builder should not affect the status of the work.

The VAT rating of remedial work to sections unapproved by a building inspector: Customs and Excise said that remedial work following an uncompleted contract will generally turn on whether there has been a separate supply of services by the second builder in addition to the original contract.

If you can show that the remedial work was necessary because of a design fault (or, possibly, bad workmanship) there might be a case. If the client had already moved into the building, the work would almost certainly carry tax.

It is surprising that the local officer suggested that all the work could be positive rated because, as you say, the structural shell served no useful purpose.

It would probably be best to try and reach an agreement with him, whereby you would agree to positive rating for work not in the original contract (of the first builder) and he would allow zero rating on that which was.

The indications are that even if your case was strong enough – and quite possibly a tribunal would find in your favour – the Customs and Excise would probably go to appeal and would probably win. Obviously the cost to your company would be totally out of proportion to the contract.

We would be interested to hear from any other readers who have been involved in similar VAT cases.

Q368: *Regarding fees for inspecting plans for Building Regulation Approval, can you tell me if there is a set method of assessing the value of a proposed application if the work is to be done by the applicant and there are no labour costs to be added?*

I am asking this because some authorities accept that labour costs need not be added if it can be proved that the applicant is doing the work, and yet others do not accept this and work on so much a square foot basis regardless of who is doing the work.

A: Since April 1981, Building Regulation departments have been charging scale fees relating to items covered by the Regulations, and based on the cost of the work to be done to the building.

When calculating the fee to be paid, the following costs can be deducted:

(a) Sanitary ware (only pipe runs need to be added to the cost);
(b) Painting;
(c) Electrical;
(d) Heating (except air supply to boiler and flue);
(e) Items covered under maintenance and repair;
(f) If the building works are to be carried out by the client and he is not going to employ any help with the construction. Most councils will accept this and the fee can be based on material costs only.

Most councils (not all) will work on a cost per square foot basis.

Q369: *Should all accidents be reported or is it merely serious ones which have to be recorded?*

A: The law, regarding construction employers, is that an accident book – Form B1 510 – should be available at every workplace. Within this book all accidents, however minor, must be recorded.

The thinking behind this is that no matter how minor the injury may seem to be, a record must be kept in case a more serious ailment develops, with the injury being a contributory cause.

Another legal requirement is that any of the following types of accident – accidents resulting in death, accidents causing absence from normal work of more than three days, and accidents resulting in injuries which may not cause three days' absence but may create a reduction of wages or restriction of normal working – must be reported in the General Register – Form 36 – and in Form 43B which is forwarded to HM Factory Inspectorate. These are known as 'reportable accidents'.

There are also items reported on the General Register and on Form 43B which should be reported to the Inspectorate. These are in part an accident report but can also be classified as an incident report.

Q370: *A contractor fails to complete the contract works by the extended completion date, and the architect issues a certificate of non-completion (Clause 22, 1963/77 Standard Form). The contract over-runs by 10 weeks for which period the contractor is liable in Clause 22 damages. During the over-run period, the contractor is further delayed by a strike and by exceptionally inclement weather. Can the contractor claim an extension of the completion date, and thus avoid some of Clause 22 damages, as a result of these later events?*

A: The architect has no power to grant Clause 23 extensions of time in these circumstances. In any case, if the contractor had completed on time, he would not have been affected by later events. The additional delay is caused not by reasons (b) and (d) of Clause 23, but by the contractor's default. The contractor cannot benefit from his own default. This situation is unchanged under the provisions of the 1980 Standard Form.

Q371 : *It is proposed to establish a small firm, employing two to five men, to undertake carpentry work for main contractors. What are the legal requirements relating to insurance and to 'statutory safety policy'?*

A: In addition to the usual insurances, such as fire insurance of building, which need to be considered there are two matters to which attention must be given when setting up the business. The first is that if private motor cars are to be used for the purposes of the business the insurance company needs to be informed of this fact since that use will alter the insurance contract.

The second matter is the requirement in the Employers' Liability (Compulsory Insurance) Act 1969. The provisions in this Act and in regulations made under the Act require every employer carrying on business to insure and maintain with an authorised insurer an approved policy against liability for bodily injury or disease sustained by employees arising from their employment. Employees are exempt if they are members of the employer's family.

The insurance cover must be for not less than £2 million. The employer must display a certificate of the insurance at each place of business. It is a criminal offence not to comply with the requirements of the Act.

'Statutory safety policy' is the term applied to the requirement in Section 2 of the Health and Safety at Work Act 1974, that every employer shall prepare and revise as often as may be appropriate a written statement of his general policy with regard to the health and safety at work of his employees. The statement must give details of the organisation and arrangements for carrying out that policy. The written statement and any revision must be brought to the attention of all the employees. Failure by an employer to comply with these requirements is a criminal offence.

In passing this law Parliament recognised that to impose this duty on small firms would be unreasonable. The Act therefore allowed exemptions to be made to this duty to provide the written statement. This has been done by the Employers' Health and Safety Policy Statements (Exception) Regulations 1975. The regulations exempt any employer from the duty if he employs less than five employees in his business.

So the employment of five or more employees means that the employer must prepare the written statement of safety policy and comply with the requirements of revising it as necessary and bringing it to the attention of his employees.

Q372: *I own some land with outline planning permission. Could you please tell me what is the maximum amount of dwellings I am allowed to build on this land without having to enter into a section 38 agreement with the authorities regarding the estate road.*

A: Regrettably there is no straightforward answer to this query, which depends largely upon the policies of the planning authorities in the area where the land is situated.

Some councils will permit two dwellings to be served by a private drive. Others may permit three. One dodge that I have seen in these circumstances is to put two access drives side by side separated only by a coloured kerbing just proud of the surface as an ownership marker. The two drives together make a paved area about 5 m wide. There are thus six dwellings in a close served by two narrow private drives. I will not argue the merits of this arrangement.

Other planning authorities may be prepared to accept a small number of houses in private courtyard developments.

However, if a conventional estate road type of development is envisaged the highway authority will require assurances that it is to be constructed to their standards with adoption in mind.

The whole process is intended to obviate the problems which have in the past, and still do, arise from unadopted roads.

The querist should consult his local planning officer and examine very closely any published policies or design guides he may have prepared.

Q373: *I was recently asked by a customer to measure up for a patio door and to give him a price for this, including fixing, and the time for completion. I obtained a price for the unit from my joiner and added to this my charge for fixing. When I told my customer the price he told me to go ahead with the work. The unit was made and I delivered it to the house.*

Later that day the customer phoned me saying that he did not want the unit, did not order it and was not going to pay for it. I told my solicitor to sue the customer. My solicitor told me I would not have a case since I only had a verbal contract. I insisted that he go ahead with the court action. The day before the court hearing the solicitor asked me where the unit was, I told him that I had sold it. He then stopped the court hearing and now has sent me a bill for his services. At no time did he tell me not to sell the unit.

A: The reader is correct in his belief that it is not necessary with building work, particularly with repair work and small alterations, for the contract to be in writing. The difficulty with a verbal contract is that there is a strong possibility of misunderstanding arising and in the event of a dispute going to court, the court has to decide which of the two parties to the contract appears to be the better witness; is his recollection of what was said the more convincing?

For this reason it is always best to confirm a verbal agreement by a letter setting out the terms on which work will be undertaken. In this way there is a written document which is evidence of the agreement. Its existence may even avoid court action arising from the agreement.

In the absence of fuller details the matter of the solicitor withdrawing the case from the court can only be answered on general principles. The sale of the unit may have meant that the reader was no longer able to show that he had suffered any real loss. Against this is the rule in law that an injured party to a breach of contract must take all reasonable steps to keep the loss to a minimum, so to have refused to have sold the unit when a sale was possible could have put the reader in the wrong.

It is not widely known that a solicitor's bill may be challenged before payment. This however is subject to the challenge being made within a stated time. In the case of a bill for a court action the bill may be examined by a court official and the amount adjusted as necessary; in the case of a bill for legal work not concerned with a court action the Law Society, the conrolling body for solicitors, will examine the bill and adjust it, without increasing it, as in their opinion is necessary.

Q374: *While tendering for works involving an improvement or repair grant I have encountered several difficulties.*

Enclosed is a typical programme of a grant application, Fig. 120, although through experience I have anticipated a lot of the requests.

Could you please provide a factual process as I believe that once a tender has been submitted to the client, that should be the end of a builder's responsibility until the Final Account and Payment.

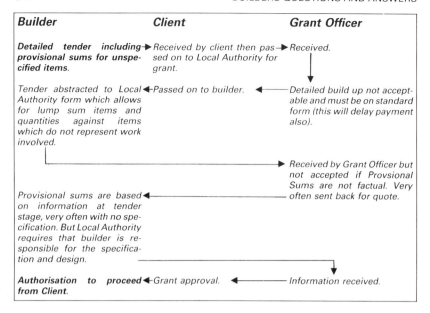

Am I correct and can anything be done about the lack of cooperation?

A: Your problems are suffered regularly by conscientious contractors used to providing estimates on a competitive basis and suddenly finding themselves required to do a great deal of additional work in presenting estimates for Grant purposes, breaking down estimates and in some cases negotiating with the local authority with no instructions having been given by the client, and much energy can be wasted in so doing.

Where the works are for an improvement grant, which require drawings, the client should appoint a surveyor or architect who will be responsible for negotiating the grant through the local authority, including provision of the specification in the first place presented in a form the grant officer is used to seeing.

You are not being paid for work which should have been done by a surveyor whose fees can be grant aided.

It may well be worth your while to establish a working relationship with a local surveyor who can assist in the preparation of this technical information.

Where drawings are not needed, i.e. for a repairs grant, the best advice is to consult the local grant officer and establish a relationship with him at a very early stage. Then his exact requirements can be clarified in advance and if the original estimate is produced in such a way that it will satisfy his requirements as well as clearly setting out the estimate for the client, less time will be wasted.

Concerning provisional sums, no grant officer will pass for grant speculative costs where the exact extent of the work is not known. Therefore it is better to add to estimates submitted a rider that states that certain works could not be estimated as the exact cost will not be known until the works are started and the problems exposed, but a further grant may well be applied for in due course.

Grant officers will set aside provisional sums from their calculations but if the maximum grant is not exceeded when the other costs are taken into account, an additional grant will be considered so long as warning is given in advance.

Whenever provisional sums can be avoided by site investigation and measurement, firm prices should be given.

Q365: *I am a bricklayer and am considering forming a partnership with a joiner with the intention of carrying out repairs and small conversions. We may also undertake work for a larger company on an occasional basis.*

In the following circumstances what would be the position regarding the deduction of income tax, (I have no 714 certificate but my proposed partner has):

i. When working for a larger company would they have to deduct 30 per cent income tax?

ii. Would the formation of a limited liability company avoid involvement with 714 certificates and tax deductions?

iii. If our partnership were to employ a third person, say a decorator, as a self-employed person, would we be under a duty to deduct income tax from him?

iv. If the joiner and I kept separate accounts could we each make use of the exemption of the liability for VAT.

A: To control the abuse and resulting tax losses which occurred with the use of self-employed persons in the construction industry the Inland Revenue has taken extensive powers. For some years there has been a system with detailed procedures whereby subcontractors either had to have appropriate certificates or suffer the deduction of 30 per cent for income tax on their labour charges. To do this the Inland Revenue has treated some matters differently. In particular a limited company is not treated as having the separate legal standing it has in other branches of law.

Dealing with the specific points raised:

i. The Inland Revenue requires a contractor who employs a subcontractor to deduct from his labour charge 30 per cent for the income tax. Failure to do this may make the contractor liable to pay to the Inland Revenue the amount he ought to have deducted. If, however, the member of the partnership has an appropriate 714 certificate then the contractor will not make any deduction for income tax from the labour charge.

ii. The formation of a limited company will not give any advantage in the matter of tax deduction. A sub-contractor who forms a limited liability company must have the appropriate 714 certificate, 714C, if the deduction of income tax is to be avoided.

iii. The employment by a subcontractor of another self-employed person puts the subcontractor in the position of a contractor to the self-employed person. If the self-employed person has an appropriate 714 certificate then no deduction will be made from his labour charge. Without such certificate the subcontractor must make a deduction of 30 per cent income tax from the self-employed person's labour charges. Care should be taken not to pay without deduction any sum greater than any limited sum printed on the self-employed person's 714 certificate.

iv. If the bricklayer and joiner do not form a partnership but operate as separate traders keeping separate accounts then each may go up to the VAT exemption limit without being registered and subject to the imposition of VAT on charges. If however a partnership is formed then there will be an exemption for the partnership.

Q376: *A large bungalow is being built for a customer on his own site and has reached the stage where the walls have reached full height.*

The bungalow is on a sloping site with over 2,000 concrete blocks under the building to dpc. Wall plates are fixed, all concrete solid floors are in, all suspended floor joists are in, all over site concrete done.

On site are all steel windows and wood surrounds primed and painted, all roof trusses and timbers and roof tiles, in fact all roofing materials. All drainage materials, flue liners, chipboard flooring materials, over £600 in kitchen fitments, all ceiling Gyproc laths, soffits and barges, two 14 ft garage doors.

In fact practically all materials to complete except internal doors, plaster and glass and bathroom suite. All materials and labour have been provided and paid for by us. One stage payment of £2,000 has been made on account.

We have now asked for a further £2,000 and been refused on the grounds that the law, the client says, makes no second payment due until the roof is complete.

The customer says he can find no fault whatever with the workmanship.

A: There is a custom whereby stage payments are made as buildings reach various heights, but it is a custom only and has no force in law, and, anyway, the custom varies in different parts of the country.

There is another custom, much more commonly observed that payments are made at monthly intervals. This particular custom carries a good deal of weight in law since it is enshrined in the standard form of contract.

There is no law which actually says that payments on account for building work shall be made at any particular intervals, the law only comes into it when the periods for interim payments are stated in the contract.

I take it that you have no formal contract with your customer. I strongly suggest that in future you have a written, formal contract. You can get out your own, modifying it from time in the light of experience, it will be quite valid and enforceable. Or you can use the standard form of contract obtainable from **The Royal Institute of British Architects**, 66 Portland Place, London W1, price £1.

There are two slightly different forms of interest to you, one is where quantities form part of the contract, and the other is where they do not. In both cases there are "private editions," and "editions for the use of local authorities." You would, I think, require the private edition, without quantities.

Press your customer for payment for work done and the value of materials on site less 5 per cent retention. You are entitled to it.

Q377: *A contract for heating and mechanical services was obtained, on a fixed price basis, for housing by a statutory authority (Gas Corporation). A contract was entered into under the green form and the RIBA Local*

Authority with quantities (Gas Corporation were nominated). Subsequently the corporation let the works to an approved installer.

The main contractor's programme issued at the commencement of the works indicated a material and labour requirement from April, 1984, to April, 1985, the period of the fixed price. Due to delays by the main contractor only 30 per cent of the contract was completed by the expiration of the fixed price period and subsequently a further revised fixed price estimate until December 1985 was negotiated by the installer to the Gas Corporation.

During the period April 1984 to April 1985 the installer through no fault of his own was unable to complete the works, thereby suffering a substantial reduction in his turnover and profit. Does his ultimate re-negotiation for the outstanding works jeopardise his right to a claim for loss incurred by the inability of the main contractor to produce the works during the original contract period, or is there in fact a basis for a claim under these conditions?

A: It seems that at the expiration of the contract period the question of frustration and determination would have been carefully weighed.

If deciding to go on with the work an extension of contract period would have been the next step, seeking payment for all preliminaries, viz. supervision, hire of plant, hutting, haulage, safety measures, protection and the like, renewal of insurance premiums (after one year) and for all uneconomic working of labour and plant etc.

To bypass this contractual procedure and negotiate fresh rates seems to me to have vitiated your rights under the old contract. It would be necessary to read all the correspondence, contract documents, original estimate and so on.

One cannot be absolutely definite and without obtaining legal advice perhaps needing counsel's opinion with its attendance cost it is unwise to take too strong a line, but it seems unlikely that there are any grounds for claim of loss of profit and reimbursement for other shortfall of turnover.

Q378: *I recall reading of the addition of 20 per cent in estimating for work where the clients were in residence* *while it was taking place and this caused unavoidable delay in completing.*

I often have, to work in houses which are fully occupied and get involved in moving furniture, etc., before I can start and would like further information.

A: A booklet published by ICI Decorator Business Advisory Unit gives the following extract:

Conditions of work	Percentage of extra cost
Room by room work in occupied and furnised private house	15%
Bed-sitter accommodation. If tenants or owner will undertake at least two adjacent rooms can be cleared and available at any one time	10%
Ditto. If no such undertaking can be given or sustained and the builder has to undertake furniture remover-cum-bailiff duties before he can commence work	39%
External painting or other outside repair work to terrace properties entailing moving ladders, materials, etc., through narrow passages daily	5%

Q379: *I am a contractor (C) under the RIBA form, with quantities, clause 31(A) deleted. An area of paving was included in the contract bills amounting to 1400 m². A "variation order" was issued for an extra area of similar paving amounting to 900 m². C had sub-let the paving work in 1984, and when the variation order was passed to the sub-contractor in 1985, he required a 30 per cent increase in his rate for the extra work due to increases in material prices. The quantity surveyor (QS) maintains that the extra work should be priced at bill rates, notwithstanding clauses 11(4) and 11(6), and that C should apply for an ex-gratia payment.*

A: This case reveals the dangers which follow when people who would otherwise be considered professional, enter into direct employment by client bodies. Contractual relationships and principles were established at a time when such people would have considered it beneath their dignity and duty to so prejudice their independence. But while times have changed, the principles have not.

The principle involved in this case is of fundamental importance, and cannot be stated too strongly. Builders should not allow this principle to be flouted as all too often it appears to be.

Neither the architect (A) nor the QS are parties to the contract. They are merely officials created by it, to perform certain specific duties for the benefit of both the employer (E) and C. E. warrants, or promises, that he will engage A and QS to perform these duties exactly and impartially, without placing restrictions or limitations of any kind at all on their independence.

This promise to give complete independence to A and QS is in no way changed by the conditions under which they are employed, or by any internal rules or standing orders of say a local authority.

In signing the contract the local authority has, in effect, suspended its standing orders insofar as they are in conflict with the contract.

If E obstructs or interferes with A or QS in the performance of their duties, he will have committed a deliberate breach of contract.

In allowing their names to be inserted in the contract, A and QS accept an ethical and legal duty to act with complete efficiency and impartiality in the exercise of their respective duties.

If either fails in his duty, or allows any consideration or pressure to interfere with the proper exercise of that duty, that would not only be reprehensible, but would also expose the person concerned to a charge of professional misconduct.

C is entitled to, and should demand, complete efficiency and impartiality from the contractual officials, no matter how, or under what conditions, they are employed by E. In default, C should take a breach of contract action against E, and report the delinquent official to his professional body for disciplinary action.

Let us see how the principle has been flouted in this case. Deletion of clause 31(A) means that C must hold his prices firm in respect of the contract works within the contract period. It does not mean that he must do so if E causes extensions of the contract period, or adds to the amount of work.

In the former case, C has his remedy in clauses 24 or 26. In the latter case, clause 11(6) is there for the specific reason that E cannot be allowed to take pecuniary advantage of C, by issuing a variation which would, were it not for clause 11(1), be a breach of contract under common law.

The duty under clause 11(6) is imposed squarely on A to consider whether a "...variation...has involved the contractor in direct loss and/or expense...", and then to order the quantity surveyor to perform the merely clerical function "...to ascertain the amount of such loss of expense". QS has no judicial function in the matter.

A has to give due consideration to the submission made by C, to determine the respective judicial manner, and to notify his decision in writing, with reasons, so that C can see whether he has grounds for challenging that decision before the arbitrator.

However, in this case, A is conspicuous by his absence! Either A has improperly delegated his duty in contravention of the principle of "delegatus non protest delegare", or QS has committed an ultra vires act by usurping A's judicial function.

Particularly in view of the fact that C has a proper basis for making a claim under clause 11(6), he should not stand for this disgraceful dereliction of duty by A. He should take legal advice without delay, with a view to taking such action as is appropriate.

By way of postscript, I suspect I know the reason underlying this case and, if I am right it is obnoxious and fraudulent. It seems that A—or QS acting in his stead—believes that C has suffered loss as a result of the variation.

But if he accepts that under clause 11(6), E will have to pay in full. This is as it should be because E is the only one to gain benefit from the extra work. However, A is allowing consideration for E, his client or employer, to override his ethical and legal duty to act impartially.

A knows that if C relinquishes his claim under clause 11(6) and applies for an ex-gratia payment instead, he will only get part of his loss, and the State will pay 75 per cent of what it costs E.

Not only is A prepared to deny C his contractual rights and rob him of moneys properly due, he is also prepared to reduce C to the begging bowl, and cause C and the State to contribute substantially for E's sole benefit.

C should resist this tactic, if only because ex-gratia payments are not intended for this purpose, and the application would fail if the full facts were known.

Q380: *A contract encountered the problem of delayed drying out, despite the use of heaters, so that a flooring sub-contractor refused to start work until the floor had dried out. The architect said that he was unable to find any provision in the JCT 1980 Edition which would allow him to grant an extension of time so as to prevent the liquidated damages clause operating.*

A: From the facts given it appears that the flooring sub-contractor has delayed in the completion of his sub-contract work which in turn has caused a delay to the main contractor. This delay would come within the definition of a 'relevant event' in the JCT 1980 Edition. Clause 25.7 includes as a 'relevant event' a delay on the part of a nominated sub-contractor which the main contractor has taken all practicable steps to avoid or reduce but which has caused a delay to the main contractor. Clause 25.1 however requires a main contractor to give written notice to the architect that the work is being or is likely to be delayed. On receipt of this notice the architect, provided he is satisfied as to the correctness of the claim, is to grant an extension of time. The use of this procedure should avoid the payment of liquidated damages.

23 Estimating/contracts

Q381: *What are the BATJIC rates of pay for working overtime, also for Saturday and Sunday work?*

A: Monday–Friday: for the first three hours, time-and-a-half of the appropriate hourly rate and, thereafter, until normal starting time the following day, at double time.

Saturday: time-and-a-half of the appropriate hourly rate up until 4pm, thereafter double time.

Sunday: any work carried out shall be paid at double time. Where work commences on a Sunday and continues until Monday then the double rate shall continue.

Q382: *Could you tell me the number of days allotted to plumbers and heating fitters for annual holidays, and are these days a right or merely a generous consideration on the part of the employer?*

A: If you are employed under the working rule agreements of either the Plumbing JIB or the H&VCA, you have 21 days holiday a year plus the eight days statutory holidays as of right.

If, however, you are not working under the above or any other working rule agreement, which would be stated in your contract of employment, your holidays would be whatever is agreed with your employer under your terms of employment.

Q383: *My problem is that I have no way of working out a fair hourly rate for a self-employed carpenter and joiner such as myself. Could you explain a method which I could use?*

A: It is an indisputable fact that a tradesman working on his own account will consciously or unconsciously work harder than an employed man. To start with you should prepare a 'Costs to Employ' table, and use this as a guide.

Such items as 'holidays with pay', 'tool money', 'redundancy reserve', etc, will not be applicable, but on the other hand 'incentive bonus' will (if calculated) be in ecxess of the published figure. National Insurance will be on a different basis.

Taking into consideration that earnings will be greater, and levies much less than shown, using the 'Costs to Employ' rate add 20 per cent for overheads, i.e. transport, telephone, estimating time, accounts, bad debts, reserve capital etc. In addition, add profit of, say, 30 per cent. This means a rate plus 50 per cent.

£250–300 per week may seem a great deal, but remember that you do not enjoy a guaranteed week; there may be slack periods when your working/earning hours may only be 10 or 20 hours in a single week. There may be bad debts or the inevitable very slow payers, and you cannot expect any compensation from Social Security for these contingencies.

Q384: *I am a small general builder doing private work from £10 to £10,000; the £10,000 I can estimate, with a reasonable amount of success, but I have difficulty with the smaller type jobs.*

I run a new vehicle and also plant such as mixers, heavy duty drills, scaffolding etc. If I was asked to give an estimate for two hours' work 10 miles from the yard what do I charge for the vehicle, plant etc and labour?

A: The cost of lorry time to and from a job 10 miles away cannot be calculated in proportion to the time involved to do the job.

For example, if the time on site is estimated to take two (or perhaps two and a half) hours, then it may be more convenient or economical to let the lorry stand by until completion.

Cost of lorry and plant calculation as follows:

	Hours
10 miles to site including loading and unloading	1
10 miles return including loading and unloading	1
Time on site for job	2
	4

Say 5 hours

To calculate the transport cost only allow £5.00 for lorry and driver.

This equals 5×£5.00=£25.00 exclusive of profits and overheads. In addition, there is the job cost—whether the job lasts two hours or two weeks.

Q385: *I have accepted early retirement after 34 years with a local authority, leaving me four years to go before receiving my state pension. I have been carrying out freelance estimating for small builders since my retirement and have now been approached by larger builder to carry out his estimating on a fee-paying basis. Could you advise me of the usual percentage paid for this type of work?*

A: During the course of estimating for larger contractors you will probably find estimates fall into one of two categories; either pricing a bill of quantities or pricing from specification and/or drawings. The latter, of course, may entail taking off approximate quantities before pricing.

The following fees are suggested: Pricing ready prepared bills of quantities, half per cent of the total estimate cost, excluding the amount included for P.C. or provisional allowance included for specialist sub-contract service.

Preparing approximate quantities and pricing thereon, 2¼ per cent of the total estimated cost excluding the amount of P.C. and provisional items as above.

If on occasions of major alteration or repair work the estimate involves a visit to site and "spot measurement", then the fee could be increased to 2¾–3 percent.

It may be helpful to the contractor if, when pricing a bill of quantities, you return some or all of your rough cost analysis notes (especially those applicable to large quantity items) when you send him the priced bill.

This will enable the contractor to make some adjustment to your rates if he deems it necessary.

Q386: *I have recently joined the Enterprise Allowance Scheme. I would like to know if there are any books to advise me how to write out estimates, i.e. replacing window frames, door frames, etc. Also what rate per hour for these type of jobs.*

A: There are a number of guides available to assist you in pricing the work you will be carrying out and I would suggest you consider the following.

BTJ Guide to Estimating £4.50; Estimating for Alterations and Repairs price £7.00; (Both published by and available from BTJ); Building Maintenance Price Book published by BMCIS, 85/87 Clarence St, Kingston on Thames, Surrey KT1 1RB.

Q387: *Could you tell me the labour only price of the work to build a brick arch. The job involves getting ground out and laying a small strip of concrete. I already have Hutchins price schedule No. 2 also Guide to Estimating Building Work by Ron Cooper but I cannot price this job, from these books.*

A: The information given with regard to specification is a little vague, however the suggested labour only price is based on excavation by hand not exceeding 500 mm deep and disposing of spoil within the work area; concrete 500 by 150 mm thick; brickwork in LBC or similar facing bricks. No height is given but has been taken as 2 metres plus the arch.

Excavation	¼ day
Concrete (site mixed approx. ⅕th c/metre)	¼ day
Brickwork (general) including screen blocks and coping	1¼ day
Arch including centre	1¼ day

The sequence of work would probably be:

Day 1: Excavate and concrete foundations; dispose of surplus spoil and construct or prepare arch centre and cut out for block bonding.

Day 2: All brickwork and screen blocks excluding arch.

Day 3: Arch and clear up.

Allowance should be made for returning to site to remove arch centre and make good pointing to soffit.

Although this work appears to require only three working days other factors may affect this i.e. access, weather, number of men working on site, loading and transporting of materials if not already on site.

Q388: *Can a written estimate be considered a contract under law without a signature, only the usual business stamp. I always believed that an estimate was only an approximate costing on materials etc. Obviously one tries to keep within the estimate figures but it is not always possible as the client may change his mind.*

A: An estimate is not legally binding, it is a professional judgement of the cost involved. A quotation, however, is legally binding.

Q389: *Could you clarify two points on pay. I am a bricklayer and work a 45 hour week of which I understand 6 hours is overtime. In BTJ Guide to Estimating book you have 9 hours unproductive pay together with the basic rates, bonuses etc. Is this 9 hours overtime in addition to my 6 hours and should my employer pay this?*

In addition am I compelled to pay a national insurance stamp on my annual holiday pay?

A: You have misunderstood the '9 hours unproductive work' mentioned in the Estimating Supplement. It comes under the heading 'Cost to Employ' and is what it costs your employer to employ you. The 9 hours overtime and 3¼ hours unproductive time is shown as an example for calculation. The employee, according to the National Joint Council should be paid a basic rate for 39 hours; the extra 6 hours is paid at time-and-a-half together with guaranteed minimum bonus.

On the second point national insurance contributions and tax is payable on holiday pay which ranks in the same way as a wage.

Q390: *I understand that one can only claim back pay for up to a six year period. Is this correct and if the sum due is recovered, is it taxable?*

A: Since pay is due under a contract of employment then if the correct amount is not paid, this is breach of contract for a writ to be issued in the courts. After this period the claim is time-barred unless in the meantime, the employer concerned acknowledges that a sum is due when time begins to run again from that acknowledgement.

If a sum is received from the employer as back pay then it is subject to income tax.

Q391: *I have had to take over the day to day running of the little firm we started in order to avoid unemployment and BTJ's Guide to Estimating is proving invaluable. I would like to know how to adjust the 'Lab' column to arrive at bonus targets for the chaps who are doing a good class job.*

The job we are on is three blocks of new flats, two storeys high and about halfway through the construction stage. My main problem is plastering and dry lining.

A: The labour rate quoted in the guide is the total anticipated nett cost based on the Craftsmen/Labourer proportions assumed suitable for the item; for example most of the brickwork rates are based on two bricklayers to one labourer.

We assume you will have added a percentage to cover your own overheads an required profit, therefore it would be in order to set the target at the same rate as shown in the guide. After measuring the work and pricing it at this rate the total is compared with the actual labour cost. If the measured value exceeds the cost the difference should be shared on a proportional basis, for example 80 per cent to the gang and 20 per cent to the company. Any arrangement should of course be agreed with the gang prior to operating the system.

Q392: *I have been told that both NHI and tax are payable on holiday pay. Is this in fact correct as I understand that only tax is due on holiday pay, as one would assume a bricklayer would be paid on the Holiday Stamp Scheme and NHI is not due under that scheme?*

A: Holiday pay attracts tax and national insurance contributions as if it were normal pay. This is true as far as employees are concerned where the employer does not participate in the holidays with pay stamp scheme—and of course with other employees e.g. clerks, managers etc—who are not covered.

However, there is no national insurance contribution for those who are within the holidays with pay stamp scheme. This is a special concession accorded by the Department of Health and Social Security. Tax is however payable.

It is worth pointing out that the employees concerned are not credited with contributions and therefore there will be a small gap in their national insurance contribution record.

Q393: *Can you please advise me what would be considered reasonable average rates for the following items in building up estimates for minor alterations and jobbing work:*
1. All-in-labour rate for (a) craftsman; (b) labourer.

2. Hourly rate or rate per mile for: (a) tipper lorry (5 tonne); (b) 15 cwt van; (c) 5 cwt van.
3. Percentage addition to materials and plant for overheads and profit.

A: This is not an easy question to answer as many factors have to be considered, for example labour availability, plus rates, type of work, travelling etc. However as a guide, and assuming the employment will be in say Kent, a reasonable all-in rate would be: Craftsman 4.73 per hour; Labourers 4.04 per hour (1984 rates).

However, do not forget to adjust these figures for your own margins to cover overheads and profit.

Plant is a rather different matter as it will depend on whether it is your own or hired, new or old, and in the case of the lorry how large. Again, assuming operation is in Kent, I would suggest the following: Tipper lorry—5 tonnes £75.00 per week; 15 cwt van £35.00 per week; 5 cwt van £30.00 per week.

The above prices exclude drivers.

Overheads and profit are very much specific to the firm in question, overheads being entirely dependent upon total annual office and management costs and the anticipated nett turnover value for the current financial year. If these are known then a simple calculation—

$$\frac{\text{office/management costs}}{\text{nett turnover}} \times 100$$

will give a percentage to work on, e.g.,

$$\frac{25{,}000}{100{,}000} \times 100 = 25\%$$

This is not absolutely correct of course; a more accurate figure can be arrived at from historical records and it is also necessary to consider whether or not overheads are likely to increase in the year due to office rent, salary increases etc.

However, as a guide and assuming small contracts with relatively high management costs, 20 to 25 per cent would not seem unreasonable.

Profit is of course an entirely different matter and will depend on the return required for future investment in the business etc; whether or not you are keen to get the job (measuring the competition) and the current state of the market.

Repair and alteration work being what it is a larger than normal risk element is involved. This should of course be taken into account in pricing the individual items of work but is sometimes allowed for in the higher than normal profit margins. Providing the work is correctly priced and overheads are reasonably accurate a 10 per cent addition for profit should be adequate.

If your query is referring to daywork then 40 per cent on materials and plant should cover both overheads and profit. Herewith, an extract on daywork rates which you may find of interest.

Q394: *A contractor was locked out for a day by a client's employees who were on strike. The contractor and his domestic sub-contractors lost a day. The contractor wanted reimbursement.*

Can the contractor recover the full cost of wages paid out for that day?

A: There does not appear to be any logical reason to suggest that if a building craftsman and labourer are locked out of a job for one day because of an internal dispute within the client company the contractor should suffer financial loss.

The minimum payment due to contractors and sub-contractors should be the net cost of employing a craftsman and labourer for a 9 hour day plus travelling time.

The PQS decision pre-supposes that some or all of contractor/sub-contractor employees could be transferred to other jobs for a day or part day. This might be so, but it is not the concern of the PQS.

If, by any chance it was the contractor/sub-contractor who had been on unoffical strike for one day it is hardly likely that the PQS would allow an extension of time, part exemption from liquidated damages or compensation for loss of profit.

Q395: *The translation from metric to imperial or vice versa can be a constant source of irritation as well as a waste of time. This must be especially true of estimators over 30, who were educated in imperial measure and are faced with a constanat stream of metric bills of quantities. Most estimators have no need to refer to a note book or reference book to ascertain quantities of component materials for a cu. yd. of concrete or a sq. yd. of brickwork, but*

translation into metric when working under pressure there is a risk of mistakes. There are, of course, many books of conversion tables, but reading through tables, which show equivalent to three or four decimal places can be very time consuming. Is there a rule-of-thumb formula which can be easily memorised?

A: The formula in Table 3 will produce a result within a 2 per cent margin of error.

A simple worked example putting this theory into practise. Item in a bill of quantities is 148 m³ concrete (1-2-6) imperial equivalent 148+one-third=198 cu. yd.

Quantities of material for one unit:

	Metric				Imperial
Cement tonnes	0.21	0.21 less	one quarter=		0.16 tons
Sand m³		0.44 0.44 less	one quarter=		0.33 cu. yd.
Aggregate m³	0.88	0.88 less one quarter=			0.66 cu. yd.

Quantities for 148 m³	or 198 cu. yd.
Cement tonnes 148×0.21=31.08	198×0.16=30.68
Sand 148×0.44=65.12	198×0.33=65.34
Aggregate 148×0.88=130.24	198×0.66=130.68

Table 3

		Approx.	Accurate
Lin. m/yd.	add one tenth	1.10 lin. yd.	1.0936
m²/yd.	add one fifth	1.20 sq. yd.	1.1960
m³/yd.	add one third	1.33 cu. yd.	1.3080

Taking the foregoing into reverse:

		Approx.	Accurate
Convert lin yd./m	Deduct one eleventh	0.91 lin. m	0.9144
sq.yd./m²	Deduct one sixth	0.83 m²	0.8361
cu.yd./m³	Deduct one quarter	0.75 m³	0.7646

Q396: *If an employee works for me for just a few hours a week am I liable to pay National Insurance contributions?*

A: The number of hours worked in a week is irrelevant when it come to calculating National Insurance charges. If the employee earns more than £35.50 a week then NI must be paid. If the wages are less than this figure then the contribution is not due.

Q397: *I have just employed a carpenter but unfortunately he has lost, and cannot remember his National Insurance number, what should I do?*

A: If he has not got a copy of his National Insurance number then he must contact without delay his local social security office and they will provide him with his reference number. For your part you should also send to the Inspector of Taxes form P46 otherwise you could get involved in some complicated problems later in the tax year.

Q398: *Very occasionally I employ workers who have passed the age of retirement and are receiving a state pension. Do I have to pay a flat rate of National Insurance for them or not?*

A: Provided their earnings are over the minimum earnings level of £35.50 you should continue to pay 10.45 per cent of wages up to a weekly earning of £265, but you should not deduct anything from the employee's wages towards National Insurance.

Q399: *Recently I had an employee give notice to leave and after taking his holiday would not be returning to work, do I have to pay National Insurance for the period he is effectively taking his holiday leave, even if in practice he has already left my employ?*

A: If the wages paid to him for the holiday period are in excess of the minimum earnings level presently set at £35.50 and the payment is not made under the construction industry's holiday with pay stamp scheme then National Insurance must be paid. If the holiday is paid under the stamp scheme this does not attract NI liability and no contribution is necessary.

Q400: *When a man reaches retirement age does the flat-rate National Insurance rate change?*

A: Basically the answer depends on whether the man can be considered to have retired from regular employment or continues working after the retirement age of 65. If he has retired then he will cease to be liable for his share of the Class 1 contributions, but you will still have to pay your share if employed occasionally. If, however, he continues to work full time then the standard rate continues until he reaches the age of 70 (65 for a woman) when he will be officially deemed to have retired and will not be liable for his contribution but as an employer you will still have to pay the employers share.

Published by Building Trades Journal

Other titles available:

Arbitration for Contractors
Builders' Reference Book
Building Regulations 1976 in Detail with amendments 1, 2, and 3
Buyers' Guide 1985
Construction Case Law in the Office
Construction Technology Guide (volume 2)
Contract Joinery
Estimating for Alterations & Repairs
Guide to Estimating Building Work 1984/85
Site Carpentry
The Small Contractors' Guide to the Computer
Builders' Detail Sheets (Consolidated)
Drainage Details
Hot Water Details
Sanitation Details (Consolidated)

Practical Guide Series

Alterations and Improvements
Setting Out on Site

For further details on the above titles or for a booklist on prices etc.
please ring the BTJ Books Department, telephone 01-404-5531.